Coffin's
SOUNDS OF SINGING

Principles and Applications of Vocal Techniques with Chromatic Vowel Chart

second edition

by
BERTON COFFIN

foreword by
Nicolai Gedda

**The Scarecrow Press, Inc.
Metuchen, N.J., & London
1987**

Other books by Berton Coffin:

Overtones of Bel Canto

The Singer's Repertoire

Phonetic Readings of Songs and Arias (co-author)

Word by Word Translations of Songs and Arias; Part I:
    German and French

First edition, 1976, Pruett Press. © by Berton Coffin

MT
821
.C65
1987
Jan. 1999

Library of Congress Cataloging-in-Publication Data

Coffin, Berton.
    Coffin's sounds of singing.

    First ed. published as: The sounds of singing. c1976.
    Bibliography: p.
    Includes index.
    1. Singing--Instruction and study. I. Title.
II. Title: Sounds of singing.
MT821.C65 1987   784.9'32   86-15491
ISBN 0-8108-1933-3

To

NICOLAI GEDDA

the most recorded of tenors
whose beautiful voice, craft, musicality, expressiveness and extended career
exemplify the vocal art as stated in the precepts of the
master teachers of the past.

TABLE OF CONTENTS

The Chromatic Vowel Chart is inside the Back Cover.

PREFACE TO THE SECOND EDITION

There is a basic reason why <u>Sounds of Singing</u> is being brought back into print. It is the pedagogical basis for both the Chromatic Vowel Chart and <u>Overtones of Bel Canto</u>. For their validation both make reference to <u>Sounds of Singing</u>. It is the primary <u>source</u> and explains in detail the Nature of sound in the human throat and gives vocalises to apply those principles. <u>Overtones of Bel Canto</u> is fundamentally a very specific book by which singers can establish and maintain their singing skills, from the amateur to the professional in the midst of a career.

This second edition of <u>Sounds of Singing</u> differs from the first in several ways:

1. I have added a Foreword by Nicolai Gedda concerning the teaching of Paola Novikova, the inspiration of this book.

2. I have used the Chromatic Vowel Chart of the <u>Overtones of Bel Canto</u> instead of the Favorable Vowel Charts of the first edition. It is still a <u>favorable vowel chart</u> which can be used by both Female and Male voices of all classifications, including Counter Tenors. The word <u>chromatic</u> means color (as in Kodachrome) and also the use of half step progressions. The basic truth is that vowels change their color for each half step of progression and can be recognized as different vowels after two half steps in some cases. Teachers and students have found it easier to use than the <u>two</u> Favorable Vowel Charts included in the First Edition.

3. I have incorporated the coupling (hookup) exercises into Passaggio Lines I and II on the Chromatic Vowel Chart and in the vocalises for Female and Male voices.

4. I have changed the word <u>Echophone</u> to <u>Vowel Resonator</u> because I have found that term is better for defining its function to singers. It is possible to effectively use <u>Sounds of Singing</u> without a Vowel Resonator, however its use accelerates the vocal training and enables a faster comprehension of the Natural phenomena involved.

5. I have also described a better, cheaper, more accurate, easily transportable, and more usable instrument for activating the Vowel Resonator - the Realistic Concertmate 200. Although it is designed as a toy, and looks like a toy, it can make a tone well suited for resonating the vocal tract and the vowels made by its different forms.

6. I have altered some of the vowels on high notes of the exercises to better conform with Garcia's vowel modification for Male voices and Female voices.

7. I have added further explanations of the phenomena of sounds in the vocal tract as they have become clearer through additional teaching and visits to Sound Laboratories.

Novikova's belief that the voice is a musical instrument was the basis of the extensive study which led to the first edition of <u>The Sounds of Singing,</u> my book <u>Overtones of Bel Canto</u> , the Chromatic Vowel Chart, and this edition of <u>Sounds of Singing</u>.

I mentioned Jerome Pruett, tenor (p. 13), in the first edition of <u>Sounds of Singing</u>. He is having a very active international operatic career in the countries of Western Europe and the United States. Together we worked out the upper extension of his voice and the professional use of the Vowel Chart to sustain his career.

Since the publication of the first edition of this text, I have observed singing in many of the greatest opera houses of the world, taught for two years in Vienna, taught within the walls of some twenty opera houses in Austria, Germany, Switzerland, Denmark, and Italy to assist young artists, to evaluate previous observations, and to find new approaches and exercises related to the singing voice as an instrument. In addition, I have consulted in Stockholm, with Dr. Johan Sundberg, Royal Institute of Technology; in Vienna with Dr. Werner Deutsch in the Recording Laboratories of the University of Vienna, with whom I made several studies reported in <u>Overtones of Bel Canto</u>; in Summit, New Jersey with Dr. Joe Olive, Bell Telephone Laboratories; and in Houston, Texas with Dr. Van Lawrence, Consultant to the Houston Opera Company, MacGregor Clinic.

In these activities I have found a validation of the principles heretofore given and many additional exercises and variations of exercises to assist in setting up the voice as an amplified musical instrument. In this journey I have taught singers of many different language backgrounds: British, New Zealand, American (they are all English with variations of vowel and prosedy values), German, Italian, French, Japanese, Spanish, Danish, Swedish, and Polish. I have found the use of the International Phonetic Alphabet, as I have defined and used it acoustically, to be very effective in establishing the vowel colorings and consonant sounds for interpretation and the control of register transitions.

I wish to express my gratitude to many participants in my vocal pedagogy classes, Master Classes, and seminars in many Universities and Conservatories in this country and in Europe. Their questions, discussions, and singing have contributed much to the thinking and research in this basic area of vowel-pitch, sympathetic vibration, resonation, and respiration.

While spoken vowel values vary according to languages and dialects, in singing they <u>cannot</u> depart from the coincidence óf a vowel pitch and an harmonic of the sung pitch. This is an <u>absolute</u> of singing. This is one of the reasons that a person can <u>sing</u> a foreign language without an accent but cannot <u>speak</u> it without an accent. I hope the phoneticists will forgive my using a great deal of license in using their tools - phonetics. Without them my work in this area would have been impossible.

Lastly, but very significantly, this work could not have been finalized without the talented ear of my singer-concert manager-wife, Mildred Coffin. We have been in 95 professionally subsidized opera houses and concert halls in Europe, and in over 76 multi-purpose opera and concert hall facilities in this country. My wife's sustained assistance in editing and at the typewriter has been a major influence in formalizing these observations of a lengthy pilgrimage of the SOUNDS OF SINGING.

BC May 1986

PREFACE TO THE FIRST EDITION

After having taught vocal pedagogy for twenty years, after having been director or co-director of no less than eight National Association of Teachers of Singing Workshops, with attendance and participation in several others, after years of private study and teaching of singing, I began to sense that what was believed to be fact was either incomplete fact or not necessarily fact. This indicated that there was a body of knowledge yet to be explored. I wanted to know more about the nature of sound in the physiognomy of the singing voice. My course of investigation was uncharted and my final conclusions were not anticipated, rather in many instances they were avoided. I had no intention of counting the visual lines of a spectrogram. In avoiding them I came upon an aural procedure of sensing the harmonic structure of singing. What we perceive from what actually happens acoustically in the voice is the psychological part of this observer's statement of the foundations of singing. We present herewith their codification for use by singers and teachers of singing.

My study of sound in the vocal physiognomy began in 1958 when Pierre Delattre who was such a figure in acoustical phonetics that a book of thirty-nine original contributions by some of the leading linguists and phoneticians of the United States and Europe are included in "Papers on Linguistics and Phonetics to the Memory of Pierre Delattre," (1973). His death prevented our concluding studies which we had begun with X-Ray motion pictures of singing in the Speech Synthesis Laboratory at the University of California, Santa Barbara. He was admitted to the Paris Conservatory at the age of ten, and although he was not allowed to attend the Conservatory because of religious reasons, a musician's ear was always present in his approach to languages and acoustic phonetics. He sensed, investigated, and codified a large bibliography in those fields. He was one of my co-authors in Phonetic Readings of Songs and Arias (1964) and my Preface represents my earliest statement of the pitch of vowels in relation to singing. Twelve additional years of investigation, teaching of singing and consultation have resulted in this book and the Singer's Favorable Vowel-Color Charts.

This is written by a teacher of singing who has done a great deal of vocal study with the teachers of the Lamperti, Garcia, and Persichini schools of teaching singing. The school of Wenceslao Persichini has been briefly described by Giuseppe DeLuca, (Brower, 1920, p. 63) who stated that he himself was the last of seventy-four artists trained in that studio. Persichini also taught Tita Ruffo and Mattia Battistini. My last teacher, Paola Novikova, was a student of Battistini and is known as the teacher of Nicolai Gedda and George London among many others I have listed on page 15. Subsequent research is based upon concepts of this and other Italianate schools of singing. My earlier training was with Graham Reed, a student of Lilli Lehmann, Jean DeReszke (a pupil of Sbriglia), and Herbert Witherspoon (a pupil of G. B. Lamperti). In fact, Graham Reed was an associate teacher in Herbert Witherspoon's school of singing. I later studied with Mack Harrell, who was a student of Schöne-René (a pupil of Viardot, Garcia's sister) and of Frances Alda (a pupil of Mathilde Marchesi, Garcia's student). Later I studied with Allan Rogers Lindquest who was a student of the Swedish school which produced

Hislop, Flagstad, and Bjoerling. I consider this background as part of my license to make observations and to write concerning the bases of singing.

I have always had a great interest in some of the "why's" which have not yet been explained. It is only fair to say that I was almost a physicist. My father was a collegiate teacher of mathematics and physics, and my early plans were to follow in his footsteps. By my second year of college I had found a part of my voice, so I changed my studies to music. However, I was later a teacher of physics in the Army Specialized Training Program in World War II, and when that was deactivated became a mathematician with the Consolidated Vultee Aircraft Corporation in the B-36 division. This may explain my interest in the aerodynamics of sound and my desire to study why various vocal phenomena exist. This was greatly stimulated by Pierre Delattre, the acoustical-phoneticist, with whom I later worked on a program which he gave before the 1968 National Convention of the Teachers of Singing in Portland, Oregon. We had a grant for continued study in 1970, but he died in 1969 and I carried out the project alone with the consultation of several authorities.

My last investigations with Dr. Delattre were with an image intensifier motion picture X-Ray in which the action of the vocal organs could be observed in their patterns in speech and in singing which included different registers, vowels, consonants, and dynamics. The pictures were amazing but my feeling was that there was little to be gained by making a singer aware of these motions. What does appear to be worthwhile is the nature of vocal sound sensed by the ear (the acoustical) and the kinesthetic sense of vibrations when certain positions are taken by the throat (the physiological). This text shows my findings in this area. Delattre made a very complete statement of the acoustical-physiological relationship in speech in an article which was published in French (French Review, O. 1968) but was not accepted for English publication because it was felt to be too elementary. Nothing could be better suited to the comprehension of those interested in the singer's art. We are dealing with unseen resonators in the teaching of singing which must be handled correctly by the senses. With the kind permission of his wife, Dr. Genevieve Delattre, his "missing link" article forms Appendix J of his book, p. 287.

The results of this study are those of a sound engineer rather than those of a scientist. It is a book of how to do something rather than a theory. Musical notation and phonetics have been substituted for frequencies wherever possible since musicians usually do not know what to do with the language of numbers. What we have done is to try to find out how the nature of sound relates to what the singing masters were writing about; what my teachers were doing; what other teachers were doing; and what present-day singers are doing.

There seems to be a widespread belief that there is less great singing today than in the past but a higher level of mediocre singing. Frequent references have been made to the lack of discipline of the vocal instrument practiced by present-day teachers of singing. Then, there is the thought that we have forgotten what to listen for in the teaching of singing, just like the violin makers have lost the art of what to listen for in violin making. To befuddle the picture, most observers acknowledge that singers are better coached in diction, style, and taste than ever before. And there may hang part of the tale - every time a coach changes diction he changes placement!

There is a quaint belief in the land that since languages are in a continual state of flux so is the diction of singing. Nothing can be further from the truth. Certain resonances exist and have always existed in the singing voice. When these were used correctly there was great singing if there was vocal endowment. When the resonances were not used correctly there was vocal decline. I tend to agree with the quote by Elster Kay (1963, p. 95), "The late Sir Thomas Beecham used to say that singers could not be trained to sing English sufficiently loudly for the Royal Opera House [Covent Garden] ... ." However, if the singer knows <u>which</u> harmonics are available in his pronunciation and how to use them, better tone, better resonation, better vowel differentiation, and better consonant articulation can be made. It is astounding what an unknowledgable diction teacher can undo if the laws of vibration and resonance are disregarded. It is amazing what can be accomplished rather quickly by knowledgable teachers when the laws of harmonic pronunciation are obeyed. Voices are <u>built</u> by utilizing vowel resonances in such a way that there is a continuing resonance from note to note, called <u>cantilena</u>, in which notes match each other like pearls on a string. One weakens a voice by allowing vowel resonances to interfere with sung pitch. Voices are built by finding the sympathetic resonation of vowels to the harmonics of sung pitch.

This opus is written for <u>all</u> singers from the beginner to the professional who **is maintaining a** career. All can probably be far better singers than they are simply because their singing does not encompass all of the basic laws of vibration and resonance in the human voice.

I must acknowledge two grants from the University of Colorado Council of Research and Creativity which enabled me to do research in Santa Barbara, California and in Europe. I am indebted to Dr. Fritz Winckel of Berlin, Dr. Richard Luchsinger of Zurich, Yvonne Rodd-Marling of Lugano, Dr. Hans-Heinrich Waengler of the University of Colorado Sound Laboratory, and the late Dr. Pierre Delattre for valuable consultations. Also I wish to thank members of the Physics Department of the University of Colorado for their advice and the use of their sound generating equipment, and the Baldwin Organ Company for the use of an electric organ in demonstrations. My thanks go to Dr. André Malecot of the Speech Synthesis Laboratory, University of California, Santa Barbara, and Martial Singher, Academy of the West, Santa Barbara, who with his artist students assisted in the X-ray motion pictures of singing which were an early part of this study.

I am grateful to Jerome Pruett, leading tenor of the Vienna Volksoper, who is also guesting in Switzerland, Wales, and England in such operas as Faust, Daughter of the Regiment, Don Pasquale, Tales of Hoffman, Magic Flute and Abduction from the Seraglio. Together we worked out the upper extension of his voice and the professional use of the Vowel Scales to sustain his career. Other students are under management but they have had additional vocal assistance by other teachers since graduation from the University and I cannot claim them as my students at this time. Nevertheless, they have also been of great assistance in the practical uses of the enclosed principles of vocal sound.

In addition, I wish to express my gratitude to my students of singing in the United States and Europe, to my many undergraduate and graduate students in my vocal pedagogy classes and seminars at the University of Colorado, and to persons in attendance at Master Glasses, Workshops, and Lecture-Demonstrations here and abroad who have contributed to the thinking and research in this basic area of vowel-tone, vibration, resonation, and respiration.

Lastly, but very significantly, this work could not have been finalized without the talented ear of my singer-concert manager-wife, Mildred Coffin. We have observed in the greatest laboratories of singing today, the opera houses and concert halls, which include over 75 in this country and 50 in Europe. Her sustained assistance at the typewriter has been a major influence in formalizing these observations of a lengthy pilgrimage of the Sounds of Singing.

October 1, 1976
Boulder, Colorado

FOREWORD

Nicolai Gedda

In my first season with the Metropolitan Opera Company I began my study with Paola Novikova and worked my vocal technique and all of my roles with her until her death nine years later in 1967. After that I vocalized and went on as she had taught me. Our association was very close and I sometimes worked with her two and three times a day. In those years my technique became very secure and I had continuing success in opera, recordings, and recitals in the United States and abroad. It was due to this security of technical knowledge which has enabled me to be in my 32nd year of a career as a leading tenor in many opera centers, and to continue my concertizing here and in Europe.

I remember Dr. Coffin's hearing several of my lessons on various occasions during those years and that he was continually taking notes although my lessons were in Russian. He was also studying and observing the teaching of other students, some of whom were his own who went on to their careers. He published his notes about the teaching of Paola Novikova in the text Sounds of Singing (1977) which he dedicated to me.

This book turned out to be very helpful for me at the age of 50, 51 or 52. I felt that things were not as easy for me as they had been when I was younger and I wondered why. I took the Sounds of Singing and restudied the details that I had learned so well some ten to fifteen years before. By restudying my voice with the exercises which Mme. Novikova used and by paying especial attention to the breath and the resonators I was able to restore my voice to what it was previously capable of doing. She was always talking about the resonators and the voice being a wind instrument. Now I vocalize the entire voice including the high notes, which have always been easy for me. But I also vocalize to the low G with the ribs expanded and lifted which gives a very full easy tone; this is because I use the resonance of the raised chest. Now I think it is the chest that saves me in the high notes, middle register, low notes, long phrases, and colorings in my roles. The chest should be up with no tensions. All of her details which are included are fantastically right when properly built into the technique.

She was very particular that the passaggio, the c to e area of the voice, should not be too heavy. It is dangerous to make sounds in this area which are too dramatic. She also taught that consonants do not hinder but assist the voice and give clarity to the text. She had a special Italianate method of teaching the consonants so that they did not get in the way. I think her teaching is tremendously important today since Italianate singing is less predominant than it used to be. The old school of singing seems to be dying out.

Not many people believe that Paola Novikova was the only student of Mattia Battistini but I believe it now. She was not a well read person on the teaching of singing, and there is no way that she could have imagined such a career-lengthening device as her breathing technique. She had something very unique - a system of inhaling with the lips together, on a slight smile and a slight yawn with a breathing-in sound that was absolutely remarkable. This she did before every exercise. I cannot explain why it gives me a feeling of buoyancy and exuberance when I use it, but it opens the throat into the perfect singing position with the right amount of mask resonance. This brings about an enormous, natural expansion of the lower ribs and is done in such a way that I can think of what I am doing when I am inhaling and what I am going to do when I sing. This inhalation had to come from someone who had a long career and I think it is that which has given me my lengthy career. How fantastic was the teaching of that lady!

She was meticulous in that the instrument always had to be right. If it was not right, I would be required to start again until the sound was right. And she was just as attentive to language accent and interpretation in my roles. She was a genius for me. One interesting thing about this method is that the technique hides itself. She taught on an Italian AH which was very bright. This makes the voice carry in the largest auditoriums and enables both coloratura and long line singing. My messa di voce and my use of the falsetto were trained by her. It is also a method which keeps the voice from becoming heavy beyond its years. I hear many singers who try to make their voices overly dramatic to their detriment; in fact their voices "dry out" and their careers are shortened. Such cannot be the case when the voice is trained as a lyric instrument whether the voice is large or small.

I heartily recommend Mme. Novikova's technical approach to those who are preparing for careers or who are in their careers. This method has served me well and I believe that it can do the same for others.

Chapter I.   THE TEACHING OF PAOLA NOVIKOVA

(A traditional Italianate intuitive approach to the teaching of singing.)

Paola Novikova (1896-1967), Russian-born coloratura soprano, studied in Germany and Italy where she achieved recognition as a singer. She maintained a studio in New York City, and held master classes in Hollywood, Vienna, and Stockholm. She was a pupil of the great Mattia Battistini who has been described as "the best Italian baritone of his day." At the age of 65 he gave recitals at Queen's Hall in England which caused such a sensation that listeners to whom his identity was unknown would not have guessed him to be a man of 65. His teacher was Wenceslao Persichini who taught Titta Ruffo and Giuseppe DeLuca (who stated he taught 74 artists (Brower, 1920, p. 63)).

Mme. Novikova received critical acclaim in her 1943 New York Town Hall recital for the "elegance, taste and subtlety" of her singing.

She was best known in this country and abroad as a teacher of singing and numbered among her students celebrated world artists at the Metropolitan Opera Company, the Vienna Staatsoper, La Scala, and the Bayreuth and Salzburg Festivals. The well-known baritone, George London, studied with Mme. Novikova for 17 years, and the famous Swedish-Russian tenor, Nicolai Gedda studied with her for ten years. Others who studied with her for shorter periods of time were Fedora Barbieri, Ljuba Welitsch, Hilde Zadek, Helen Donath, Irmgard Seefried, Hilde Gueden, Pia Tassinari, Delia Rigal, Erich Kunz, Ferruccio Tagliavini, Kim Borg, Elisabeth Hoengen, Mario Berini, Mona Paulee, Frances Yeend, Inez Matthews, Wilma Lipp, Richard Manning, Belen Amparan, Janine Micheau, Kerstin Meyer, Aase Nordmo-Lovberg, Valorie Goodall and George Hoffmann.

It was my privilege to have taken several lessons annually with Mme. Novikova over a period of ten years during which time I made copious notes of her teaching. In addition, I was able to observe her instruction of many lessons with several of her world-famous artists. I have taken time so that her instructions and procedures can be placed in true perspective. They are an outgrowth of the schooling which she received as a singer, of her highly intuitive nature, and her experience as a vocal technician and coach. I present this in a spirit of devotion to a person who demonstrated and clarified the pedagogical concepts on which much of the research and writing in this book is based. Hers was a recent, Italianate, first line school of the teaching of singing. I will give an overview of her approach before I take a look at the vibrator of the vocal "trumpet," the resonator of the vocal "trumpet," and the interaction of the vibrator, the resonator, the breath, and articulators. The following are quotes of Paola Novikova.

THE INSTRUMENT

"I consider the human voice to be a wind instrument. Our resonators are mask, teeth, and chest; to coordinate these resonators is the job of the teacher." [The resonators are the air spaces which are enclosed by those members mentioned.]

"Work only for the schooling of the machine (ribs, abdomen and mask). There are no good sounds that come by chance!"
"Points to watch."
    1. Mask position [the cheeks should be up];
    2. passive palate;
    3. collar bone support for below the passaggio; and
    4. flexible rib support for passaggio and above.
    [As though the chest were opening up.]
"It is absolutely necessary that a singer have a strong machine, if he is to support the voice. The machine must be healthy and strong." [The breathing machine becomes stronger through good singing.]

"The correct functioning of the machine will give correct tone, the ear will not." [The unaided ear may not but the Vowel Resonator will tell which way the pronunciation should work - good singing is like a massage of the voice.]

"Never look for quality in a beginner. None of them know how to breathe and they control the sound through their muscles."

"We must learn to train our breathing and resonance machine. Voice development is a training of the machine - not the sound." [This book goes by sound to tell the machine what to do.]

"If it feels wrong that is bad - if it sounds wrong that is a matter of opinion. " [If there is pain there is an improper relationship of pronunciation and the breath.]

"Please command - don't allow. Please command the machine so that the sound does not become bad. " [But the sound can tell when the machine is working improperly.]

BREATHING

The following inhalation was used for all vocalization.
1. Inhale with the mouth closed but with the teeth slightly apart.
2. The vocal cords should be closely adducted with the lips closed enough to make a snoring sound as in deep sleep where the vocal cords are completely relaxed and the glottis is not as open as for breathing while conscious.
3. The nostrils should be enlarged and the cheeks wide so that there can also be a sound made behind the soft palate.
4. The corners of the mouth should be elevated slightly as in the Mona Lisa smile.

She also recommended the independent use of the above inhalation to develop strength of the chest. Keep the noise of "deep sleep" when inhaling in recital or in opera whenever there is time - otherwise, use the catch breath.

She seated students so that they worked only from the waist up - this demanded much more effort from the ribs. De Reszke used the same approach (Leiser 1934, p. 311).

"To obtain the connection between the voice and its support. . . . he would make the pupil sit down in an attitude of complete relaxation, round shouldered, elbows on knees, hands hanging down in order to relax all of the muscles of the chest, and prevent the use of any others except those of the diaphragm. Then, in inhaling, the lower ribs were to be expanded without raising the chest:-'Imagine yourself to be a great church bell, where all of the sonority is round the rim.'"

All the work was in the tank - didn't bother with the larynx itself. "The muscles get stronger through the preparation. " [The larynx was drawn downwards by the inhalation. Luchsinger (1965, p. 76) called this "the trachea pull. "]

"The action of the flexible ribs is up at the end of a phrase and when singing a descending musical passage."

"When the breath drops and the chest falls, firmly hold the hands up under the chest and help the muscles of the collar bone and chest to hook up until they become strong by themselves."

"If the back is killing the singer, it indicates that he is keeping the support."

For more space in the throat [sombre timbre], she asked that the lips be closed and puckered while inhaling through the nose. This was followed by an attack with a smile in which there was a two-pronged air-space through which an attack could be made into both cheek-bones.

"Take a full breath for each exercise in vocalizing - throw away unused part." F. Lamperti (1890, p. 23); Garcia (1855, p. 10); Caruso (Marafioti, 1922, p. 158) used the full breath.

"She frequently used stretchers [muscle building springs] - used in a sustained manner when singing over the passaggio [passaggio circa B-flat - d in low voices; B - E medium; C-sharp - F in high voices] to induce action of the flexible ribs."

"Don't command the broad back - only the flexible ribs."

"Mobilize the ribs for high notes, economize the ribs for low notes."

"The less sound you give in the passaggio, the more strength demanded of the ribs."

"The chest must never drop - it is held up by the low ribs."

"Give abdominal support before, not with high tones. The greatest intensity of the machine is on the way down, not on the way up."

"Breath control differs with the disposition of people - the excitable people tend to have a bumpy breath - the calm people have a calm breath. There is great difficulty in training an excitable person in a calm breath."

"We have only one muscular thing to think about in singing: the muscular control of the machine (abdomen and ribs). One sings on the focus but without muscular pressure except at the breath in support and control. If support is dropped, then the tone falls back on the throat, and other muscular support steps in." (I find the focus by means of the Vowel Resonator.)

Novikova did not use the word pressure with energetic people. "Instead of pressing air down - open up the ribs." [At the same time there is a thin waist.]

"Hold back the breath, not the sound. After rib expansion, let sound go! It will find its way into the mask where focus is. The mask is the keyboard; play on it. The breath opens it up." [Holding back the breath was called "vocal struggle," F. Lamperti, 1877, p. 25.]

"Watch sensations; let them be your guide. The sensation of fixing or holding is at the breath. The chest must never drop; held up by ribs. The tone hangs suspended on the breath. Less effort; more sonority!" [Sympathetic vibration, not forced vibration.]

"The chest [rib cage] must function throughout the whole voice."

"Don't inhale half-heartedly, don't inhale without thinking of the mask."

"Never classify voices until the breathing is set, never before 5 or 6 lessons. Impossible to classify by sound. Get it on the breath then it will show."

"The lifted up chest should never drop during the exercises because when the chest drops, it squeezes the air out of the lungs in an artificial sudden way. The chest lifts up everything that it finds in its way. If the chest does not lift up then something is tense."

"Singing is how to breathe and what to do with the breath." [In relationship to how to pronounce.]

"The legato is of the breath - the sound is a consequence." [Also of reverberating vowels.]

"The moment you sit down on the breath it cannot be lifted up."

"Sing with breath and not voice."

"Too narrow on inhalation. Inhale as through the back of the ears to give the width of the mask." [This also calls into action the downward and widening influence of the omohyoid muscles and the widening muscles between the hyoid muscle and the tip of the chin as well as the hyoid bone and the mastoid process. These can be felt with the fingers. These opening muscles become strengthened in singing.]

"Before singing and during singing think up the expanded ribs. The muscles of the back get stronger."

On hearing a demonstration lesson. "The students do not always inhale. They go through the motions but they don't inhale. Keep them close to you so that you can hear the inhaling noise." [The sound of deep sleep and the noise behind the soft palate. The lips must be closed for this inhalation.]

"The opening of the space behind the ears makes the whole head feel empty." This brings into action the muscles which elevate the veil of the palate.

Sitting backwards on a chair for vocalization gives fantastic results. "Pour the sound - it can be a thin stream but the breath is always turned on." [Or she would have a singer sit with his/her back against a straight chair in such a way that he/she could feel the widening of the flexible ribs.]

RESONANCE, THE MASK

"The cheeks should be widened and raised on inhalation and in this position the attack is made into the mask." [This creates the musculature of the cheeks of the "natural singer."]

"Open the mask on inhalation and sing as though continuing the inhalation."

"The instrument is the mask, but do not try to sing there directly. Open up and let the sound in from the larynx. Don't try to sing in the mask - let it." Gatti-Casazza, 1941, p. 80 speaks of Tamagno's problem with high notes when he could not use mask resonance because his nose was stopped up.

"One must have a feeling of interior smile on every note."

"Never keep the corners of the mouth lifted after the cheeks are lifted up."

"Show the lower teeth to stay off of the throat and to free the jaw." [The lips mute the voice - cover the lips only for muted effects and the muted vowels.]

"The less effort at the throat, the more the sonority."

"The sound should always be bright and not dark. Even the darkest voices should vocalize very bright."
(Italian a not ɑ. She also used ɛ and ɔ.)

"Drop the chin but never the jaw." (That was below the passaggio! Above the passaggio pictures of her singers reveal that the jaw was often unhinged.)

"In singing one should have the sensation of a fork (breath passage) into both cheek bones."

"It frequently helps to lift up the mask with the fingers when singing. This helps if the mask is lazy." [This also lateralizes the mouth so that the resonance has a higher pitch. The change of color is instantaneous - because the teeth show.]

"The mask is the keyboard; play on it. The breath opens up the keyboard."

"Pay attention to lifting up the cheek muscles. Anglo-Saxons and Germans have trouble in speaking with high muscles, but not Italians and some Slavs."

"If palate and mask do not feel open, don't go on. It is useless."

"When singing [u o a ɛ i] the mask must be open for every vowel." [Line up the vowels.]

"NO HUMMING." [Humming mutes the voice - not used by Garcia, Marchesi, or Lamperti schools.]

"Who does not know how to breathe well never knows how to sing. When we train our breath we form the inside of our instrument in a way that we do not disturb the air going through the whole pipe from the diaphragm to the head." [Standing wave in the vocal pipe.]

"On down-scales, keep high on focus. On first low tone of ascending scale, keep sound light; otherwise it might pull tone off the focus."

"The cheek bones should be more lifted up since the tongue is still heavy." [The student was singing ɒ or ɑ; she wanted the Italian a which Helmholtz said had a pitch of d³. She would frequently lift the singer's cheeks with her finger.]

"Be asleep in the throat but energetic in the mouth and lips." [The pipe stays close to ɤ, ɔ, ʌ, ʊ.]

"Don't hold mask open after breath has found its channel. It will govern automatically."

ATTACK

"Attack is for you, then everything else is for the audience - not one vowel wild."

"Inhale, wait, then attack. The "wait" after inhalation is to let the breath take possession of all the spaces it can in the body."

"Inhale and then imagine you go back the same way with the breath in your attack."

"Start right and it is there, and all we have to do is play the machine. Give the "house" [space] to the whole musical phrase from the beginning."

"Sing phrase mentally. When the sound is heard, it is only a continuation of what was done mentally."

"Attack should be higher in imagination with supporting instead of pushing."

"Pull in stomach before attack and not with attack. The first makes a beautiful sound - the other does not." [The waist becomes thin before the attack if a full breath if taken. Some dramatic singers use a downward thrust against a wide belt around the waist for high notes.]

"Start first note high. Always vocalize open and bright, on the breath." [High and intense overtones.]

"Attack - start with the point, not with the pitch."
[Start with high overtone on the sung pitch.]

"Watch that the tongue is wide and upon the teeth when
you start [an exercise]." [This was to get away from the
effect of the thick-tongued American-English. Start the
tone frequently with dental d, n, t, l's, and rolled r's.]

"Too low a production gives throatiness." [Low and weak
overtones muffle the voice so that it will not carry.]

"This kind of work is imperative at the beginning of
study - the intake, the expansion of the ribs, the mask
all followed repeatedly by the attach on the vowel ah."

"See the ah before you attack." [The vowel pipe must
be formed by the time the pitch is sung - otherwise
there will be a vowel glide at the onset.]

"Make no point of opening the throat while singing. It is
already opened by the inhalation of the breath."

"There is no such thing as a white sound in my system -
with mask resonance there is a bright sound. Lift up
the voice and give the mask."

PRONUNCIATION

Vowels

"Form the vowels on the outside of the mouth - not inside.
The focus is formed inside, the vowel outside. Smile for
[a ɑ ɛ e ɪ i]. Pucker for [ɔ o ʊ u] and [œ ø ɤ y]."

"Move the tip of the tongue, lack of it is what makes
voices throaty."

"The vowels should never be independent of the mask.
The open mask is a must at the start of every phrase.
When this occurs it will serve as a mirror for the vowels."

"Ah [a] should be sung forward and not back and spread.
There is usually too much action inside the mouth and
not enough outside." Italian [a] rather than American
[ɒ].

"The covering or coloring of a vowel must be done from the front and not the back."

"Do not become angry with the throat, pay attention to the vowels."

"No sleepy mouthed people - this is where the quality comes from."

"What many do not understand is that the bright vocalization sound becomes very resonant when they sing." [High overtones.]

"Keep the resonance "point" on each vowel." [High overtones.]

"In changing vowels on top notes, change only the lip position. Word changes are made at the lips and teeth and with the tip of the tongue."

"If ee is pinchy, put a little oo in it, let it float out." [High resonance vowels must also have some low resonance in them.]

"The pronunciation is done by the movement of the lips, remembering that there are only five vowels which form the real pronunciation. They are oo, oh, ah, e, i; all the other languages are just based on those five vowels but they are mixtures, an oo and an ee makes a French y, and oh and an ε make a German ø, etc." [Brought about by playing the various vowel resonances.]

"Be careful of the English diphthongs. The oh and the e are very dangerous matters. Make your pupil always aware of the fact that in the oh, there are two vowels, oh and oo, which need two formations of the lips. Now, all the formations of the lips in pronunciation have to be very exaggerated when we are training. The moment this becomes a part of the body of our student, he doesn't need to exaggerate any more. If the student is trained to pronounce right, his face will be absolutely calm and the movement of the lips will be very slight. But without this exaggerated way of getting the elasticity of the muscles we will not achieve the results we want." [She frequently got this action, and vowel tuning by manipulating the corners of the student's mouth with her thumb and middle finger. She was tuning by her very sensitive hearing.]

"Search to see what the machine wants. What does the
voice agree with? Find out the medicine then make the
voice ready for the basic rules. There must be the
complete freedom of sound from the machine." [Sing in
such a way that the vowels agree with the pitch, thus
avoiding muscular and acoustical interference.]

When a student was singing "Where'er You Walk," she manipulated the mouth
with her hand. "And all things flourish" - "all" - not inside mouth, but outside.
She pulled the lips forward for [ɔ], apparently the amount of movement was
governed by her ear.

"When you feel that the tube, the pipe is all one, then
you may begin to train the voice as such, which means
you are giving the sounds into the right resonator."

"I would suggest to train the voice on a smile until the
passaggio, then comes the vowel oo, then comes the
head register." [Male voices.]

"The less the mouth opens, the more the mask chamber
opens. You may have to drop the chin on the top."

"You still have a desire to project ee - don't. Let it
float out - put more oo in ee - the same space of oo has
to be filled out with ee." [Keep the lower resonance in
the two resonance [i] vowel by coupling [u] with [i]].

"The base of the tongue should move forward to prevent
disaster." [With the tongue backward there are only
the single resonance vowels ɒ, ɔ, o, u. They need
overtones.]

"Keep the jaw still without chewing around." [It is very
difficult to keep a continuity of sound when the jaw is
continually moving around because some spaces will
have sympathetic resonance - others will not.]

"You thought the ee was broader than ah, but it is not."

"Be vowel conscious and not sound conscious. Every
phrase is a compilation of vowel sounds."

"There is no such thing as wrong intonation, it is always
a wrong position of the instrument; never try to correct
the pitch." [She could correct the student's intonation
by moving the corners of the mouth with her hand.]

"Speak perfectly, clearly on the pitch. There is no
legato of the sound - it is an intangible thing."
[Legato is a phenomenon in which overtones are continuous from tone to tone. When vowels are changed,
various overtones are amplified and weakened by the
echoing vowel pipe.]

"When the tone is spread, work for point, point, point.
Still too much action inside mouth and not enough on the
outside. Use lips to help with the focus."

"Don't worry about the vowels; worry about the point.
If the right point is there, the right vowel will be there."
[The fixed resonance, "2800" assists in lining up the
vowel resonances.]

"The less we allow the lower jaw to help, the more we
can play on the point."

"Always show the lower teeth for the correct opening of
the hinges." [She had them sing on one tone - oo - aw -
ah - eh - ee.]

"Don't ever 'cover' the sound; it is the vowel that is
covered." [Check with the Vowel Resonator to find the
particular sounds which will amplify the voice in the
passaggio.]

"Some voices are pitched but not focused." [Vowels
are not tuned.]

PRONUNCIATION

Consonants

"You are afraid of interrupting the line for consonants.
The opposite is true - by lips and tongue interrupting the
tone, the throat is rested."

"Even in dramatic singing in middle and low voice there
is not the low support. Do it with diction, consonants,
vowels, the mask and collar bone support."

"Always pronounce outside of the instrument. If you
pronounce inside, it is only for your royal pleasure and
no one else's for the voice will not project."

"The 1 - n - d - t consonants should be with the tongue wide and slightly between the teeth." [This is needed to overcome the American consonants. The Russian fronts his tongue more than the Italian but the exercise is a great one for the American singer to get his tongue forward from the alveolar ridge.]

"The consonants have to be pronounced by the tip of the tongue in order not to disturb the construction which we fix already inside of our mouths. The ch sounds in German affect the throat, even if one is a great singer. I do not advise singing in Italian opera in two days after having sung Wagner. The Italian followed by the German is o. k." [There are fewer acoustical interferences in the consonants of the Italian language than in the other languages. Marchesi italianized French and German in her teaching, 1905, p. 6.]

"Lyric singing is more a matter of liquid pronunciation; dramatic singing is a matter of more incisive pronunciation."

"Be careful of the English "l," which is wrong because it is pronounced with the middle of the tongue." [X-Ray pictures show that there is also a constriction at the back of the tongue which muffles the higher overtones.]

"Practice with dah - not duh - to loosen the tongue and get a brighter color." [This is the same as Caruso, (1929, p. 192) in Fucito book.]

"Sing n drah 1 on d ohn on the same pitch to train the tongue." [The symbol ‿ means tongue slightly over the lower teeth, allowing resonation of the complete vocal pipe.] The tongue lies on the pedestal of the lower front teeth for [d n, t and 1].

"Your "t" has a tendency of h behind it - it should not. This is important for diction and for vocalizing." [The Italian p, t, k are not aspirates.]

"The European pronunciation of l - n - d - t allows the vowel sounds to be made in the mask whereas American l - n - d and t destroy the vowel positions for wideness in the mask." [The American d, n, t, l disturb the tongue channel resonance; the Italian d, n, t, l trigger it. Hence the use of these consonants brightens the voice.]

"ENUNCIATION should not be confused with hitting the walls of the throat." [Enunciation should avoid a poor relationship between the resonation by the vocal tract and the vibration by the vocal cords.]

The words she used for blending pronunciation with vocalization were usually sung on the same pitch, varying up and down the middle voice from word to word, with attention paid to the different pronunciation of single and double consonants as in Italian. (The sign ⌢ means to dentalize the consonant, the sign ˅ means to roll the r.) See the list on page 143.

REGISTERS

"Registers do not exist if the voice is treated correctly."

"Do not train on the high register, it is a consequence of the light, bright, middle register." [In men and women train the middle voice bright; round for the top. See Garcia (1894), p. 16. I suggest whistle register in both Male and Female Voices.]

"For top notes, spread the ribs and give a more open mouth." [Frequently gained by unhinging the jaw.]

"When you go very high, exaggerate the mask at the start of the arpeggio."

"Both rows of teeth should be showing in high notes."

"Sing aw or oo on top but move only the upper lip - do not touch the machine."

"For the passaggio, it is imperative to train on oo." [oo - for men, aw - for women.]

"In the middle register the mouth is open only slightly, with the upper and lower teeth showing."

"On the middle and low voice it is like the support is at the arm pits. When the voice goes high, think the support down about 12 inches."

"Low voice is gained with mask open and closed mouth."

"Don't spend too much support on low tones, then nothing is left for the high."

"Don't let the tongue go back when coming down scale.
Give the tongue more flatness when you come down."

"Never cover a sound but don't keep it from being covered." [To men on top voice.]

"No chesty sounds for any reasons and for any voices."
[I have found it necessary to use them and blend them.
I have found that extending the middle voice both ways
will not work. Middle voice cannot be extended to high
voice nor can it be extended to low. Find and develop
the high and low registers, then the middle voice can be
blended into them. A voice trained only in the middle
register will always have severe limitations in range
and dynamics.]

PASSAGGIO

"In the passaggio, the voice goes from oh to oo even without saying it." [Fiberoptics reveal that an unsensed
movement of the tongue brings about the change of vowel
color.]

"Never try to give more space at mask for high tones.
Give space at the start, and forget about it."

"Training the passaggio with the [u] may give a throaty
sound. Get the [u] from the [α]." [The [u] vowel has to
be mixed with a.]

"The less sound you give on e-f, in the passaggio, the
more strength is required in the ribs."

PLACEMENT

"One sings on the focus but without muscular pressure
except at the breath support. If support is dropped, then
the tone falls back on the throat and other muscular
support steps in."

"When going down scales, keep high focus. On upward
scales have the position of the mask before the attack."

"Basses must establish the high register in order that
the low register may be open and the quality retained

- not the sound of an empty barrel which is not heard beyond the third row." [The bass must have high overtones to be heard.]

"The e, f, f# should be absolutely under the eyes - you are still back on the palate."

"Forget soft palate and uvula - sing from front teeth to mask." [Use tongue channel resonation.]

"Feel high on low tones; feel low on high tones." [High vowels [a ɛ] on low notes, low vowels [ʊ o ɔ] on high notes.]

THE JAW

"Show the lower teeth to free the jaw, however, the lower jaw should always be hanging."

"Drop the chin for passaggio and high notes, never the jaw."

"It is a must in coming down the scale to close the mouth." [This gives higher resonation of overtones necessary for low notes.]

LOW NOTES

"Tenors on low tones should keep "ah" bright, but mouth must not be too open; it should be almost closed." [See Garcia, 1894, p. 17.]

"Low tones must not be too heavy; they cause a throat pinch, then the high tones seem not to find their right place. [In practice] if palate and mask do not feel open, don't go on. It is useless."

"This is how to develop the ringing part of the lower voice - be sure that the tongue is forward and that it is relaxed under the chin when singing [a and ɛ]." [The hyoid bone raises on [a] and lowers on [ɛ].]

"High tones must have depth; low tones must have height." [Low vowels on high notes, high vowels on low notes.]

"Each time you go down with the sound, the support should come up higher on the chest."

"On lower notes, mouth almost closed - tongue on the edge of the teeth - the width of the instrument - never have any pinching of the sound as you go higher."

"Why do you work so hard to support the low notes? Casa harmonica should not drop; if you keep the chest lifted up there is a natural resonance."

"Make sure to give the maximum of height on the ending low note - then on the next attack you already have the position." [Have high harmonics in ending a low note so that you are prepared for the next attack.]

"On the attack, a low note needs high focus and the high note must have a low quality."

HIGH NOTES

"Give abdominal support before, not with high tones. The greatest intensity of machine is on the way down, not on the way up."

"In changing vowels on top notes, change only the lip, tongue, and jaw positions."

"You hurry the tempo because there is no support. Concentrate on the attack from the middle of the back for highest note. Now the whole bell is functioning. Don't be afraid, just set down on that point - the whole bell expanded."

"Be sure there is outward pull of the flexible ribs for the high notes."

"In covering or coloring a vowel, it must be done from the front of the mouth, not the back."

"Lean on the chest. Don't step back when taking high notes."

"Watch when singing high notes not to try to open the throat more. It is already open."

"Don't command the broad back - only the flexible ribs."

"Passaggio is knowledge. High register is support [and pronunciation]."

"On top notes you need depth, you can go to <u>aw</u> or depth on <u>ee</u>. Depth is not a quality of sound but is a sensation of the instrument."

"After enormous top notes and returning to middle voice, if the chest wants to fall, help hold it up by the hands - it looks like interpretation."

"Have depth in top on attack, otherwise the tone will be white." Mix [a] with [ʌ or ʊ] vowels.

"Let the shoulder blades go together more on the top." [Activates omohyoid muscles.]

"To avoid pushing of the high tones, feel low."

WIDTH - NARROWNESS

The beginning and ending of exercises must be authentic - same width, same power, same color - same position. If we begin with a 3-inch width and end with 1-1/2 inch width, our work is nil.

<u>Ah</u> forward in the mask, neither back nor spread.

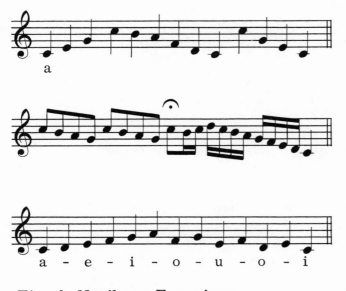

Use this exercise "to preserve the width of the palate and the throat."

"The mask has to grow so that it goes behind the ears, then the mask will have the maximum opening."

Sing this from the collarbone so that the coloratura is always clean and neat. Attack it behind the ears.

The [u] should have the space of the [o]. Otherwise this becomes dipthongish. Keep the width of the palate on [u].

Fig. 1 Novikova Exercises

"Keep a sense of great width of mask. To overcome nasality, concentrate on the width of the mask and of "ah" at the teeth. Watch to not narrow the palate on nasal voices. Imagine two points, like a pronged fork, going into the cheekbones for nasal voices. This will help them to keep from narrowing to the nose."

"Don't give the mask in an artificial way. Open up the mask and forget about it."

"During the inhaling the throat opens, so no change is necessary afterwards. The opening of the throat gets wider with deeper inhaling, causing growing volume of voice."

"When one covers the sound, one narrows the position of the mask."

"Falsetto narrows the opening of the mask and doesn't have quality. Then the voice needs security and space in the mask [ah]."

COLORATURA

"Every aspect of virtuosity should be built on the attitude of joy and happiness, not hard work."

"In making scalewise movement, repronounce the vowel on each note - a a a a a etc." [We will see that no two half steps on a vowel will have the same vowel color.]

"Use flexible mouth on the way up and down, closing when one comes down. If the jaw is not flexible it is hard to repronounce the vowel." [Tune the vowels when going up and down.]

"Coloraturas cut off the volume by depending on collar-bone support instead of diaphragm, thus allowing ease of fast emission. In olden days, all voices from bass to soprano, did this." [The resonators are smaller in coloratura passages than in cantilena.]

"No matter if the voice is light and flexible, don't neglect the setting of the machine; otherwise the throat becomes more and more narrow and the voice is lost in a few months, and in the case of light voice it becomes falsetto."

[All voices must find their resonation on long, slow exercises; to work only on fast scales entirely causes loss of resonation. Tosi (1723, tr. 1743, p. 57) stated that if agility is continually practiced too fast the voice "becomes an indifferent one."

"When going from coloratura to cantabile, "hook in" to the strength of the diaphragm." Also practice starting with cantabile, then go to fioratura with the shift of support from the diaphragm to collarbone support. This should eventually be automatic. This is the reason that some coloraturas have poor cantabiles and the fuller voices have poor agility.

"To go fast you must go slow. The less we interfere with nature, the more grateful nature is and the more the growth." [We find the natural phenomena of vibration and resonance more readily in slow passages and exercises. Then alternate coloratura exercises with slow.]

"Heavy voices need coloratura singing. Don't give in to slowness with them."

"Everything that has to do with fast singing is done with chest held high so that the diaphragm will not interfere."

COLORS OF VOICES

"When the voice is fixed in the mask, the voice can be allowed to brighten or darken automatically as the song calls for particular colors."

"Even the darkest voices should be vocalized very bright."

"Think staccato and sing staccato - the chest should not drop or dance."

"The larger a voice, the more elastically it must be trained to keep it from getting hard."

"Don't cover the sound. It is the vowel that is covered." [Modify the vowel instead of covering.]

"Bright vowels give lyric singing; darker vowels give dramatic singing."

"When the big voice is fixed in the mask, let them open up or darken automatically." [Small voices have less range of clear and sombre timbre.]

"What teachers do not understand is that a bright vocalization sound becomes very resonant when a singer performs."

"Lyric singing is more a matter of liquid pronunciation; dramatic singing is a matter of more incisive pronunciation."

INTONATION

"There is no such thing as incorrect intonation - the situation is actually a wrong position of the instrument. And usually the high tones are flat or sharp when the passaggio is produced wrong. In a scale, listen to the vocal line slowly to see where the voice drops and suddenly gets heavy. When the sound is sung into the mask correctly, the pitch will correct itself."

TECHNIQUE

"A singer must be a slave to his technique - if his mind wanders even once, the palate is happy to go astray."

DYNAMICS

"Mezza voce is the whole resonance with a small amount of tone."

"The voice always needs help on pianissimo; use brains; instrument can take only so much."

"The diminuendo doesn't mean that the sound has to leave the point and fall down. There has to be a much bigger control of the breath when we sing the diminuendo because we give more space inside of our mouths so that the sound remains in the same pitch. It has the same point but the size of resonator that we offer to it is larger. Consequently the same amount of breath is distributed in a bigger space and the sound gets smaller because it is in a bigger space." [Motion picture X-rays indicate the

laryngeal cavity contracts for forte and enlarges for
piano! Film by Delattre and Coffin.]

"For forte, have more sensation of opening or expanding
the chest, not pushing the tone."

"Never crescendo with 1) the power of the sound, but
2) with the expansion of the ribs. #1 annihilates the voice.
The sound is a consequence. Never do anything with the
sound. No right to change a throat or uvula - only change
in the chest and open up the mask."

"You have no right to touch the soft palate, uvula, hard
palate or base of the tongue."

With a rough singer she had to cut away volume - 1/3rd part of his voice. She
manipulated it to get it all cleaned up.

"It is much easier to sing forte than to sing piano."
[Most of the vocalization was between mf and forte.]

"When the instrument is ready, which means the pipe is
unified [standing wave in the vocal pipe] and always the
same, when there are no tensions, we think piano and we
sing piano. We think forte and we sing forte. The concentration of the breath control is in the piano much
harder than in the forte because we have to diminish
the amount of sound, keeping the sound in the same
point, the same resonator, and this we must achieve
with tremendous support of our breath." [This is done
by the contraction of the retaining muscle, the diaphragm,
which in its contraction pulls upon the lower ribs. They
must resist falling. A collapsed chest will not resonate.]

"Now the crescendo and diminuendo. Crescendo does
not mean that the sound has to lose the focus, the point,
when it gets bigger. In crescendo we give only a bigger
amount of vibration which we achieve exactly in the same
way as the string instrumentalists do. He presses his
finger more upon the point and he gives a crescendo of
his sound, controlling very much the bow. This is
exactly with us, we just concentrate more on the point,
pressing more upon the bow which is in this case our
breath."

INTERPRETATION

"Sing words, not syllables - exactly with the same accents as in the spoken word. These accents have to be put into singing. First recite the poem, then study the music, vocalizing, then comes the song."

"Place the voice on the heart but only after the machine is perfect. This is the end of our work."

"In singing, just keep the position and pronounce."

TALENT

"Talent is when there are brains, heart, machine and drive."

"One must always know what one is doing."

"In selection of students, give preference to the poorer instrument with better brains and better drive than fantastic instrument and no brains."

"Rossini - voce, voce, voce. Novikova - brains, brains, brains."

END OF PHRASE

"The action of the flexible ribs is up at the end of the phrase."

"End the phrase without a grunt."

"Every phrase should be finished in the direction of the mask - never towards the chest."

"Watch focus at finale - the resonator should not change, and the mouth opening does not need to change at the end."

"The last note was not high enough and not focused. If the last note is not focused and in tune, the exercise does not have any value - watch the last tone."

MISUSE OF VOICE

"The good voices can take the most beating. The mediocre voices give in immediately."

"It is nonsense to talk about people losing their voices; it is simply a result of the instrument being used badly. To sing well is easy, to sing badly is hard work."

PERFORMANCE

"Chew an apple to moisten the throat before and during a performance. The chewing flexes and refreshes the throat. One will not be bothered by dryness."

"Never sing any part of what will be done before the public the day of performance - if not learned by then it will never be learned. The singer may look at the score when resting, but not sing any of it."

VOCALIZATION

She frequently taught singers seated on a straight chair - men backwards on chair - women as usual in chair. The reason people are kept seated is to get them relaxed; when they are relaxed they can stand if they so desire.

"More effort is demanded from the ribs when a student is vocalized when seated."

"Don't give in to the student's desires - they should sing only that which is good for them at a specific time."

"If a note bothers, have the student actually seat himself during the singing of that note in a song or passage - the relaxation of the leg muscles will frequently help."

"Never do consecutive exercises of the same kind. Continually alternate types of vocalization; this helps the throat to be elastic."

"After an exciting exercise use a quiet one to see if the student has forced."

"Use muscle builders during singing over the passaggio (either heavy rubber belt or spring stretchers) to stimulate flexible ribs. [This gives the feeling of leaning against the chest as well as holding the breath back with the flexible ribs. See "appoggio of the voice," F. Lamperti, 1890, p. 22.]

"Do not overburden the instrument. The secret is to leave it contented. Never ask too much."

"No falsetto - nonsense."

"No humming." [See G. B. Lamperti (Brown), 1931, p. 104.]

"Never have weight on sounds. When you feel it has weight, it will not carry. Five vocalises with concentration are better than 30 with no knowledge of the machine."

Summary. Paola Novikova's teaching was based on two of the fundamental principles of the great Italian masters of singing. First, there had to be good breathing - she taught this by the inhalation described on page xxx. Second, there had to be a full and bright vowel sound which she obtained by the deep breath and high cheeks with the teeth showing. If her students had problems they were usually related to the concept of "full and bright vowels."

This book is a continuation of her work in that it is a study of vowels used as resonators in the instrument of the singing voice.

The patterns which she used for vocalization are shown on the next two pages.

Diatonic exercises (alternate with arpeggios),
On [a] unless marked otherwise.

Fig. 2. Novikova Exercises.

Arpeggio exercises (alternate with diatonic exercises).　　Paola Novikova
On [a] unless marked otherwise.

ra ———— ro ———— a ————

Words which she used to join vowels with the singing of single and double
consonants.

dormire	addio	il raggio
donare	il sole	Der Gott [ɔ]
dannaro	la collera	Die Götter [œ]
lampadina	il cuore	Der Hut
lubricare	la bocca	Die Hütte
la face	durezza	Die Wand
la faccia	vendetta	Die Wände [ɛ]
il Dio	il rogo	Die Heimat [ae]

Pierre Bernac has written:

"The first condition to sing effectively in any language is
to be intensely aware of its vowel sounds. I dare say that
this knowledge is particularly important for English-
speaking singers, who are not accustomed to pure vowel
sounds in their own language. [The vowel resonances

move in English on the diphthong vowels - other vowels also tend to move whereas vowels in the Romance languages are more stable.] This is why I believe that it is only by precise principles of phonetics that one can overcome the difficulties raised by the marriage of words and musical sounds." The NATS Bulletin, February 1962, p. 5.

How can speech be turned into the language of a musical instrument - that of the singing voice? Let us first look at a few pertinent elements of speech.

Chapter II. Classical Principles of SOUNDS OF SINGING

Mettete ben la voce
Respirate bene
Pronunciate chiaramente
Ed il vostro canto sarà perfetto.
    Gasparo Pacchierotti (1740-1821)

Pacchierotti was probably the greatest of the castrati. He sang at San Carlo, at the opening of La Scala (1798), and at the opening of La Fenice in Venice in 1792. (Quote collected by Philip A. Duey.)

Translated by Francesco Lamperti (1890). Introduction, "He who knows how to breathe and pronounce well, knows how to sing well," commenting... "and this is one of the greatest truths which study and experience have ever suggested to the successful cultivators of the art of singing."

"Quality is closely allied not only with vowel and consonant sound, regarding their own individual pitch, both of these phenomena being more or less radical and unchangeable. Because of pitch, which must be perfect, we shall see that vowel sounds and colors for expression are modified in relation to pitch. This is an important factor in pronunciation and expression much neglected and too often only partly understood."
    Witherspoon (1925, p. 74) who later became General Manager of the Metropolitan Opera Company. The underlining is this author's.

The contagion of diction books giving vowel values of speech has misled many singers and teachers of singing so that the phenomena of vowel and consonant pitches are less understood today. In our Phonetic Readings of Songs and Arias (1964), we stated the pitch value of vowels and that vowels must frequently be modified for sung pitch. Since that time we have found that consonants must be modified very carefully because of explosiveness and airflow, both of which can interfere with the vibrating vocal cords.

Teachers of the bel canto (beautiful singing) have been heard to say that the basis is pure vowels. My observation is that they wish to have pure tone rather than fuzzy and out of focus tone. These are photographer's terms which lead me to the observation that there are many similarities between light and sound. Vowels become resonators in singing and when their relationship to sung pitch is right, the tone is good; if not, the focus is soft and fuzzy.

"I purposely use the term "singing diction." This book [Phonetics and Diction in Singing] is not concerned with

speech as such and the elements of speech are treated
only as they are related to singing. One of the most
widespread errors is that spoken and sung sounds are
the same. Nothing is further from the truth. To sing
the way you speak may be advisable for popular music,
but it would make the voice sound brittle, harsh, and
uneven in opera, song, and choral music. The adjustment of phonetics to the vocal phrase is the real
problem for any accompanist and coach and the solution
constitutes a very important part of his art." Kurt Adler
(1965, p. 5). [The underlining is mine. Mr. Adler was
formerly a conductor and chorus master of the Metropolitan Opera.]

"The motives and movements of your mind and body make
up only half of the proposition of singing. Natural phenomena of vibration and resonance contribute to the other
half." G.B. Lamperti as quoted by William E. Brown
(1931, p. 22).

"He who knows how to pronounce (with the spaces of the
mouth and throat vibrating sympathetically to sung pitch),
and control the breath, knows how to sing."
W. Shakespeare, 1921.

"It is a strange fact that the throat is controlled by what
happens above it, in the acoustics of the head, through
word, vibration and resonance." G.B. Lamperti (W.E.
Brown, 1931).

"The secret of the phenomena met with in passing from
one register to another is to be found in the Resonator
of the vocal organs." Mathilde Marchesi, Opus 31. (In
ascending scales, close the vowel at the register transition, in descending scales - open the vowel.)

"It has become the habit of considering the breath as
the only cause for bad or good tone. This is the cause
of the eternal breath pressure with which so many singers
produce their tones and ruin their voices." Lilli Lehmann,
1914.

"The study of all the vowel forms is indispensible for
beauty of tone. The one-sided method of practising on the
open A (ah) is insufficient, because the voice also requires
for its perfect development a careful husbanding of the
breath, and a peculiar position of the larynx, and the play

of the tongue and lower jaw, which cannot be acquired by practicing only on A...." (Julius Stockhausen 1884, the teacher of both of the teachers of Dietrich Fischer-Dieskau).

"I should recommend to philologists who wish to define the vowels of different languages to fix them by the pitch of loudest resonance." Delattre has done that, I have determined their pitches for singing.

<u>What is Singing?</u> The best definition I have found is by the noted music critic, W. J. Henderson (1910, p. 1). "Singing is the interpretation of text by means of musical tones produced by the human voice." He later stated that if the singer "cannot fathom the secrets of his own throat, he must stop at the very threshold of his art." He believed that it was right that the singer should first learn to make <u>musical tones</u>, but if the singer stopped there without using them for interpretation, his art was incomplete. Henderson considered one without the other to be inadequate.

<u>What is Musical Tone?</u> That which is a musical tone to one person may not be a musical tone to another. We may be misled into believing that musical tone is a subjective perception. To the sensitive ear this is not the case. I quote Mancini (1777, p. 96):

> "If the harmony of... the mouth and 'fauces' is perfect, then the voice will be clear and harmonious. But if these organs act discordantly, the voice will be defective, and consequently the singing spoiled."

The best test of whether a tone is musical or not depends on whether it is "harmonious" or "discordant." A good tone is in <u>concord</u> with itself.

<u>What is a "bad tone?"</u> A "bad tone" fights with itself. It is actually a situation where two vibrators <u>interact</u> badly with each other. In stringed instruments the <u>conflict</u> is between a string and the resonator; in the organ the <u>conflict</u> is between the reed and pipe. In brass instruments the <u>conflict</u> is between the lips and the "trumpet." In the voice the <u>conflict</u> is between the vocal cords and the vocal tract.

<u>Purpose.</u> <u>The purpose of this text is to show how to bring the frequencies of the vocal cords and the vocal tract into concord on the various notes and vowels.</u> I believe that this book, the Chromatic Vowel Chart, and the Trumpet Principle exercises will enable singers and teachers of singing to "fathom the secrets of their throats" so that many more singers can cross the thresholds of their art and truly realize the vocal talent and musical art with which they are endowed. I agree with Benade's philosophy (1973, p. 35):

"Whether one is physicist, a musician or an instrument maker, one tries to make use of any tools at hand to provide an instrument that helps rather than hinders the creative effort of music making."

I hope that these efforts will be accepted as an aid to creative music making!

CHAPTER III.   THE VOICE AS A MUSICAL INSTRUMENT - BEL CANTO

There is a fundamental precept of learning - knowledge must be built on knowledge. The brain cannot perceive a new idea unless it is related to something it already knows. In light of this truth, I will mention a few characteristics of instruments, which all musicians know, and compare them with those of the voice. All instruments have an activator, a vibrator, and a resonator (or resonators). I will describe the phenomena of sound in as visual a manner as possible. Sound, of course, is unseen but there are many visible parallels.

First of all I must refer to Manuel Garcia as stating that the voice can transform itself into a multitude of instruments (Memoire sur la Voix Humaine, 1872, Paschke, 1984 tr. p. xxvi.)

PIANO

Activator.   There is a hammer which makes the strings vibrate. In singing there is the breath which causes the vocal cords to vibrate. The touch of the pianist gives the dynamics of the melodic line - that means that there are various touches controlled through the imagery of the pianist. In singing there are various breath "supports" which are used in voicing the height and dynamics of the melodic line.

Vibrator.   In the piano, the strings have different lengths and thicknesses from the lower notes to the higher notes. In the voice, the vocal cords vary in length and thickness from the lowest to the highest note of the range. This has been referred to as the thick and thin. This is only partly true since the vowels are involved with the shortened/lengthened and thickened/thinned vocal cords. They also vary with the registers which have long been defined in the classical schools of vocal pedagogy.

Resonator.   In the piano, there is a sounding board. With a poor sounding-board a piano has an inferior tone - it is the resonator of the instrument. In the voice, the chest is the sounding board up to the area between c^1 and e^1 in all voices, Male and Female. This has been called Chest Voice.

Birgit Nilsson speaks of the sound banging into her head (Hines, 1982, p. 200). When this occurs she says that she is singing into the mask. The Head Voice begins in men and women around d^2 according to Garcia (Paschke, 1984, tr. p.18) or f^2 according to Marchesi (reprinted 1920). The Head Voice is known to those teachers who train Rossini, Donizetti, and Bellini tenors with the high extension. Other male voices do not sing in this register. It is actually supported falsetto and was taught by the Neapolitan tenor, Sbriglia, who made his debut in America with Adelina Patti in Bellini's "La Sonnambula." He was

a Bel Canto artist himself and used the Falsetto in finding the high voice of
Jean de Reszke who sang as a baritone before coming to him.

Thus the Falsetto, Head Voice diagonals of the Chromatic Vowel Chart (inside
the back cover of this book) are confirmations of the teachings of the Garcia -
Marchesi schools of singing. Both registers are related harmonically to the
vowel pitches on the chart. It is known today to teachers who have taught both
Counter Tenors and the tenor extension of the Bel Canto period. Incidentally,
I have heard teachers argue about whether registers exist; I have never heard
them discuss WHY and HOW they exist other than in relationship to vocal cord
activity.

JEW'S HARP

Jew's Harp. To understand the resonance characteristics of the vocal tract let
us think about this toy which is a rather primitive instrument. Although the
Jew's Harp, [called jaw's harp in German] has not yet been called an orchestral
instrument, it shows very clearly the resonance of the vocal tract (although the
movement of the jaw is denied). If the lamina of the Jew's harp has a frequency
of 100 Hz the interger muliples of that frequency will be heard which are in the
vowel resonator of the throat. This has been described by Dr. Schubert
(Juilliard Symposium, 1982). Players of the Jew's Harp are playing the
overtones of the lamina as a melodic line.

FRENCH HORN

The natural French Horn, without valves, was controlled in pitch by the use of
the hand in the bell. That means that pitch was controlled by the lips, by
varying the air pressure within the instrument, and the opening at the bell by
the use of the hand. The singing voice does the same by the vocal cords and by
various positions of the tongue, jaw, lips, and soft palate. This positioning
involves the use of phonetics which has been a major study of mine since the
research and publication of Phonetic Readings of Songs and Arias (1964).
Delattre and I made a preliminary definition of the pitch of vowels (p. v) at
that time. At present the public hears computer voices daily on the telephone,
radio, and television, due to the developments in the fields of acoustical-
phonetics and synthesized speech.

Another fascinating attribute of the French Horn is that the piping is so long
that the high and close together harmonics (modes of vibration) are used a
great deal in performance. In contrast, the vocal tract is so short that only the
low Male voices are singing with a large number of high harmonics. On spectrograms the sung pitch appears to be missing. The sung pitch is a "phantom
fundamental." In reality it is not there but the ear hears it by means of the
overtones (Potter, Kopp, Kopp 1965, pp. 377 - 400; Coffin 1980, pp. 206 - 226.)

C. Johansson, J. Sundberg, and H. Wilbrand (STL-QPSR 4/1982, p. 117) have reported the most intensive acoustical investigation of the Female voice to date. The Female high voice has very few harmonics and the lowest one is tuned to the sung pitch (fundamental) by the opening of the mouth (the "bell" of the instrument), the positioning of the lips, and, in contrast to many statements to the contrary, the raising of the larynx. I would add that there is another control which is very observable on Television, the raising of the head.

PIPE ORGAN

First of all we have inherited the term "registers" from the organ which have been defined in singing as being "a series of consecutive and homogenous sounds produced by the same mechanical means" (Garcia, 1872, p. 6). It is interesting that the early organ builders, who were extremely knowledgeable about acoustics, named many of their sounds after the various instruments because of the timbres of the stops, viz. trumpet, strings, flute, reeds, vox humana, etc.

We can see on the organ that the shorter pipe gives a higher pitch and a longer pipe gives a lower pitch. In the singing voice, this can be seen in the Back series of vowels [u - o - ɔ - /a/], the Umlaut series of vowels [y - ɤ - ø - œ - /a/] but not on the Front series of vowels [i] to /a/ since the tuning is primarily done by the tongue and the jaw. It can be seen on the Neutral series of vowels [ə - ʊ - (ʌ) ʌ] by lip and jaw movement. The rounding of the lips and the closing of the jaw lower the pitch of the resonator. The spreading of the lips and the opening of the jaw raise the pitch of the resonator.

There is a most interesting phenomenon in the manner by which the reed stops are tuned on the organ. The technician first tunes the reed and then tunes the resonator to the reed. If the resonator is not in tune with the reed the pitch is unstable and the sound is unresonant. In the terms of the acoustician, there is negative interference. When the resonator is in exact tune with the reed there is positive interference and maximum resonance. This same acoustical condition exists in the singing voice. When the resonator of the vocal tract stands in a position where there is harmonic agreement with the pitch of the vocal cords there is maximum resonation and an easy support of the breath. This is called "sympathetic vibration." This penomenon of the voice has been overlooked by most otolaryngologists, researchers, observers, and writers of the voice being mentioned only tangentially in the Juillard Symposia, Care of the Professional Voice, (1971 - 1982). In my opinion, this is one of the most important facets concerned with the care of the Professional Voice - the sung pitch/vowel pitch relationship in singing. When the relationship is good - the voice will have its best health; when the relationship is poor - the voice is beaten and becomes unhealthy, fatiguing quickly. In this situation singers begin looking for ways to relax! Relaxing usually implies being phlegmatic.

TRUMPET

In the trumpet, as in other brass instruments, there are the two vibrating lips brought together and placed against a pipe. With the proper movement of air through them they are brought into vibration. The same occurs in the voice.

If the lips are drawn tightly and vibrated, a higher pitch will result; a comparable use of the vocal cords exists in singing. If the lips are placed too tightly together, there will be no vibration; the same is true in singing.

If the lips are puckered into the mouthpiece the 'thickened' lips will give a low tone. The same is true in the singing voice, but the thin vocal-lipped brighter and open vowels near /A/ are more effective for low notes.

Without moving keys on the trumpet it is possible to change height of pitch. I have chosen to call this "bugling." The same occurs less obviously in the voice (yodeling) and is related to its register changes. This is because in the trumpet the tubing is significantly longer than in the "horn of the voice" [usually called "vocal tract" by those studying the singing voice as an acoustical phenomenon]. The vocal tract (resonance pipe) length varies shorter and longer than 16 centimeters (about 6 inches) depending on voice classification (in the German system known as "Fach").

As a trumpet player must learn to vary the length of his tubing by use of fingering the valves on that instrument (or the trombone by the use of the slide), for best tonal results the singer must be able to vary the effective length of his instrument by the use of various vowel colors. These are formations of the vocal tract caused by movements of the lips, tongue, depressor, and/or elevator muscles of the larynx, and action of the soft palate. This is the basic thrust of this text which is an extension of the vowel modifications of Garcia (1984, p. 46), Stockhausen (1884, p. 8), Delle Sedie (1885, p. 46), Witherspoon (1925, p. 92), Appleman (1967, p. 235), and others.

I would like to highlight in a dramatic way the trumpet principle as it applies to the singing voice.

Sound the Trumpet. Let us begin by discussing the sound of the trumpet in a dialogue between a salesman and a boy. This will be followed by a dialogue between a singing teacher and his student.

Boy: I would like to buy a trumpet. What do you have?

Salesman: Here is one, a beautiful model.

Boy: May I try it?

Salesman: Yes.

Boy: P h g r m p h Squawk. I don't like the vibrator. May I have another one?

Salesman: My son, you see the vibrator is made up of your upper and lower lips; obviously we cannot give you new lips.

Boy: Well, what do I buy when I buy a trumpet?

Salesman: All you buy is a resonator.

Boy: But I want to play different notes.

Salesman: If you press your 1st, 2nd or 3rd valves in different orders, you will find that you make different notes.

Boy: Why did the notes change?

Salesman: Because you changed the pitch of your resonator.

Boy: How interesting! But I do not want to move my fingers.

Salesman: Then you press your lips differently to get higher and lower notes.

Boy: What are those notes?

Salesman: They are modes of vibration of a resonator yet each pitch you play has its own overtones.

Boy: When I glide from one mode of vibration to another, what is that called?

Salesman: It is a lip slur. These devices sound all of the pitches on the trumpet.

Boy: Thanks. I think I'll take it.

Sound the voice. Ten years later the boy studied singing.

Singer: I would like to have a voice like Enrico Caruso.

Teacher: I am sorry but you must use the voice with which you were born.

Singer: I really do not like the vibrator.

Teacher: Sorry, you must learn to vibrate the vocal cords which are in your throat.

Singer: What happens when I learn to vibrate them?

Teacher: You will find that you have more registers than you knew you had.

Singer: What are registers?

Teacher: Different ways in which the vocal cords vibrate. Sometimes your vocal cords act as though you are pursing your lips so that they become thick; at other times the vocal cords are pulled in a way to give higher pitch. Then there is another way - the vocal cords, after they are pulled tight, come together touching each other in the front and back allowing a very small part of the cords to vibrate. Sometimes they can be used in such a way that there is a whistling sound.

Singer: Can I have all of these?

Teacher: Yes, all these different ways of vibrating are usually attainable in all voices.

Singer: What did you say they are called?

Teacher: They are called registers. For men they are called Chest, Mixed, Falsetto and when above c^2 Head. [Based on the Garcia definition of registers (1872, p. 9)]. For women they are called Chest, Middle, Head, and Whistle voice.

Singer: Can you make something out of the vibrator I have?

Teacher: Yes, it can be developed so that it will be a good singing vibrator.

Singer: Fine. Now I must tell you I do not like my resonator. Can I have a new one?

Teacher: No. You must use the one with which you were born but you must learn to use it in an instrumental way in singing, somewhat like a trumpet. This is especially so in large halls.

Singer: Why is that?

Teacher: Because in singing you must pronounce vowels on a sung pitch.

Singer: But I can sing any vowel on any pitch in my voice.

Teacher: In the first place I must tell you that you do not have as many pitches in your voice as you will eventually have, and that you are not resonating the vowels very well on the pitches which you do sing.

Singer: Why is that?

Teacher: Because vowels have pitch and your vocal cords have pitch. If they are in synchronization with each other, you will have a full sounding, resonant, and free sounding voice. At the present time you do not know how to pronounce when singing.

Singer: That is very disturbing to me because I consider myself to be a linguist and that I know exactly how to pronounce when I sing.

Teacher: You are to be congratulated on being linguistic. It will help you in your singing languages. However, you must know how to modify your vowels in singing.

Singer: Do you mean to say that I cannot pronounce in singing the same way I pronounce in speaking?

Teacher: Yes. I repeat, that the language must be slightly changed. It is somewhat like the scale of the piano being tempered so that there can be many key centers. When a piano is in tune, it is slightly out of _tune_ and because of this it allows us to perform the music of western civilization with its harmonies and sonorities.

Singer: So if I change my vowels slightly, I am supposed to resonate better?

Teacher: Yes, and you will also sing higher and lower. It is a very sensitive situation and is now notated so that you will know exactly the color of vowels you should pronounce on the various notes to have the sympathetic resonance which amplifies the classical singing voice. This is the reason for the Chromatic Vowel Chart.

Singer: How does this relate to a trumpet and vibrating lips?

Teacher: Unlike your trumpet, where the resonator has great control over the vibration of the lips, the trumpet of the voice (the vocal tract) is so short that it is almost independent of the vibrations from the vocal cords. However, a positive effect of the vibration of the vocal tract on the vibration of the vocal cords is observed through good intonation, good tone, easy vibrato, and a forward, full sound of the voice.

Singer: Is there a bad effect on my vocal cords if my resonator is not right?

Teacher: Yes, there is. Poor intonation, a weak sound, and a poor vibrato. The vibrations from the trumpet of the voice tend to cancel or alter the vibrations from your vocal cords.

Singer: Is this a new idea?

Teacher: No. It is a very old idea which can be better understood today.
            Pacchierotti over 150 years ago said, "He who knows how to breathe
            and pronounce well [resonate], knows how to sing well." Garcia
            and the Lampertis were aware of this effect.

Singer: Have people ignored this in the art of singing?

Teacher: They may have consciously ignored it but subconsciously the
            successful teachers have listened very intently in training voices
            and have gradually found the correct relationship of vibrator and
            resonator for the best singers.

Singer: This sounds very technical. Are there better words for describing
            this relationship?

Teacher: Yes. It is called focusing or placing the voice; training the voice
            so it makes big waves.

Singer: But I do not want to make big waves all of the time.

Teacher: Of course. You see, you must know how to make big waves so that
            you can control the smaller ones. Soft singing with good resonation
            requires a great deal of physical effort. The best singers become
            quite athletic in their vocal technique.

Singer: Are you saying that I do not have vocal talent since my range is
            short and I do not have much resonance?

Teacher: No. I will say that your talent is not fully evident. You study so
            that you can realize your talent. You may sing for years before
            you attain your potential. Only those with excellent material and
            perseverance can get to the top. You may need to work for some
            time before you will know the vocal and musical talents with which
            you are endowed.

Singer: Should I practice the "trumpet" and vibrator exercises regularly?

Teacher: Yes. It is a sure way by which you will find the individual quality
            of your voice. You are simply obeying Nature's law of the har-
            monic series in a musical instrument when you practice in this
            way. As G. B. Lamperti said, "The great need of a teacher of
            singing is the ability to individualize voices." So, take your
            vibrator and your resonator and practice the relationships about
            3 or 4 times each day for periods of 5-10 minutes. In this way
            your voice will show its individuality and have a healthy

development. Remember, take care of your vocal cords. They are the <u>only</u> vibrators you will ever have. No hoarseness ever, no allergies, no colds. Health is a basis of your wealth as a singer. Much of your health is dependent upon your developed breathing and developed throat musculature.

Singer: Must I memorize all of the relationships of the Chromatic Vowel Chart to sung pitch?

Teacher: No. Most of your memory will be muscle memory with your ear rather intuitively telling the throat what to do. You will eventually memorize certain phonetic relationships to the various pitches in your singing voice.

Singer: If it eventually becomes intuitive, or almost intuitive, why should I know what goes on?

Teacher: Your knowledge of what occurs will give you greater security and concentration in your singing. This enables you to become more absorbed in your roles and in the musical nuances of your songs.

Singer: Does not this take a great deal of work?

Teacher: Yes. It calls for discipline and dedication. In any sport or in any physical art, great concentration and dedication are required to reap significant rewards even by the most talented.

Singer: What do consultants who work with the instrument companies say about this?

Teacher: Arthur Benade in his <u>Fundamentals of Musical Acoustics</u> (1976, p. 382) tells of hearing a recording of Teresa Stich-Randall singing <u>Porgi amor</u> from Mozart's <u>Nozze di Figaro</u>. "Whenever a note of the aria persisted a little, she seemed to be "tuning" one or another of the vowel formants [resonance] matching already complete, but the adjustment would take place rather quickly, making the tone "bloom" in a most pleasing way. Enquiry among singers shows that this mode of singing is not in general consciously cultivated." [The Chromatic Vowel Chart was formed to assist in consciously cultivating this resonance of a voice on all of its sung pitches.]

The Trumpet Principle. The trumpet principle is stated by Arthur H. Benade (1973, p. 24) who has written for the C. G. Conn Ltd. Technical Reports and has been involved in the study of mouthpieces for King Musical instruments.

Of the brass instruments, I use the trumpet as an analogy of the voice because the "tonal resonances" of the vowels fall within the range of the B♭ piccolo trumpet, whether a singer is a coloratura soprano or a bass. I have enclosed in brackets the vocal terms which describe the relationships in the singer's throat.

> "A trumpet [voice] produces musical tones when the vibration of the players lips [the singer's vocal cords] interact with standing waves in the instrument [the vocal tract]. These waves are generated when acoustic energy is sent back by the instrument's bell [the opening at the lips and teeth]." Benade (1973, p. 24)

If the poor trumpet player does not adjust his lips exactly to the pitch of the resonator, the quality and intonation will be bad. A system of practice is to "buzz" a mouthpiece at a certain pitch and to slowly insert it into the trumpet which is at that pitch. That condition will give the best quality and resonance.

The singer, however, varies the resonance of the vocal tract so that it synchronizes with the composer's pitch which signifies a particular vibration of the vocal cords. His pronunciation echos the "trumpet effect" in singing. This is acoustical effect in singing. This text will show how that phenomenon can be heard and used.

In a practical way a singer can "buzz" his throat by thumping it on the side, or by playing pitches into the front of the mouth by means of a Vowel Resonator hooked up to a Concertmate or some similar instrument. When the singer tunes the throat to a resonant vowel, he should immediately sing that vowel on that pitch. It can also be sung an 8ve below or two 8ves below. Singing a particular pitch is no problem to a singer - it is almost intuitive. Tuning the vocal tract is the part of the vocal instrument which needs instruction; that tuning is by harmonic pronunciation.

Fathom the secrets of your own throat. What is the mysterious secret of the throat? Twenty-five years of work in the area of vowel pitch has led me to believe that a basic secret of singing is the harmonic interaction of sung vibration and vowel vibration. My first statement on the pitch of vowel resonances was made with the collaboration of Dr. Pierre Delattre in the Preface to Phonetic Readings of Songs and Arias (1964 p. v.) The following values were given:

Frequencies of the pharyngeal cavity for the various vowels in male and female throats are

æ	a	ɑ (750 cps)	roughly	g^2
ɛ	œ	ɔ (600 cps)	roughly	d^2
e	ø	o (456 cps)	roughly	a^1
i	y	u (350 cps)	roughly	f^1

I   II   III   Series (Modified from Howie and Delattre.)

Fig. 3. Delattre and Coffin Vowel Frequencies

This utilized the following symbols of the International Phonetic Alphabet.

THE INTERNATIONAL PHONETIC ALPHABET.
(Revised to 1951.)

Fig. 4.

VOWELS

	Front	Central	Back
Close	i y		ɯ u
Half-close . . .	e ø		ɤ o
		ə	
Half-open . . .	ɛ œ		ʌ ɔ
	æ		
Open		a	ɑ ɒ

The pronunciation of vowels used in this text is as follows:

u **u** as in English, *pool*, (dark U).
ə **ə** rounded (close) schwa, Fr. *le*.
ɯ **ɯ** [u] with lips either drawn back or neutral, (bright U).
ʊ **ʊ** half rounded (half close) schwa *pull*.
o **o** The German O, *ohne*, (dark O).
ɤ **ɤ** O with lips either drawn back or neutral, (bright O) *jovial*.
ʌ **ʌ** lateral (open) schwa, *fun*.
ɔ **ɔ** as in American, *awe*, (dark *awe*).
ʊ **ʊ** our coinage of the lateral ɔ , rotated 90 degrees, (bright *awe*), *joy*.
ɒ **ɒ** dark ah, *father*.
ɑ **ɑ** lateral Ah, corners back, and jaw down, *shout*.

a **a** front ah, Italian A, corners back, *mine*. without diphthong ending.
æ **æ** as in American, *fast*.
ɛ **ɛ** as in American, *met*.
e **e** first sound in *may*, American, *mitt*.
ɪ **ɪ** as in American, *meet*.
i **i** as in American, *meet*.
œ **œ** lips rounded ɛ, Ger.*Götter*, Fr. *coeur*.
ø **ø** lips rounded e, Ger. *schön*, Fr. *peu*.
ʏ **ʏ** lips rounded ɪ, Ger. *Hütte*.
y **y** lips rounded i, Ger. *fühl*, Fr. *du*.

Subsequent research, investigation with Dr. Delattre until his death in 1969, and consultations with Dr. Fritz Winckel of Berlin, Dr. Richard Luchsinger of Zurich, and Yvonne Rodd-Marling of London have led me to enlarge the 1964 values of vowel frequencies to the following notation which varies slightly with voice classification:

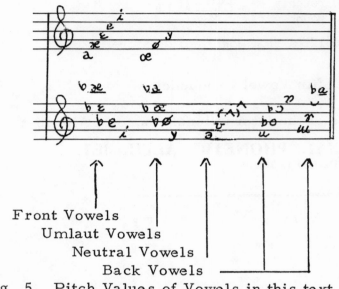

The upper resonances of vowels, R^2. It has been found unnecessary to tune them.

The lower resonance of vowels, R^1 is heavily underlined on the Chromatic Vowel Chart on the Front, Neutral, Back, and Umlaut vowels. They are doubly underlined on the charts on pp. 152 and 165.

Front Vowels
Umlaut Vowels
Neutral Vowels
Back Vowels

Fig. 5. Pitch Values of Vowels in this text

It is interesting that some half-steps in some singing voices feel like they are "a mile wide." Because of this sensitivity, it was necessary that vowel pitches be defined chromatically for use with the singing voice. The Chromatic Vowel Chart has been created to stand behind the piano keys (of a Steinway Grand Piano, other keyboards may vary in size) to give the vowel color-sung pitch relationships with greatest exactness. The lower vowel resonances, R^1, are notated on the treble clef in Fig. 5. and are heavily underlined on the Chromatic Vowel Chart. The upper resonances of the Front and Umlaut vowels are indicated on the Vowel Chart between Notes #41 and #59. There is little advantage in tuning them.

Can every vowel be sung on every pitch? Since vowels have pitch and vocal cords have pitch there is a problem. In the instruments, the pitch of the reed or vibrating lips is controlled largely by the resonator. With the voice, the vibrator is almost independent of the resonator. However, Chiba and Kajiama (1958, p. 195) state:

"When a vowel is pronounced at a very high pitch the vocal chords cannot completely perform their functions and the larynx is not in its normal condition. This also accompanies a deformation of the vocal cavity. Thus, in order to observe the change of vowel quality occurring according to the pitch of the voice, it is necessary to use artificial vocal chords or an artificial larynx. These make it

> possible to get rid of the effect produced by the vocal
> cavity being deformed on account of an effort to emit a
> high voice." [The underlining is mine.]

Singers cannot avoid the changing form of the vocal cavity in singing songs of
extended ranges, so there is a physiological law. The deformation of the vocal
tract results in the brightening for low tones and rounding for the high tones
(Garcia, 1894, p. 16). For the "trumpet effect" to occur there is also an
acoustical law which must be obeyed. The pitch of the vowels involved must
also be harmonic with sung pitch or there will be a weakening and/or distuning
of vocal cord vibrations. These modifications are notated in Chapter VI. xxx

I must conclude that the basis of "instrumental" singing is the
harmonic series. The more ringing and vibrant the singer
wishes his voice to become, the more he should utilize the mar-
monic values of the Chromatic Vowel Chart. The more a singer
wishes to approximate the sounds of speech, the more he can let
his voice become non-harmonic. There will be a reduced size
of voice and carrying power in the process. (How often we have
heard a spoken explanation of a song in a weak voice and then,
when the song is begun there is a singing voice which carries.
This is a definition of the voice used in speech and as an instrument. The voice carries in singing because of harmonic amplification.) This means that as the painter has dark and light
colors with which to paint, the singer has harmonic and nonhar-
monic sounds with which to sing. The more the loud nonhar-
monic sounds are used, the more wearing it is upon the vibrating
vocal cords. The singing-actors who use a large amount of non-
harmonic sounds in their voices do not last as long as those who

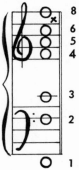

The Harmonic
Series

Fig. 6

are noted for their beautiful singing. There are singers who are noted for
what they can do with voice; there are those who are noted for what they can
do without voice. The Chromatic Vowel Chart is concerned with the formation
of the voice as a musical instrument. The degree to which a singer desires to
deviate from the harmonic is at his own artistic discretion. However, Nature
does not allow the vocal cords to be treated roughly over a very long period of
time without penalty.

How is it possible to hear the harmonics of the singing voice? By a better
technique of hearing, just as a microscope enables the eye to see more. The
vowel-pitch phenomenon can be heard by sympathetic resonance to any external
vibration (that has pitch) played either into the front of the mouth by a Vowel
Resonator or against the side of the vocal tract by a vibrator used as an
artificial larynx. The technique is very simple - hold the vocal cords together
while holding the breath and mimic vowel sounds until you hear an increase of
resonance (loudness of sound). Immediately sing on that vowel. The various
vowels can be pronounced in such a way that the harmonics and their vowel
colors can be heard loudly and distinctly felt. What benefits can be gained by
practicing with such an instrument?

1. A singer can play the actual pitches of his song on the organ and at the same time pronounce the vowels, note by note. Some vowels will resonate - others will not. The singer can stop and search with his lips, mouth, and jaw until he finds the resonant vowel. If he immediately sings that vowel-color, the voice is "focused." Invariably it has a different pronunciation from that which he uses in his speech patterns.

He finds that he must slightly alter his pronunciation for resonation. How can he remember what the pronunciation sounds like? He can simply write a phonetic of the vowel color over the note he was singing. A whole new world is opened up to the singer, and he often finds that he/she has several options from which to choose. In order to resonate, the tone must frequently be given a slightly different color from that shown in our Phonetic Readings of Songs and Arias (1964). Hence the Chart is an addenda to that book. This is the art which one must use for good singing and for good diction - the art of vowel modification.

2. No person's voice can be recognized when pronouncing with an "artifical larynx" or with a Vowel Resonator with an electric organ hookup. Even a man's voice is no different from a woman's voice which means that the overtone-vowel relationships are not only impersonal, they are sexless! By its use, male voice teachers can feel what the pronunciation of female singers must be in various arias. An appropriate transposition downward for a few semi-tones is indicated by the Chromatic Vowel Chart arrow placement as noted in the upper corners of the chart. This is related to what the arrow placement should be for the voice classification of his student. Furthermore, women teachers can feel what it is like for men to pronounce their words in songs and arias.

3. Diphthongs can be heard immediately by the diminishing of resonance on the vanish. The student soon learns to maintain the vowel. If he then sings on that vowel-color, the vibrato will spin because the tone is "in the groove."

4. One of the most fascinating things to me has been that the student almost reflexively states what he has done to find the resonance. This is all to the good because he has verbalized his sensations and in the process

brought to his conscious knowledge what has happened.
All that the teacher needs to do is to nod his head to
indicate that he understands. Thus the student does the
verbalizing from his senses, which is a much better way
of transferring learning to his brain than for a teacher to
describe a sensation and hope the student can bring it
about by an inefficient monitoring process. In the study
of melodic and harmonic pronunciation, both the student
and teacher have the joy of discovery.

Vocal Fatigue. The great teachers of singing have clearly stated that singing
should be restricted to two or three short periods a day of a half hour or so.
Garcia (1894, p. 15) stated that beginners could sing for four or five minutes at
a time "but this may be repeated three times a day. If it causes the slightest
fatigue it must be stopped at once for the rest of the day." Chevalier Jackson
(1940, p. 463), the great American specialist on diseases of the throat stated:

> "About 95 percent of the aspirants for a career in vocal
> music are compelled to give up because of myasthenia
> laryngis. [The muscular disability of the vocalis muscles
> which is evident in a chronic hoarseness.] The damage
> is usually done by the training necessary to increase the
> range upward."

He states that "prevention is better than cure," and that treatment is absolute
rest of the singing voice for three to six months with only a limited use of the
conversational voice, say 500 words a day. He found that under all lies the
fundamental fact that most persons who have myasthenia laryngis are incessant
conversationalists!

What should one do? Watch with care long practice sessions, extended periods
of choral singing, opera performances on consecutive nights, and extensive
talking. Talking where the decibel level is high is especially fatiguing, such as
on airplanes, on subways and at parties. At the height of a career when the
voice is mature, schedules rarely call for more than three performances a week
and there are "covers" when the singer is indisposed. When one fatigues or
loses his voice the vocal cords change their mass and the muscles within the
vocal cords must do extra work to maintain the height of pitch. Eventually they
lose their ability to contract the vocal cords to the usual vibrating pitch of the
voice. If the muscles are overworked, they may permanently lose some of their
ability to contract. There is also the possibility that the vocal cords will have
their mass permanently enlarged. Thick vibrators give lower pitch than thin -
look at strings and reeds.

All of this pertains to one thing, the primary vibrator and the muscles within the vocal cords themselves. Transplants are unavailable, the pair with which the singer is born are his only ones. If opera directors, musical directors, conductors, accompanists, singing teachers, and/or choral conductors think the singer is protective and egocentric about the care of his voice, so be it. One thing for sure, whether taken away by someone else or by the singer himself, the cords cannot be restored by exercises or medication.

Jackson states (1940):

> "No training or special exercises can be carried out without working the already jaded muscles....the muscles must be allowed to recover from the damage previously done."

As a principle of practice, be careful of how much you sing even if it is great singing. This traditional advice applies even to the most healthy voices and the best singers.

Since singing is the combination of languages with the vocal instrument let us study the pertinent elements of language and see how they can be combined. Needless to say, some singing requires more of the instrumental aspect. I would call this the bel canto. Other types of singing demand more of the language. Some singers are adept in combining the instrumental with one language, some with many languages, and too many with no language. If a singer expects to have a significant career in today's market he/she should have great skills in combining the linguistic and instrumental elements of expression.

CHAPTER IV. LINGUISTIC ELEMENTS OF SINGING

The Classification of Vowels

All <u>spoken</u> languages have vowels and consonants. Some of the ancient languages were <u>written</u> only with consonants. For sounds to carry there must be vowels and the inflections, rhythms, and emphases which can be placed upon them. Language is altered in singing because the pitches affect the vowel resonances and some of the consonants. The inflections, rhythms, and emphases are musically notated by the composer, making words less easily understood - especially in the higher pitches.

Vowels are changes of timbre brought about by the articulators of the vocal tract. Delattre (1965, p. 47) in Fig. 7. shows the formations of the vowels which outline the vowel quadrilateral. We will see later that for most spoken vowels there is a resonance formed behind the tongue hump which has been called R^1 by Chiba and Kajiama, and a resonance in front of the tongue hump which they called R^2. There are other vowels which lie at about every point within these bounds in singing. These are variations and mixtures of the Cardinal Vowels shown. Delattre (p. 284 of this text) states there is another manner of forming R^1 when the throat is formed as a stopped pipe.

The vowels on the [i - æ] series are called Front Vowels and on the [u - ɒ] series are called Back Vowels. The Umlaut Vowels are the Front Vowels with rounded lips. In singing most vowels seem to approach a lessened tongue hump, so I have constructed a Neutral (Mute) series based on the schwa vowel /uh/ which I have (in Helmholtz terminology) defined by pitch of loudest resonance for use in the Chromatic Vowel Chart.

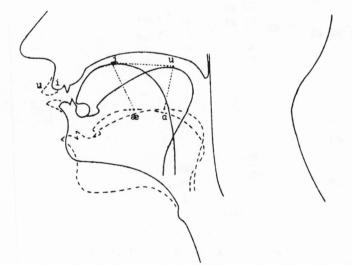

From COMPARING THE
PHONETIC FEATURES by P.
Delattre.   Permission Julius
Groos Verlag

Fig. 7. The Physiological Basis of the IPA

There are those who believe that vowels are made by the vocal cords. If that is true, how is it possible to speak by means of an artificial larynx?

Scripture (1906) formed artificial throats in which he used rubber bands for vocal cords. The artificial throats were formed to create different vowel sounds. Through a plastic window on the side of the throats he was able to see that the rubber band vocal cords operated differently for the various vowels. This was their <u>reaction</u> to the resonating air in the artificial vocal tract. They did not <u>make</u> the vowels. The vowels are made by the different resonances (basically R^1 and R^2) of the vocal tract. Delattre confirmed this by speech synthesis on the Cooper Pattern Playback at Haskin's Laboratory (1952).

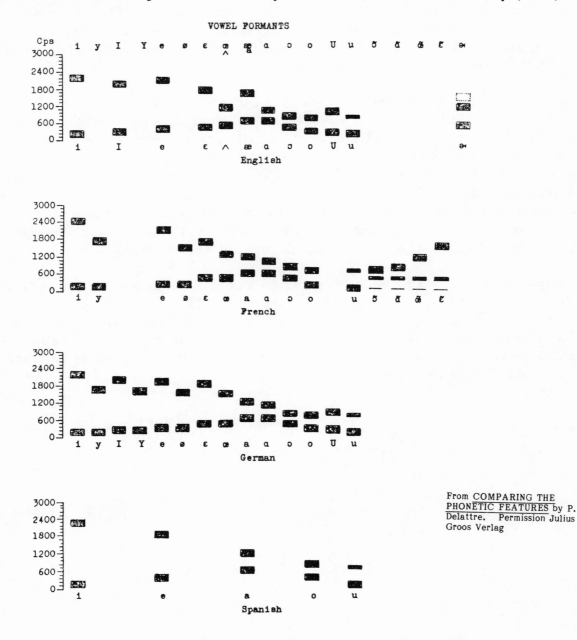

From COMPARING THE PHONETIC FEATURES by P. Delattre. Permission Julius Groos Verlag

A presentation of the musical relation among vowel formants in English, French, German and Spanish, as they would appear on the average sound spectrograms of a male voice. These formant frequencies will produce satisfactory synthetic vowels only at a standard voice fundamental of 120 cps.

Fig. 8. Delattre's Vowel Formants for English, French, German, and Spanish

In Fig. 8 Delattre (1965, p. 48) has illustrated many of the acoustical values of vowels in English, German, French, and Spanish.

The frequency numbers can be thought of as pitch by using those on the Chromatic Vowel Chart when it is placed on the piano with the arrow on f^1, or by simply looking at the Chart away from the piano.

Fig. 8 shows that vowels have different resonance (formant) values in the different languages. It also shows that vowels are essentially two-part chords for all vowels but the [ɤ] and the Nasal vowels. The example is with a Fundamental pitch of B♭ in a Male voice with overtones at each 120 Hz above it. It shows the ascending and descending pitch of the vowels as used in the Chromatic Vowel Chart. Very important - it shows that certain vowels have common lower resonances - [i, y, and ʊ], [e, ø, and o], [ɛ, œ, and ɔ], and [æ, a, ɑ, and ɒ]. You and I will use this phenomenon to help place the voice and to equalize the vowels.

Since the upper resonances are in the high harmonics which are very close together, I have found that it is <u>not</u> necessary to have a vowel scale for their use. Their waves can easily super-impose upon the waves of the lower harmonics.

VOWELS AND CONSONANTS IN SPEECH

Delattre's schematics from spectrograms show how vowels juncture with consonants in speech. In this example each syllable is closed since it ends with a consonant. It will be seen that the resonances (formants) are in transition going to a consonant.

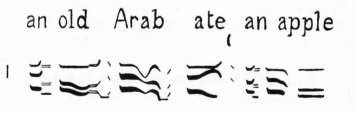

From <u>COMPARING THE PHONETIC FEATURES</u> by P. Delattre. Permission Julius Groos Verlag

Fig. 9. Vowel Formants in Speech

The "pure" sound of the vowel is at the beginning of each syllable, all of which begin with vowels. It is interesting to note the relatively low pitch of the underlined consonants as follows - "a<u>n</u> ol<u>d</u> Ar<u>ab</u> ate a<u>n</u> ap<u>pl</u>e." The plosive [t] is shown by a high frequency sound after the word "ate." The same high frequency sound would occur after [p] and [k] in Teutonic languages. It would be absent in the non-plosive Italian, French, and Spanish languages as in the word "apple."

There are very low sounds on [b] and [d] (and would be on [g] if it were present) which are followed by the low frequency vibrations of their small explosions. The liquid [n] and [l] have a sustained vibration in each of their resonances. The glottal stop on the beginning of each word is hardly seen, meaning that they were soft attacks - probably the "coupe de glotte" for which Garcia was maligned. In this case it gives firm vowel sounds. With more emphasis, the sounds would be more percussive.

Reinald Werrenrath, a famous American baritone of the early part of this century, said:

> The German, the Frenchman, the Englishman and the
> American strive first for an intelligent interpretation of
> the text. The Italian thinks of tone first and the text
> afterwards, except in the modern Italian school of
> realistic singing. (Cooke, 1921, p. 288.)

This needs to be kept in mind constantly when vocalizing for the various languages. To do this it is necessary to practice the unique consonants, singly and in combinations. Add to this list the troublesome consonants you find in your singing.

VOCAL GESTURES

Paget (1930) was of the opinion that the gestures of the articulators were essential to the comprehension of languages. He thought that movements which took place in the sound-stream from the larynx in some way carried meaning to the listener. Delattre was not entirely satisfied with his speech synthesis and felt that in the consonants there was an awareness of place of contact. We know that the deaf can lip read a speaker by sight; perhaps we can lip read by sound. I know that Sundberg's experiments with artificial singing (by electronic devices) of a soprano voice in which the resonator was made to match the pitch of the played tone (resonance tracking) has been interpreted by voice teachers as having the mouth too open at the top of the arpeggio. This was in spite of the fact that there was nothing resembling a mouth in his equipment. By other teachers the sound has been described as being spread.

With the extensive number of live television performances of opera, and fewer of recitals, we should become much more aware of the outward gestures of vowel and consonant gestures. There must be artistic, facile and unobtrusive forms and gestures for both - and related to pitch height. As Novikova said - no sleepy mouthed singers. No drawling and slurred speech. It will simply not carry in a large auditorium or over a loud accompaniment.

The gestures of the articulators are of utmost importance to understanding the words in singing. When they are slow, the voice is slow moving and awkward; when the gestures are fast, the singer can be on the vowel longer. Of course the speed and strength of the gestures will vary with moods, height of pitch, languages, etc. The gestures of articulation of the consonants in the Table on p. 143 should be practiced frequently in middle voice, the area where recitative takes place. Care should be taken that Italian, French, and Spanish consonants are non-plosive and that the aspirates, fricatives, buzzes, and plosives are given due attention in the Teutonic languages. When handled well consonants help the voice. Exercises with consonants should be practiced daily. In addition to the Novikova consonants (p. 41) the following selected words should be practiced for certain characteristics of the various languages.

VOCAL GESTURES PRACTICE

ENGLISH
Voice the buzzes, v, z, ʒ, th.

| love | was | azure | with | his | zebra | has | vanished | with | this |

| pledge | weds | Pronounce | vs | pronouns | spasms | bounds |

Voice the final consonants (closed syllables).

| thing | name | win | land | wag | judge | wings | wrench | Bob | did |

GERMAN
Unvoiced final fricatives, sibilants, and plosives - c, t, p, k, x, s, sh.

| Wind | hinab | dank | Weg | ich | ach | nichts | falsch | fest |

Practice the double consonants.

| fliessen | Mutter | stille | Blicke | hast du | Tag ging | leicht zu |

| verliebte | Morgens zu | Hoffnung |

FRENCH
Practice the closing consonants c, r, f, l.

avec   plaintif   mer

Pronounce alternately /i y i y i y i/ then pronounce nuit, depuis, suis.

ITALIAN
Practice the closing consonants m, n, r, l.

The consonants d, n, t, and l should be dentalized, the r is double at the beginning and ending of words.

reposar   almen   andiam   nel   par   cor

Practice the following consonants with the tip of the tongue against the lower front teeth and the blade of the tongue touching the aveolar ridge.

egli   ogni

Practice the personal pronouns.

io   mio   tuo   suo   miei   tuoi   lei   suoi

ADVANCED CONSONANT PRACTICE

ITALIAN

Practice the alternating tongue and lip exercises of Sieber. Dentalize the tongue consonants

la   be   da   me   ni   po   tu   (ba)

ENGLISH
Practice uniting closing and beginning consonants.

his son	come morning	not taught	his thin	stand when
Ted did	take cake	with them	help plan	and he
taught them	told the	this saw	his zeal	at the
small lamb	take care	Bob belts	ten tables	and low
him most	heart's desires	darkness	oats (vs)	hosts
None now knows his name		and he	would not	want them

an ice man   a nice man
an aim   a name
great eye   gray tie
house add   how sad
it swings   its wings

Use mute (schwa) vowel for final /R/ in English

her   never   word   Hermann   roar

An |old |Arab |ate |an |apple

GERMAN
Practice the glottal stop for different meanings (indicated by |).

zu meinen	zum |einen	er |ist es	er |ist's
wo leben	wohl |eben		

zollen   lengket

FRENCH
Practice the French Nasal Vowels.

Pendant que l'enfant mange son pain, le chien tremble dans le buissons.
Leiser (1935, p. 314). These were Jean De Reszke's phrases for teaching the
mask resonance by use of the French nasal vowels.

Practice the sudden gestures of beginning consonants.

Alternate the syllables in the upper and lower lines, then read laterally.

lɑ me va pɔ re e su frɑ̃ tə, la mə du sə, lɑ mɔ dɔ rɑ̃ tə,

de li   sdi vɛ̃, kə ʒe kœ ji   dɑ̃ lə ʒa rdɛ̃, də ta pɑ̃ se,

From Romance, Debussy (Phonetic Readings of Songs and Arias, 1964, p. 287
by Coffin, Errolle, Singer, and Delattre). This is written so that the closing
consonants of syllables and the opening consonants of the next syllable are not
anticipated as in English.

Now pronounce a few French lines - no glottal attacks or stops, no plosives, no
double consonants, and no anticipated consonants!

Avant de quitter ces lieux   ə vɑ̃ də ki te se ljø,
Ce breuvage pourrait me donner un tel rêve   sə brœ va ʒə pu rɛ
                                      mə dɔ ne œ̃ tɛ lrɛ və
Printemps qui commence   prɛ̃ tɑ̃ ki kɔ mɑ̃ sə

Now you know that consonants and vowels both differ with languages. I have
spoken of a few relevant characteristics. There are more vowels in some
languages than others. And the type and number of consonants differ. Why is
it that Italian singers wish to sing only in their own language? I believe that
they feel a secure voice placement only in their language which has very
variable vowels and few consonants. Also the vowels are centralized to such an
extent that the vocal tract acts more as an even stopped pipe. Therefore the
throat is a better organ for them.

This means that singers from other countries must learn the centralized vowels
and the liquid consonants to sing Italian well. Of course there must be a good
vocal sound by nature. It is impossible to resonate a sound that does not exist.
I will show how many of the linguistic sounds can be transformed and used in
the singing voice.

It will be noticed in Delattre's Fig. 274 that the epiglottis and larynx are not
shown. His picture is concerned with the positions which give vowel resonances
[formants]. There is a fixed resonance called The Singer's Formant.

The Singer's Formant (Resonance).   There is a resonance just above the highest of the vowel resonances, Note #59, which is present in good voices when the pitch is below c^2 in mezzo forte to fortissimo singing.   According to Professor Winckel, Berlin (1971), this is "dependent on the shortness and sharpness of the pulse at the output of the larynx." It increases with the length of closure time of the vocal cords in their vibratory cycle.   When the vocal cords do not close, as in sotto voce, this resonance is not present.   This has been called "the fixed formant," "the singer's formant," or the "2800" ring. Since it is a fixed resonance it does not pertain to the Chromatic Vowel Chart and is not notated.

The following figure shows graphs of singing by Fischer-Dieskau and Maria Callas with the upper line indicating the total energy of the voice and the lower line the amount of energy of the fixed resonance or formant.   It will be noted that in the crescendo and diminuendo about half of the energy of Callas' voice was at the fixed resonance area, while much more of it was present in the male voice of Fischer-Dieskau.   Let it be said that the amount of energy at the 3,000 Hz (Dr. Winckel's terminology) may distract a listener from the intonations of a singer; it never gets to the place where vowel resonances are made less important.   One listener may be awed by the ring of a singer's fixed resonance, while another says, "yes, but he was out of tune." I have had the experience of singing with Prof. Winckel's electronic instrument for the fixed resonance and I found that while I was singing I could in some way control the amount of 3,000 Hz in my voice by watching a meter.   Perhaps we will eventually have video-feedback assistance in finding and controlling the fixed resonance of the singing voice.

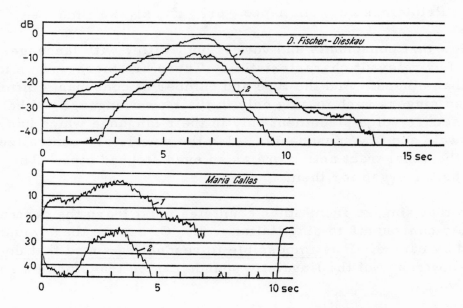

Level recording of the swell tone of 2 first class singers.   Curve 1: total energy of the voice; curve 2: portion in the area of 3,000 Hz.

Fig. 10. Winckel's Fixed Resonance Values

Winckel (1971) Folia phoniat. 23: p. 231.

CHAPTER V.   COMPARISON OF SPEECH AND SINGING

Researchers have been greatly interested in the differences between speech and singing. Some singing teachers have said, "Sing as you would speak." To what extent is this true? Can the statement be true? In Fig. 11. I show speech of a man and of a woman.

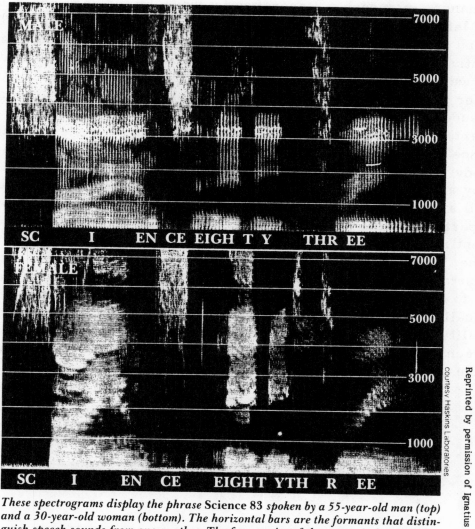

These spectrograms display the phrase Science 83 *spoken by a 55-year-old man (top) and a 30-year-old woman (bottom). The horizontal bars are the formants that distinguish speech sounds from one another. The frequencies of the woman's formants are higher. The long i in science, for example, shows formants at 400, 1,200, 2,000, and 3,500 cycles per second for the man, but 500, 1,800, 2,800, and 4,000 cycles per second for the woman. The higher the frequencies in a voice, the harder it is to synthesize.*

Spectograms – Science 83
Reprinted by permission of Ignatius G. Mattingly.
courtesy Haskins Laboratories

Fig. 11. Spectrograms of Male and Female Voices in Speech

Vertical lines (striations) can be seen in the male voice. They are the glottal pulsations which are almost constantly changing in the drone of speech, coming closer together in the rising inflection of a question and the emphasis of a word and becoming further apart in the falling inflection during the conclusion of a sentence. The inflections can best be heard through a wall or sound barrier in which the articulation has been filtered out.

Speech can not be defined in Hz or cycles per second - the basic pitch is very much in transition; in singing it is not, see Fig. 9. Notice that in the Female voice of speech that the striations are so close together that they cannot be seen. The vertical lines, again, are glottal pulses and are completely independent of the resonances in speech. Resonance is shown by the dark broad bands, reading from left to right. The bottom straight line is the zero line. The lowest broad band is the lowest resonance, R^1, and is seen only in vowels and voiced consonants. The broad band above R^1 is the second resonance of vowels, R^2. Delattre was able to synthesize speech with these two resonances (Formants) on the Cooper pattern playback. He was also able to paint the consonants which are the sudden "breaks" in the resonance lines in Fig. 8. Both R^1 and R^2 are in constant transition in speech. These are called "transients" and are of vital importance to intelligibility. In both the Male voice and the Female voice there is a steady resonance between 2800 and 3200 Hz. It is believed this is the frequency amplified by the cavity of the larynx or the piriform sinuses which are small swallowing troughs on either side of the larynx. This resonance is very important for the carrying power of the voice and is a sound which is almost entirely eliminated in "soft" voice. When a person is told to "speak up," this is the resonance which is added to the voice. It is higher than the overtones of orchestral instruments, which allows the singing voice, with the aid of the vibrato, to be heard through an orchestra. The resonances above R^1 and R^2 are basically timbre or voice resonances which allow us to recognize the individuality of voices. We need not chart them for singing. The consonants can be seen interrupting the vowel bands and, in this case, have very high frequencies.

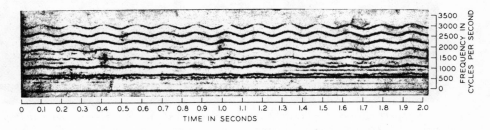

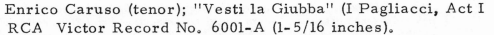

Enrico Caruso (tenor); "Vesti la Giubba" (I Pagliacci, Act I
RCA Victor Record No. 6001-A (1-5/16 inches).

From Visible Speech. Potter, Kopf and Kopf. 1966. Permission granted by Dover Publications.

Fig. 12. Spectrogram of Caruso

In Fig. 12. of Caruso the bottom line is again the zero line. In spectrograms all harmonics are equally distant from each other. The wave-like lines are the play of the vibrato on the harmonics. Notice the density of harmonics in the area of 2800 Hz. They are playing in the area of the singer's formant. But most intriguing of all is that when we look for an harmonic which is equal distance above the zero line, it is missing. The vocal tract was not long enough to resonate the sung pitch! The sung pitch is heard even if that frequency is not in air or is not resonated. It is what I wish to call "the phantom fundamental." The ear creates that pitch when it hears any three consecutive overtones. See <u>difference tone</u> on page 267.

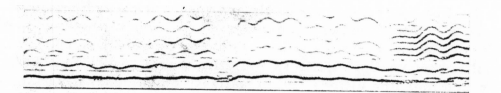

Frances Alda (soprano) followed by Enrico Caruso (tenor); "Qual Voluttà 'Trascorrere" (I Lombardi, Act III). RCA Victor Record No. 16-5002-B (1-15/16 inches).

Fig. 13. Spectrogram of Alda and Caruso

In Fig. 13. we see the harmonics of the voice of Frances Alda. Her sung pitch is resonated, she has wider spaced harmonics, and a fewer number of harmonics which seldom appear above 3000 Hz in singers. At the end of the example Caruso's voice enters, identifiable by the closeness of the overtones and the missing fundamental.

In both examples we see only one consonant - where the harmonics are interrupted. Is there a reason why Verdi was always telling his librettists, "Too many words, too many words?" Mind you he was setting Italian words to music which are less obtrusive to the singing lines than those of the Teutonic languages.

I show the positions of the tongue to orient the terms Front, Umlaut, and Neutral vowels. Placement of the different members of the vocal tract is by the speaker's/singer's concept of vocal sound. If he is Italian - the sound will be an Italianate sound. The phonatory gestures are learned and monitored by ear, even though no one hears his/her own voice as well as others. To isolate the movement of the tongue, soft palate, etc. is quite likely to interfere with their coordination. To see the articulatory movement in X-Ray photography is astounding. There is a gestalt of activity - the whole of the parts - which must be maintained. The Vowel Resonator can show the quality of vowel which is necessary for resonation. It is by the sense of vowel color and vibration in the vocal tract and head which guide the singer. "To know the result before we act is the 'golden rule' of singing," (Brown/Lamperti 1931, p. 28).

The close /O/ sound is dangerous because it is back and gives heaviness to the voice. I have seen Alfredo Kraus in a Master Class in which he had Male voices use the Nasal open AW [ʊ] for Oh in the <u>Passaggio</u> in the area of Note #22. To be specific it was the phrase in the Germont aria of <u>La Traviata</u> - "Dio mi guido, Dio mi guido, Dio mi guido." Where is the baritone who has not strangled on these phrases because of the weight if sung with true vowel values. <u>This is vowel substitution!</u>

Vowel Substitution.   There are optical illusions and there are aural illusions in which vowels can be substituted and the listener hear the written vowel. This is especially true for Male voices on Note #22. Mr. Kraus also used nasal UH for AH and [ʊ] as in pull and nasal [æ] as in fantastic for [e]. It will be noticed on the Chromatic Vowel Chart that Gold nasalized vowels are substituted for Green vowels on that note. The nasalization is related to the "mask resonance" exercise of De Rezske and gives a feeling of resonance which would be covered by an eye shade - in the area of the eyes and the bridge of the nose. Why would mask resonance be taught by De Reszke's teacher, Giovanni Sbriglia, who was a Neopolitan tenor (Coffin, NATS Bulletin, Nov/Dec 1983)? The answer is simple. French meaning differs with nasalization and denasalization, Italian, English, and German do not.

The physiological cause of vowel nasalization can be seen in Fig. 57. The nasal port is open. The acoustical effect can be seen in Fig. 8, the lower resonance of the vowels is reduced and the upper resonances increased. This has the effect of giving an "overtone boost" to the voice. Dr. Van Deinse, of Holland, stated at the 1979 Vienna Congress of COMET that sopranos and tenors who had nasal obstructions had difficulty in the transitions to their high voice. He advocated surgery for those who had serious deviated septums. The discussion of "mask resonance" will not die away when outstanding singers are using it successfully. There is much unknown about it. Why are there so few good French singers? Because their language teaches them denasalization - other languages do not.

QUESTIONS AND ANSWERS

Q. Do some choral conductors wish to have a straight tone from the singers in their choirs? (We do see the vibrato in the spectograms of great singers shown in this chapter.)

A. One answer is yes; there are still a few of these conductors. These conductors are usually instrumentalists or singers who have never had a good vibrato in their voices. It is my belief that a choral conductor should be a singer so that he/she has some knowledge and feel for the use of the voice. The voice does not need to be a great one. There is another answer usually given - blend.

Q. Is that valid?

A. No. Neither acoustically nor vocally. Why can string players be seen using vibrato in orchestras? To get the choral effect! Beethoven's symphonies were never heard originally as we hear them today - the string sections were very small and the totality of a large section was not heard. Allow the vibrato to play, but keep the singers near the same dynamic! Ethically it is wrong to demand a straight tone from a gifted voice - it can be reduced to mediocrity very quickly. If the demands are too severe the singer should make his exit as soon as possible.

Q. But what about intimate music like madrigals?

A. Let the less talented voices with good musicality participate. As Lamperti said, the first responsibility of the voice teacher is to individualize voices. Choral singing is the opposite - make everyone alike! A strong voice can color a choral section, but the reverse should not be the case.

Q. What effect do vowels have on voice placement?

A. Front vowels have an upward and forward pull on the larynx and the Back Vowels have a back and downward pull on the larynx. The most Central pull upon the larynx is by the Neutral Vowels and a combined front and downward pull is activated by the Umlaut Vowels.

Q. How can this be applied in singing?

A. In sotto voce high tones, vowels from the diagonals of the Front, Umlaut, Neutral, and Back vowels can be sung. In full voice the pulls upon the larynx by the Front and Neutral vowels are most favorable for the highest tones. In other words, certain vowels place advantageous pulls upon the larynx and assist it in giving the most acute pitches, others seem to interfere. In vocalization and in performance modify to the vowels which can be sung and avoid those which disrupt the singing.

Q. How can a singer get the airflow type of vibration into the voice?

A. First of all, it exists quite naturally in young Female voices. It can be kept by vocalizing downward slurs on little /u/ from Note #36 on up the scale ending on /AH/ an octave, 12th, or double octave lower. Starting on this for a few minutes every day will sustain the Female Head Voice. When this is missing, the voice can become very hard and strident.

Q. But this seems to be a false voice.

A. Yes, it is. I believe it was called voce finta [feigned voice] by the old singing masters.

Q. What about Male voices?

A. In Male voices, do the same thing beginning on Note #23. Sing downward on little [u] or with the "open mouth hum" (m). Continue up the scale in a supported, mixed voice. Doing this will assist in finding and maintaining the Mixed Voice. I have little faith in the falsetto sound which has been called "witch voice." I have been unable to make significant gains through its usage.

Q. Are all languages the same as far as the Front and Back vowels are concerned?

A. They are not. The Italian is the most <u>central</u> of the singing languages. /I/ is not so fronted, [U] is not so backed and /AH/ is more of a composite of all vowels. Italian is an open syllable language, never ending on a stopped consonant. The ending consonants m, n, r, and l frequently have a voiced sound after them. Consequently, the Italian language is a loud language which carries well and their opera houses are large. The German and English houses are smaller because so much of the singing of those languages is with the house closed to make plosives, etc.

CHAPTER VI. THE VOWEL RESONATOR - FINDING SYMPATHETIC
RESONATION

Components, connections, and usage.

The Vowel Resonator is a two-inch speaker which can be wired to a source which
will give as many pitches as possible of the human voice from the highest
coloratura soprano to the lowest bass. The most convenient source is the
Radio Shack Concertmate - 200 (formerly the Casio VL Tone 1) which is small
enough to be carried in a brief case. Larger models of electronic sources can
be used. The two-inch speaker should be 8 ohm and the source should match it.
A newer Casio PT 1 has an output jack but does not have as pure a tone. I have
found the best source is a straight flute tone whether a small instrument, such
as a Concertmate, Casio, or a large instrument, such as a home organ, is used.

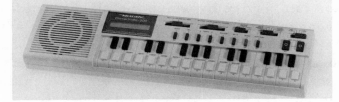

Fig. 14. Radio Shack Realistic Concertmate 200
Courtesy of Radio Shack, a Division of Tandy Corporation.

Most sources need to be amplified for use with a Vowel Resonator. I have used
an Archer Mini-Amplifier which is available at Radio Shack stores. The wiring
should be sturdier than speaker wire and have the ability to withstand flexible
usage. I have used regular electric-light wiring. The components should be
soldered with care that <u>plus</u> is connected to <u>plus</u>, and <u>negative</u> to <u>negative</u>.

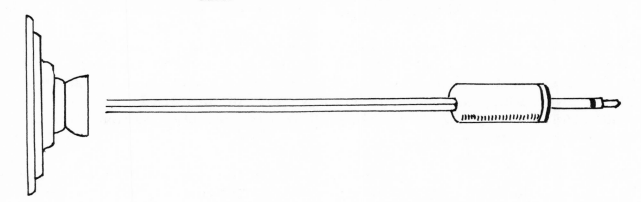

Fig. 15. VOWEL RESONATOR

<u>WHEN USING THE VOWEL RESONATOR IT IS IMPERATIVE THAT THE VOCAL
CORDS BE HELD TOGETHER AS IN THE START OF A GRUNT.</u> Play a note on
the Concertmate and hold the speaker in front of the mouth. Adjust the mouth
and throat until the loudest resonance is heard. Sing on that pitch, keeping the

throat in the position which gave the peak resonance. Resonating vowel colors are indicated on the Chromatic Vowel Chart when the Chart is correctly placed on a piano keyboard for the singer's voice classification. Use the flute stop, preferably without vibrato. It is also preferable to use an electric organ which extends to the f above high c $[f^3]$. This height is necessary for the resonation of the high pitches of many sopranos. The Casio PT 1 does not have the high octave, or the low octave of the Male voice. It has a vibrato and the flute stop is not a sine wave. Other sources are on the market and will be coming on the market from time to time. In my descriptions of ways to proceed in the resonance studies I will use the term Concertmate since it is the most desirable instrument I have found on the market today. Also, it is readily available at Radio Shack stores.

VOICE PLACEMENT BY THE VOWEL RESONATOR AND A CONCERTMATE

The Vowel Resonator is a device by which the singer can find the sympathetic resonance of the throat in his/her vocalises, songs, and arias. The other kind of resonance is forced resonance, which the singer should avoid as much as possible because it leads to physical forcing, extraneous noises, tensions, and fatigue and, in many cases, the throat doctor. When the Vowel Resonator (any 2" speaker coupled with an amplifier to a Concertmate 200 or similar electronic device) is held about 1/2 inch in front of the mouth and the vocal cords held together (as in the beginning of a cough) a c^2 pitch, ca above middle c, can be played into the mouth and its LOUDEST RESONANCE found. This is found by slow movements of the lips, tongue, and jaw on the vowel OH (some kind of an OH is on that pitch for all voices, Male and Female). When maximum resonance is heard, sing on that position of the vowel pipe (the formation of the throat between the vocal cords and the lips). It seems that there is a feedback of vibration between the VOWEL RESONATOR and the vocal cords. The pitch of other vowels can likewise be found by referring to the Chromatic Vowel Chart.

The objective is to have the vowel "zero in" on the pitch so that the sound is amplified. (This effect is best heard when the Concertmate has been computed to have a straight flute tone on the ASDR position. Instructions are given below.) Other vowels which will resonate on the various pitches are found on the CHROMATIC VOWEL CHART when the Chart is correctly positioned for the singer's voice classification.

There are High, Medium, and Low positions of the scale on the Concertmate. I have found the Medium position of the scale is best most of the time because the pitches of the vowels lie on the heavy lines on the Chromatic Vowel Chart between Notes #23 and #40, with the usable vowel resonances being between Notes #23 and #37. (The Vowel Chart was formed in the first place by this procedure with a Sine Wave generator, amplifier, and a two-inch speaker. These were too cumbersome for mobile usage. Later, an electric organ was used with an 8 ft. Flute stop - still too large for travel! The use of sympathetic resonation is a continuation of Helmholtz' investigations with tuning forks and Helmholtz resonators (found in the translated and interpreted edition by the noted English physicist, Alexander Ellis, 1885, pp. 104 - 118).

CONCERTMATE STRAIGHT FLUTE TONE HOOK-UP

1. Place upper right switch to Cal.
2. Place next switch to the left, to ADSR.
3. Press MC (below and to the left).
4. Press the computer numbers 33099100.
5. Hit the M+ button (in the middle row at the right).
6. Move upper right switch to Play.
7. All tones played should now sound like a straight flute tone.

WHEN THE VOWEL CHART IS PLACED ON THE PIANO KEYBOARD APPROPRIATELY FOR YOUR VOICE CLASSIFICATION, THE VOWEL RESONATOR WILL REINFORCE THE VOWELS ON THE CHROMATIC VOWEL CHART ABOVE ANY PITCH YOU WISH TO SING.

THE USE OF THE VOWEL RESONATOR WITH MALE VOICES

Male voices should sing the desired vowel on any desired pitch AFTER having found the vowel pipe position by resonating a pitch an octave higher. The Open position relates to what has been called Upper Register on the Chart, and is called Open Voice (Fr. Voix Claire). The Close position relates to what is called Mixed Voice or Covered Voice (Fr. Voix Sombre). Thus the opening and closing of vowels control register changes. This is seen in the Caruso scales on pages 97 and 98 in my book Overtones of Bel Canto. These show that the voice is closed in an ascending scale and reopened in descending so that an easy transition of registers can be made. This is one of the reasons for vowel modification in singing exercises, songs, and roles. Many of my American and European artists are using the Vowel Resonator with the Chromatic Vowel Chart and my books as their teacher in my absence - it will tell them the exact opening of the vocal pipe for any troublesome tones and passages.

Question. Which pitches should be played into the mouth, since all, or almost all, of the Vowels have pitches higher than Male Voices can sing?

Answer. For Upper Register and Mixed Register (indicated by U and X in Overtones of Bel Canto) you should play an octave higher than the pitch you wish to sing. When this resonates, sing the vowel on that formation of the vocal pipe. The Open position sound is in the Upper Voice and should not usually be sung higher than the upper loop of the Passaggio (Notes #21, #22, and #23). From there on up, sing on the

Green vowels. On the highest notes, the Front and Neutral vowels work best. The close sound is Mixed Voice. (It can be called Male Head Voice since it can be one of the vowels on the Vowel Chart an octave above the pitch to be sung. The Vowel reads like it is Female Head Voice.) If this is difficult to find at first, resonate on the pitch to be sung. The Close position should be cultivated beginning on Note #19. The placement of the Voice by closing in this area enables the Male Voice to be extended to very high notes.

Q. What if the Vowel on the Chart does not match the vowel of the song?

A. That is the point of vowel modification. The desired vowel is not quite right for that note. Sing the vowel which is closest to the vowel in the word in the song. This is the compromise made to maintain both resonance and intelligibility.

Q. Is it necessary to make all vowel sounds agree with the Chart?

A. No. Very fast notes and passages do not have the time to resonate - why bother? Another thing. Voices cannot be built by singing fast vocalises entirely - in fact the voice will lose in strength. In longer notes, the standing wave can occur which gives maximum resonance. This is true for both Male and Female voices.

THE USE OF THE VOWEL RESONATOR BY FEMALE VOICES

Female Voices should play the pitch in the song which they wish to sing and try to resonate the printed vowel on that pitch. This is especially true for those vowels of the Head Register and many of those of the Vowel Register on the Chart. For the mixed Register, the octave above should be played and resonated. For the Chest Register, the 12th above (third harmonic) should be played and resonated.

Q. What about opening and closing the vowel in scales?

A. Mathilde Marchesi, the greatest teacher of female voices, said the voice should close in going to Head Register (e^2, f^2, and $f\#^2$) and open when coming down the scale. The same things should happen at the passaggio in the e^1, f^1, and $f\#^1$ area of the voice as marked in the lower loops on the Vowel Chart.

NOTE: The basic thing new in this statement is that for Mixed Voice, in both Male and Female voices, the vowel should be tuned at the octave because of what is known as "the missing fundamental" - the tone is sung but it hardly shows on spectrograms (sonograms). See pages 11 and 222 in <u>Overtones of Bel Canto</u>.

Q. Why is it that Female voices are less clearly understood than Male voices?

A. The pitches of Male singing are low enough for good vowel differentiation but the higher the sung pitch, the fewer the harmonic overtones for differentiation. In fact, above Note #34 the Front and Neutral <u>Green</u> vowels are best. If composers insist on writing words above this note they can expect to hear nonsense syllables. Back and Umlaut vowels tend to bother American singers.

LISTEN TO YOUR THROAT WHILE SINGING!!

How does one hear? Even the most knowledgeable scientists know very little about how we hear while singing (Schubert 1983 Juilliard Symposium). By using a throat microphone we can hear the throat resonate <u>while singing</u>. This is <u>very different</u> than the way it resonates while speaking. It is largely the throat which must be trained for singing since an instrumental standing wave is necessary for what is known as beautiful singing (bel canto).

You can use the following components
1. A RadioEar Bone Vibrator - see Fig. 16,
2. A small amplifier such as the Archer from Radio Shack,
3. A set of Headphones, and
4. An adaptor which will allow both of the Headphones to hear the throat vibration.

Use of the RadioEar hookup is simple. When the RadioEar is used as a throat microphone and heard through the headphones the singer can hear when there is a constancy of vibration. This is the basis of Bel Canto. How simple! How unscientific! No meters to read! Simply go by the sound and the sensation in the throat. The singer will become much more aware of how he sings and what he does to sing well.

The basic problem can be shown by the Delattre vowel form illustrations on page 274. He has shown by the hash-marks that there are different resonators in front of, and back of the tongue hump. In singing, X-Ray studies reveal the tongue hump is changed in such a way as to allow the entire vocal tract to vibrate as a whole. At the same time it allows the higher overtones to vary for vowel recognition. This can be done very effectively by listening to the throat while singing. Following is an illustration of the RadioEar Bone Vibrator which probably can be found at a hearing aid store.

Fig. 16. RADIOEAR B-70-A BONE VIBRATOR   P-3024-A Cord 72"
Subsidiary of Esterline Corporation
375 Valley Brook Rd., Canonsburg, Pa. 15317

HEARING OVERTONES - "HARMONIC UNDERTONES OF A RESONATOR"

Much valuable information has come to us
through the principles which can be verified
with a Helmholtz Resonator such as is
shown in Fig. 17. These come in various
sizes so that harmonic overtones of all notes
can be clearly heard when an appropriate
resonator is inserted into the ear. A bb^2
resonator will show that bb^1, eb^1, bb, gb, eb,
and Bb, have overtones, which in Helmholtz'
terminology, will make the bb^2 resonator
"bray." Helmholtz/Ellis tr. (1886, p. 110).
The sound is definitely loud and unmistake-
able. These pitches are "called the harmonic
under tones of the resonator." One of the
"Ah" vowels has this frequency, so all of
those pitches have that vowel on them. This
and the harmonic overtones are the bases
of the CHROMATIC VOWEL CHART. The
Chart can be checked out by this method.

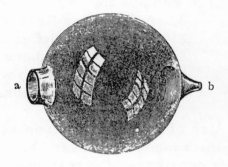

Fig. 17. Helmholtz Resonator

It has been said that the mouth acts as a Helmholtz Resonator in singing since
it is able to amplify the harmonic overtones of a sound and filter out, or erase,
the non-harmonic overtones. This is as good an explanation as any in explaining why a singer's rather loud announcement of his song does not carry but a
piano sung tone carries well.

THE KORG TUNING TRAINER

Seeing is believing to many people. For those, a Korg Tuner can be used to see vibrato and to see intonation (based on whether singers are singing on their resonance peaks). Use the control on the Korg Tuner which indicates the frequency of a note and watch the swing of the needle for good intonation and rate of vibrato. For good intonation, the needle should swing equally on both sides of the indicated pitch. I have done a limited amount of observation of this type but it can probably be utilized to assist singers who have slow, unpleasant vibratos and pitch problems. Whereas the Concertmate flute source gives mostly the prime (or first harmonic) the Korg Tuner gives the odd numbered harmonics and, as a consequence, is not wholly satisfactory as a source for a Vowel Resonator.

THE TWO OPENING POSITIONS OF RESONATION

When working with the Vowel Resonator, it will be found that two openings of the mouth can be used for the high notes. Usually the first one to be found is the most open one in the Fig. 23. by Manén. The more close form is gained by placing a /y/ [j] before the vowels attempted. This is what I call a "Silver Ah" and moves well in fast runs. This was probably the /A/ used by the castrati when they were singing with a "smile." There should be no trouble in finding the more open position. If so, it can be gained by preceding the vowel with a [w]. Both openings are available - use the one which best suits the throat, the emotional coloring, and artistic taste.

THE SILVER AH

In some Female voices the Middle Voice sounds like a whisper (Sir Thomas Beecham said that it sounded like the singer had been eating sea-weed!). I have also found that in some voices there is a heavy vibrato, verging on a "tummy vibrato" when singing notes in the middle and low voice after working with the Vowel Chart. To offset this I have used what I call "the Silver Ah" and the reason I have done so is because Helmholtz (1954 p. 106) said that the Italian AH had a frequency at d^3 (probably the 2nd Formant). I have found that Ah on Notes #41 to #45 can be resonated in a position in which there is a slight smile and the teeth fairly close together (preferable to a position in which the mouth is more open). Female voices can sing this AH a 12th below this note to find the clear phonation of the Middle Voice. It is close to the position of speech and is best phonated with a high collar-bone breath support.

Male Voices can sing a pitch either 2 octaves and a 5th or 3 octaves below the Italian Ah to brighten and clearly phonate the middle and low voice. I do not think this form should be carried above about Note #13. This has added great vibrancy to bass and baritone voices and will eliminate hollow, non-vibrant tones. I believe this technique should be a part of daily vocalization. Male voices are mainly heard by their overtones - the sung pitch is several decibels down from the energy of the overtone resonance peaks and is heard by a unique phenomenon of the human ear - the difference tone. See Appendix J.

The Silver Ah gives an overtone to the voice which will cut the curtain of orchestral sound and is probably related to the so called "smile" on which the castrati were taught. Because of its strong overtone it will not blend in quiet choral singing but is probably of use in singing dramatic music with orchestral accompaniment.

THE MUSCULATURE OF THE VOCAL TRACT

By "vocal tract" I mean the throat between the vocal cords and the lips which forms a reverberating tunnel. In reality the voice is a unique pipe organ which has many colors called vowels. The different contractions of the walls of the throat, tongue position and jaw opening are involved with the pitch which comes from the vocal cords in singing. And the muscles of the larynx which form the pitch are effective on some notes and not on others. The relationship is so involved that I will not make a blanket statement until later. This means that the outside (extrinsic) muscles of the larynx are involved with the inside (intrinsic) muscles of the larynx and that that relationship should be used to the advantage of the singer.

The favorable vowel pitch/sung pitch relationships are incorporated in the exercises of Sounds of Singing and Overtones of Bel Canto. One law can be stated - EVERY VOWEL ON EVERY PITCH HAS A DIFFERENT RESONATION. Assisted by the Vowel Resonator and the Chromatic Vowel Chart this relationship can be automated. That is, it can be established in the ear as vowel color and in the kinesthetic feel of the throat so that it can happen subconsciously. It has been called the sixth sense by Elster Kay (1963). Brown/G. B. Lamperti stated in Vocal Wisdom (1931 p. 91), "Tone and breath 'balance' only when harmonic overtones appear in the voice, and not by muscular effort and voice placing." That is why teachers and singers can use a Concertmate or a similiar electronic device effectively.

I have heard it said that there can never be too much space--how can a person look at a rank of organ pipes and believe such a statement! Pipes vary with pitch. The question is always how much space. Find out with a Vowel Resonator.

Good luck with the Vowel Resonator or RadioEar and best wishes for your career. It is the best way I have found of imparting the technique of the passaggios to singers. Someone has said that this technique is a sure way of finding the true color of a singer's voice. Historically, many singers have been misled by trying to imitate the vocal timbres of other singers. That probably is an eternal truth! Make the most of your own voice! Your voice is an original. There is no other like it!

CHAPTER VII.   THE CHROMATIC VOWEL CHART

Derivation.   The Chromatic Vowel Chart is a plotting of the vowels of loudest resonance.   They are related to Delattre's schematic of vowel resonances in Fig. 58.   The Chart is based on the lower vowel resonance, R^1.   As the Front Vowel progression [i, e, ɛ, æ] goes up in his schematic, it also goes up on the Chart in the heavily underlined vowels on the Vowel Diagonal between Notes #23 - #40.   It is also shown in musical notation above Note #50.   The Back Series [u, o, ɔ, ɒ], the Umlaut Series [y, ø, œ, a], and the Neutral Series progress in like manner.

Definition of Vowel Colors.   Vowels are defined linguistically at the right end of the Chart.   They can and should be checked out with the Vowel Resonator to see which colors of vowels are intended.   It can be seen from Delattre's Fig. 8 that vowel values vary between languages.   In singing, the value should be taken which is nearest to the language value and which has a loud resonation.

Map.   The Chromatic Vowel Chart is, in effect, a map which can be read up and down, from left to right, and from right to left.   It has been designed to stand behind the black keys of a standard grand piano in the location as noted in the upper corners of the Chart.

Vowel Lines.   There are horizontal lines which are numbered on the left of the Chart.   Vowel Line I is for Front Vowels, Vowel Line II is for Neutral Vowels, Vowel Line III is for Back Vowels, and Vowel Line IV is for Umlaut Vowels.

Actual Vowel Scales.   The pitches of the lower resonance of vowels are indicated above the heavily underlined diagonals between Notes #23 and #40.   These form the Vowel Register.   The diagonals to the left of the underlined diagonals are harmonically related to the Vowel Register.   To be specific, the small numbers at the end of each diagonal indicate which harmonic of the sung pitch vibrates the vowels in the Vowel Register.   I call them Harmonic Diagonal 2, Harmonic Diagonal 3, 4, etc., on the Chart.

Diagonal Lines.   The diagonal lines of I indicate the modifications of the lower vowel resonance of Front Vowels.   The diagonal lines of II indicate the lower resonance of Neutral Vowels; those of III the lower resonance of Back Vowels, and those of IV the lower resonance of Umlaut Vowels.

Columns.   There are vertical columns in Lines I, II, III, and IV over each note. They are the harmonics of the pitch over which they stand except when the vowels are below the heavily underlined diagonal.   I have no explanation for the diagonals marked as 1.5, .67, .5 and .33 at the right of the diagonals other than they can be heard with the Vowel Resonator.   They can be used with or without the Vowel Resonator.   The vowel colors above or below each note will vibrate sympathetically with a sung tone on that note when the arrow on Note #23 is correctly adjusted for voice classification as directed.

<u>Color Code.</u> The vowels are coded for openness. <u>Red</u> means so open that there is danger of trouble or a break. <u>Yellow</u> means that the vowel is so open it may disrupt the vocal cords, <u>except</u> in the lower voice where brightness is desired.

<u>Green</u> vowels are mid-open or mid-close and are safe (and are coupled). <u>Blue</u> means very close with a danger of losing resonance.

<u>Technical Function.</u> The vowels are also color coded for technical function. The Chromatic Vowel Chart indicates the vowel colors which have resonance peaks on each note of the singing voice, Male and Female. The colors are a bit like traffic lights - <u>Green</u> is for <u>go</u>, and <u>Yellow</u> is for <u>caution</u> (in the <u>upper</u> voice - the vowels will have a tendency to spread and interfere muscularly with vocal cord vibration). <u>Yellow</u> is fine for low notes which need to have higher overtones to be heard (the curve for acuity of hearing falls off quite fast below 1000 Hz - roughly c^3, see Fletcher's curves for acuity of hearing in <u>Overtones of Bel Canto</u>). <u>Red</u> is to be avoided, take a side street to a <u>Green</u>! <u>Red</u> is only for a scream after which there is little singing. <u>Blue</u> is for vowels which are quite close and need to be mixed with auxiliary vowels for better resonation.

<u>Registers.</u> When working with artists in Europe, I have asked what difficulties they have had and how I could be of assistance to them. The areas in which they usually desire to work can be easily notated and are shown below:

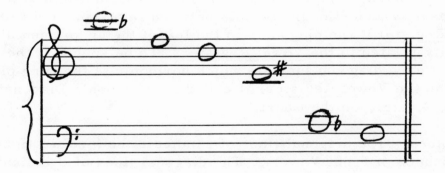

Fig. 18. Register Transitions. The circles (not notes) are areas of vocal difficulties.

In actuality, they have defined acoustically the <u>passaggios</u> of the voice. These are areas where voices change from one register to another. These changes are indicated by small arrows in the Vowel Lines. The traditional names of the registers are given at the upper end of the diagonals on the Chart when they exist. The registers below Mixed Voice are all Chest Register. It is the professional singers definition of registers with which I have concerned myself; certainly the principles are the same for the non-professional.

<u>Covering</u>. The term covering usually is applied to the Male voice. The place where covering should take place is usually at Note #22. For Female voices, a closing of vowels must take place at Note #22 or below in going from Chest voice to the register above it. <u>The arrow is 1/2 step above "the break."</u>

<u>The Loops</u>. I have placed loops on Notes #21 - #23 indicating how the voice should close at this <u>passaggio</u>.

<u>Passaggio Lines I and II</u>. These are vowels which have the same lower resonance on the pitches indicated. By singing them alternately on the pitches indicated they equalize the voice and assist in making register transitions. These will be discussed more fully and utilized in the vocalization chapters.

<u>Caruso Vowel Scale</u>. The vowels on this line are formed from the Caruso vocalizes in the book by Fucito and Beyer (1929).

<u>Resonance Schematics</u>. The Delattre schematics of resonance spaces in speech (see p. 274) should convey a concept of total pipe resonance (the pitch of the total pipe from the vocal cords to the lips) and of the tongue channel resonance (the pitch of the cavity in front of the tongue hump). The "hash" marks indicate speech resonance. Instrumental resonance comes about when the opening approaches those of [ε] and [œ] which are without "hash" marks. This is probably what teachers of singing refer to when they say, "Sing with an open throat." It is more open than speech.

<u>One Chart</u>. The Chromatic Vowel Chart is one Chart for Female and Male voices. The lower resonances for ALL voices are above middle c. Male voices resonate these vowels by the harmonics of their sung pitch. Contraltos, when singing their low notes are in the Male baritone range and resonate on the same vowels as do the high Baritones; Counter Tenors, when singing their high notes, sing on the vowels indicated for the Female voice in that range. All available modifications are on the Chromatic Vowel Chart.

<u>Pitch Frequencies</u>. I have placed the frequency of pitches on the Chart to serve as a bridge between researchers and musicians. There has been a vast amount of research since 1800 from which we can borrow. There is little gained by re-inventing the wheel.

<u>Contra Bass Register</u>. Basses can extend and maintain their low voice by octave leaps downward in that area. Vowels are the same at the octave. Leaps from eb downward as far as Ab will assist in establishing the contra-bass Register described by Manuel Garcia II (Paschke translation of 1841/1984, p. xlviii). It does not rumble the chest but is felt at the larynx. It is probably a type of "vocal fry." Sometimes this aids the low notes of Male voices.

VOWEL PARADOX

Q. Why is it that the /A/ vowel stands at the top of the register diagonals and /U/ at the bottom when the /A/ is better for low notes, and vowels toward /U/ are better for high notes?

A. This is a paradox with which we must learn to live. The muscles of the throat must serve two masters. 1. They must form vowels and consonants. 2. They must also assist in height and depth of pitch, dynamics, and the dull and clear timbres. The diagonals on the Chromatic Vowel Chart indicate the different registers formed by the vocal tract (which also have an effect on the vibrating vocal cords).

The vowels in Blue and the lowest Green vowels are considered to give dark color or Sombre Timbre. The high Green vowels and the Gold vowels give bright color or Clear Timbre. (For further discussion see Appendix G, p. 257 in this text.)

Q. Why is this important?

A. Timbres are important for expression and for proper use in progressions between registers. This seems to be the most prevalent problem in the singing of extensive ranges as in opera. The difficulties appear where the /A/ vowels are shown in Red on the Chromatic Vowel Chart.

Q. What does the Vowel Chart have to do with the thick and thin mechanisms referred to by Vennard and other investigators?

A. The vocal cords function in two ways in good singing. The low pitches are gained by a shortening and thickening of the vocal cords somewhat similar to the brass player's pursing of the lips into a mouthpiece for low notes. For higher notes the vocal cords are lengthened and thinned by the set of muscles called Stretchers. This is akin to the stretching and thinning of the lips by brass players. A third type of vocal cord closure in speech has been found in fiberscopic observations. Dr. Van Lawrence has called it the pharyngeal squeeze. This has a bad effect on the singing voice. It is due to a weak muscular action which causes a person to speak in a grunting fashion. It is a function of the larynx which requires the assistance of a knowledgeable vocal teacher or a vocal therapist.

Q. Does this have anything to do with vowels?

A. Yes. According to Husler and Rodd-Marling (1965, p. 98) the /A/ vowel requires the Tensor mechanism and the [u] and [i] requires a Stretching action upon the vocal cords. Hence /A/ is best for low notes and the [i - a] and [ʊ - ʌ] series are best for the higher notes. They do not address the Neutral series which is Central and works well for high notes and high note mixtures. This thinning-to-thickening occurs in ascending in each register. Peculiar? Yes! The Tensor vowel /A/ is at the top of each diagonal and the Stretcher vowels /u/ and /i/ are at the lower end. That is the Vowel Paradox!

Q. What does this mean?

A. This means that the upper end of a diagonal (register) must be sung for low notes and the lower end of a diagonal (register) must be sung for the high notes. A rule of thumb - Yellow for low notes and Blue or Green for high notes. High sopranos should be cautious of singing into the Yellow for the highest notes, although it is sometimes required.

Q. Is all of this necessary?

A. Yes. If you wish to sing well you must have a technique which will enable you to sing in an extended range. The public would not be interested in a three stringed violinist. Neither are they interested in short voices.

CHAPTER VIII. HOW TO USE THE CHROMATIC VOWEL CHART

Phonetics of the Chromatic Vowel Chart. New symbols beyond those used in Phonetic Readings of Songs and Arias (Scarecrow Press 1964, 1983) by Coffin, Errolle, Singer, and Delattre are all International Phonetic Alphabet symbols except [ʊ] which is my coinage of [ɔ] of aw to the extent that it would sound like joy if one really were "joyful." I have also used the accented schwa [ʌ] with parentheses e.g. (ʌ) to indicate that the lips should be slightly rounded. ALL PHONETICS ARE DEFINED BY PITCH ON THE CHART, LINES I, II, III, AND IV above the heavy underlining, on Notes #23 - #40. Singers should broaden their linguistic value of vowels into a vowel scale. In so doing they will lose their regional accents in singing, although they may be evident in recitative and speech.

The following vowel values should be learned since they are unknown, even to most phoneticists:

[ɯ] is lateral "oo" - with spread lips. This is a modification between [u] and [o].

[ɤ] is lateral "oh" - with spread lips. This is a modification between [o] and [ɔ].

[ɒ] is a dark "ah" very much like we pronounce "father."

[α] is a lateral "ah" which is brighter than usually found in American speech. The lips are spread and the jaw down.

[ʌ] is the carat, "open schwa" - usually the accented neutral vowel. I call it the covered /A/. It has a pitch higher than the close schwa [ə], which is referred to as the unaccented neutral vowel by phoneticists.

(ʌ) is the rounded lip "open schwa" which has a lower pitch than [ʌ]. It appears on Line II, Notes #30, #31, and #32 and those pitches which are harmonically related.

The Trumpet Principle. Form the vocal "trumpet" of the voice by singing the given phonetics on the indicated pitches. These are the vowel-colors which have harmonic resonation that can be heard and felt while singing. How does one practice with such a Chart?

Method. The minute I say how, I will be expounding some kind of a method. I will suggest a few procedures and relate a few comments from the writings of the vocal masters. It is my belief that as singers and teachers of singing work more and more with the Chromatic Vowel Chart they will develop methods of their own to incorporate the Trumpet Principle into procedures they already employ. They cannot misuse the Chromatic Vowel Chart significantly unless they practice the extremes of the voice, a particular series of vowels, or a specific area of the voice too much or too long at a time. If they sing too long in a particular spot, the group of muscles involved will become fatigued; this must be avoided. Favor the resonations which can be found with the cheeks raised while opening the sides of the mouth. Garcia's basic rule concerning brightening the low notes and rounding the top notes should be kept in mind while using the Chromatic Vowel Chart.

Breathing. Since we are dealing with sympathetic resonation, the breath effort is reduced (see Appendix xxx). Forced resonance requires more effort because the breathing muscles must overcome the conflict between vibration of the vocal folds and the pulsation of air in the vocal tract, the frequency of which is controlled by the various vowels.

Rotate the Vowel Series. PLAY ROTATION! Since singing is a form of athletics, because it is an activity which can play only by muscular activity, continually rotate or alternate the vowel series to activate and strengthen the musculatures of vocalization. By rotating the use of musculatures, the singing mechanism becomes more facile in its gestures, gains more strength, and becomes more adroit in finding the various resonances quickly. This can also involve register change, and in most cases, a subtle change in breath flow and breath pressure. The basic objective is to get the voice all together so that the singer can go quickly and easily from any part of the voice to any other. A change of a half step requires a change of activity in the laryngeal and articulatory muscles, even if the vowel apparently remains the same. That is one reason why vowels should change in melismatic passages in vocalizes, songs, or arias.

Instructions. Get the Feel of it! Place the Chart behind the black notes of the piano, then

> Place the arrow sign $^{2}\!\!\downarrow^{3}$ in its proper place for your
> voice classification, as indicated in the upper
> corners of the Chart. Before reading further,
>
> 1. Sing some 4-note scales on the diagonal Vowel Rows in Lines I, II, III, and IV written over the notes you are singing.
>
> 2. Sing and pronounce vertical columns over notes in your voice. Find the maximum resonance of each vowel by playing the lips, tongue, and jaw until the maximum tone is felt. The tuning is very subtle.

3. Sing the vowels note by note on Passaggio Lines I and II, alternating the two vowels shown.

4. Female voices, sing the Caruso scale from Note #17 upwards. Start in Chest Voice.

5. Male voices, sing the Caruso scale through the passaggio. Always round gently on Note #16 and close on Note #20. Sing as high as comfortable.

THE USE OF THE CHART IN SONGS AND ARIAS

Letter Name the Chart. Singers who are using the Chart only with their own voices frequently mark the letter name of pitches on their Chart. For example, a soprano would mark Note #23 as g, Note #24 as a♭, etc. They can then score the vowels in their music away from the piano. Thus they know how to place their voices before they sing. On exposed and extended high notes it is best to stay in Head Voice. Try to pronounce the indicated vowel when singing. The lower and faster notes will not need to be scored.

Recitative. There is less concern for sympathetic resonation and modification of vowels in recitative which lies nearer to the speaking range of the voice. The larynx is less concerned with attaining an unusual height of pitch and by a less dense accompaniment.

USE OF THE VOWEL RESONATOR WITH THE VOWEL CHART

Learn How to Sing. It is my belief that many can teach, place, and develop singing voices by the use of the Chromatic Vowel Chart with artificially generated pitch - an extension of the Electric Larynx. The phonetic symbols on the Chart are written sounds which will echo the various pitches in the singing scale when the arrow is properly placed for the singer's voice classification. The Chart and these exercises will make many more resonant colors of voice, better intonation, better quality, a more distinguishable diction, and a more robust voice available to a singer for his or her interpretation. There are many books on interpretation. It is the intent of this book to deal primarily with providing the instrument and colors for the interpretative art of singing.

The Vowel Chart was built by means of the Vowel Resonator. The Chart and Resonator can be used together in training the singing voice. They will tell the exact color of vowel which will maximize the voice on any pitch. Perhaps a few suggestions on how to tune to the Vowel Resonator are in order. Everyone has tuned in to a radio station. It comes in loud and clear when the scanner comes into the correct frequency. Use of the Vowel Resonator is quite similar. While holding the Vowel Resonator in front of the mouth with the vocal cords together as in a cough or grunt. Slowly and <u>silently</u> mouth between the vowels indicated below until the loudest resonance is heard on the vowel you wish to sing. <u>Sing on that position.</u> To find vowels on the

Front series - do a <u>slow</u> scan by going slowly from /i/ to /a/.

Neutral series - do a <u>slow</u> scan by going slowly from [ə] to /uh/.

Back series - do a <u>slow</u> scan by going slowly from [u] to [ɒ].

Umlaut series - do a <u>slow</u> scan by going slowly from [y] to [œ].

<u>Control of the Voice.</u> Since the earliest writings, singers and teachers of singing have been concerned with the control of the singing voice. Possibly the greatest of them all, according to Henry Pleasants (1966), was Gasparo Pacchierotti (1740-1821) who said, "Mettete ben la voce, Respirato bene, Pronunciate chiaramente Ed il vostro canto sara perfetto." Collected by Phillip A. Duey. Francesco Lamperti in his preface (1875) translated this statement as being, "He who knows how to breathe and pronounce well, knows how to sing well [he continues] and this is one of the greatest truths which study and experience have ever suggested to the successful cultivators of the art of singing." Admittedly breath is a control but very few persons speak of pronunciation (resonance) as being the other control. G. B. Lamperti in Brown's <u>Vocal Wisdom</u> (1931) states, "It is a strange fact that the throat is controlled by what happens above it, in the acoustics of the head, through word, vibration and resonance." The Chromatic Vowel Chart tells the singer which vowel-colors to use for proper throat space control for each step of the singing voice. The only thing new is that I have, in the process of studying this phenomenon, found a way by which vowel resonances can be heard, felt, notated, and used. The procedure is simple enough so that any one can hear it and feel it, and can apply those vowel colors during the training of the singing voice as well as during professional performance, stage center, in any opera house or concert hall in the world.

There is a unique advantage to the teacher in using the Vowel Resonator/Concertmate or Electric organ combination. The male-voiced teacher can feel and hear what it is like to make vowels like a soprano. A female-voiced teacher can instruct a man on how to "cover," "darken," or "round" the tone with the feel of the lower <u>Green</u> vowels over Notes #22 to #28. Garcia said it this way in his <u>Memoire</u> presented to the French Academy in 1840, Paschke Translation (1984, p. lii):

> "The tones included between e^1 and b^1, when one gives them some full vigor in the chest register and sombre timbre, acquire, in men and women, a dramatic character which has led to an error in the very appreciation of their nature. In place of recognizing in them the

influence of the sombre timbre, joined by intensity, in
conditions of effect more favorable than anywhere else,
people have seen in these tones an exceptional case, and
they have designated them by the name mixed tones, or
mixed voice, darkened (sombrée). The A string of the
violoncello, although weaker, reproduces rather well
the same effect. "

Please note that the lower Green vowels on Notes #20 and #26 bring about this
condition in either Male or Female voices, concert pitch. Acoustically speaking,
the vowels over a broken line have a pitch exactly a 5th above the sung pitch and
when one pronounces them exactly, both the sung pitch and its 2nd harmonic
(octave) are reinforced. Said in another way, this pronunciation seems to cause
the voice to sing in two registers at once!!! No wonder it is called Mixed.
This (1.5) series is quite unstable and the pitch will wander either to the sharp
or flat side depending on which side of the 5th the singer pronounces the vowel.
If the singer resonates that vowel on the Vowel Resonator he will find a resonating vowel color and when singing the pitch a 5th below the vowel, dead center,
will have good resonance, focus, and good intonation. This reinforces both the
sung pitch and the octave. If the singer resonates the vowel at the 8ve, the 8ve
will be reinforced and the sung pitch will not be reinforced but it will be heard
as a phantom fundamental. (See Difference Tone, p. 267.)

RadioEar - hookup. Young singers are not frightened by the "gimmick" of a
RadioEar - headphone hook-up (used as a throat microphone) if they have had
any experience with microphones. The microphone has had enough bad effect
on singing - we might as well use it to our advantage.

Everyone has seen the exploits of those who ride on surfboards. They simply
wait for a large wave to come along and then they ride it. The lower formant,
R^1, is something like a large wave of sound. With the RadioEar-Headphone
hook-up, simply find one of the large waves and sing up and down the scale on
4 or 5 note exercises. You will become aware that in ascending, the mouth will
open and in descending the mouth will close. It will also be noted that the vowels
you are singing are those on the Chart if it is correctly placed for your voice
classification. Also, you can change waves (registers) by closing while going
up, and by opening when coming down. Likewise you can change Vowel Series
at will in the exercises. However, you can not change to any vowel value you
wish without losing resonance on some of them or by going through low troughs
of resonance.

QUESTIONABLE THOUGHTS THAT BEAR SCRUTINY -

Q. Is it true that any vowel can be sung on any note?

A. No. This is more nearly possible in Male voices than in Female voices.
Because of the pitch of the lower resonance of vowels, most Male singing

is done <u>below</u> the pitch of the vowels. They also have more harmonics with which to make vowel differentiation. It appears that most vowels can be sung in fast moving passages in the middle of all voices when there is not sufficient time for a standing wave and amplification of the voice to occur.

Q. Since a person can <u>see</u> into the throat, is it true that the pressures of the vibrating air can be disregarded?

A. No. These pressures also assist, amplify, or interrupt vocal cord vibration.

Q. Is it true that a singer should sing only on the pure Italian vowels A, E, I, O, U?

A. No. First of all, Italian is a <u>central</u> language - nearer to the Neutral position than other singing languages. So all vowels should be blended towards [ʌ] as in "pulse" or [ʊ] as in "pull." Furthermore there is only one /EE/ vowel and only one /OO/ vowel in Italian. Also, I think what is meant is to sing vowels which give a pure sound and to sing them without diphthongs, as is our tendency in English. Of course /E/ and /O/ have open and close sounds in Italian. Lilli Lehmann said that the best Italian artists used mixed vowels. They still do! Vowel modification came from Italy!

Q. Why do some teachers believe that Female singers should not sing Chest Voice?

A. A person who believes this was probably a Lyric or Coloratura Soprano. These classifications have light low voices and those teachers have not experienced that register significantly in their singing. I do not believe it is possible for those teachers to form the voices of Italian Lyrico Spinto, Dramatic or Mezzo sopranos. They would deny Contraltos their voices. There is also the possibility that those teachers have not yet learned how to blend the Chest voice into the register above it.

Q. Why do some teachers believe that the Head Voice should not be taught?

A. Those teachers probably have robust voices and think that the <u>larger</u> the tone the <u>better</u> the tone. The result is that when the singer comes to the area at the top line of the treble clef there is a shrillness and a type of vocal clutching which sets in. Sometimes there is a crackling sound and the vocal cords stop in their vibration. This is due to the type of sharp vocal cord vibration

which will be discussed in the next Chapter. The same thing
can occur at the top of Male voices which do not cover
properly in the area of d^1 to f^1.

In conclusion, all of the vowel values have been derived by means of the Vowel
Resonator - electric vibrator hookup. They may be used by singers, students,
and teachers "to find" and maximize the voice in the same manner. I firmly
believe that we are training the vocal cords at the same time we are training
the spaces above them.

We are at a time in history when the subject of acoustics is not taught in some
of the better universities and Schools of Music. Acoustical phonetics is usually
not involved with the singing voice. Even the Bell Telephone Laboratories have
made little study of the singing voice; and very seldom is the acoustical basis
of phonetics taught to those who use them in the pronunciation of French, German, Italian, and English. Is there a reason why some of the findings of this
study happen to be unusual? Also, in some Schools of Music the traditions of
the great singing masters are not studied in vocal pedagogy classes. Does
there happen to be a reason why the relationships between their precepts and
the nature of sounds in the singing voice are largely unknown? With a Vowel
Resonator and Concertmate hookup any teacher or singer can quickly gain an
enormous knowledge, through his senses, of the uses of pitch-vowel-register
relationships. Yes, we are in an age of discovery which should lead us again
to the great singing of the past.

Why not a Stradivarius? People speak with pride of owning a Stradivarius, a
Steinway, a Baldwin, a Selmer, or some elite kind of a musical instrument
which has been constructed by specialists in sound. Is it not just as important
to take natural materials of voice and construct them into a superb musical
instrument? The artist's craft of creating and maintaining an harmonic vocal
instrument of living members is just as distinguished as that of creating an
harmonic instrument of inanimate members. Somewhere along the way a lack
of perspective has arisen in the evaluation of this creative process.

Lilli Lehmann (1914, p. 104), said of maintaining a singing voice,

> "... the motto must be always, practice, and again,
> practice to keep one's powers uninjured; practice brings
> freshness to the voice, strengthens the muscles and is
> for the singer, far more interesting than any musical
> composition."

Isn't that an odd twist? How often today do singers want to perform now and not
take time to form their instruments? Unfortunately, they cannot buy a vocal
Stradivarius to play upon - they must form it as they play upon it. How exciting
if they follow a procedure based on the acoustical laws of sounding the vocal
instrument!

Persons who do not learn the technique of teaching singing, are not willing and/or do not have the time to learn the craft. They may be fine for coaching but there is a danger that they will create more problems than existed. Some teachers have been known to say that if a singer has any vocal problems, that teacher will not accept such a person as a student. The art of singing cannot endure unless <u>native talent</u> is sustained by a dependable technique.

Alfredo Kraus, noted Lyric Tenor, states the situation very clearly (Opera, January 1975, p. 19):

> "The stage forms the artist, but ruins the singer. And
> I, by profession, am a singer. To be a singer you need
> a technical knowledge which you cannot have at 20, 22,
> or even at 25. Technique is the basis of everything.
> You cannot be a singer if you are not first a vocal tech-
> nician, and you cannot be a good artist unless you are
> also a good singer."

Let us study further vocal principles which have been handed down to us!

CHAPTER IX.   THE RELATIONSHIP OF PHONATION AND COLOR IN SINGING.

SING ON THE BREATH [FLOW]

There is a traditional saying, "Sing on the breath," but one word is missing - the word [flow]. This is indicated by the figures below with description of the actions and sounds.

Singers should thoroughly understand that "the ringing and dullness [of vocal sound] are produced in the interior of the larynx, independently of the position high or low, of this organ; the open or closed qualities of the voice require the bodily movement of the larynx and of its antagonist the soft palate. Hence, any timbre may be bright or dull. This observation is most important for the expressive qualities of the voice." Garcia (1894), p. 12. I show the Glottis-Opening and Air-flow graphs of Chiba and Kajiama (1953) with my explanatory comments of their meaning. The lowest lines are the zero lines.

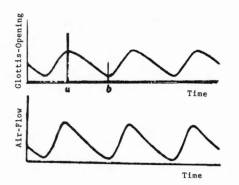

Glottal action - Smooth pulsations, vocal cords waving at each other.

Vowels - Diluted, "like a beverage with added water."

Acoustical characteristic - Little interference of waves of glottis and vowels, some trumpet effect.

Quality - Flute-like, whispery, Garcia's "dull timbre."

Registers - Female: Vowel, and Head. Male: Falsetto and sotto voce Mixed Voice.

Wave form - Sine, almost all low frequency, R^1, very little 3000 Hz.

Air flow - Takes a great deal of breath. In Head voice Garcia said at the ratio of 4 to 3. Bernoulli effect.

Fig. 19. SMOOTH VOICE
Slow motion sound
"ffuff-ffuff-fuff."

Chiba & Kajiyama, 1958

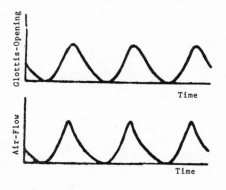

Glottal action - Soft explosions, vocal cords closing each cycle, some 3000.

Vowels - Distinct - stopped pipe - R^1, R^2, R^3, and 3000 Hz.

Acoustical characteristic - Positive interference (trumpet effect - wave reinforces wave), or Negative interference (resonance wave disrupts glottal wave).

Registers - Chest, Mixed, Middle (Upper) Vowel, and Head.

Wave form - Triangle wave, rather rich in harmonics.

Air flow - Economical air flow.

Fig. 20. SOFT EXPLO-
SIONS. Slow motion
sound "popopop."

Chiba & Kajiyama, 1958

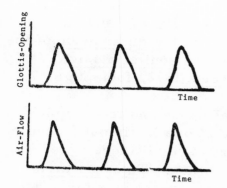

Fig. 21. SHARP EXPLO-SIONS. Slow motion sound - "ppopp-ppopp-ppopp."

Chiba & Kajiyama, 1958

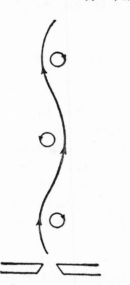

JET FROM A SLIT SHOW-ING SINOUS FORM AND VORTICES (A. WOOD, 1962). THIS IS THE BA-SIS OF THE "WHISTLE" REGISTER AND THE FLUTE SOUND IN THE SINGING VOICE. EDDIES ARE FORMED ON BOTH SIDES OF THE MOVING AIR. THE NUMBER OF EDDIES PER SECOND GIVES THE PITCH.

Fig. 22. Whistle Vibration

Glottal action - Sharp explosions - prolonged closure of vocal cords in each cycle.

Air flow - Great economy of breath, long phrases.

Vowels - Very distinct with vowel modification unbelievably critical on high pitches. Very strong 3000 Hz.

Acoustical characteristic - Strong trumpet effect. Positive interference (wave reinforces wave) or Negative interference (wave wipes interrupts wave). Pressures frequently alter the sung pitch (sharping or flatting) and influence the vibrato, usually slowing it.

Quality - Reedy because of high harmonics, metallic (gold, silver, bronze if good, brassy if bad).

Pronunciation - Extremely sensitive vowel modifi-cation is required, especially at higher pitches.

Register - Chest, Mixed, and Vowel.

Wave form - Triangle wave - very rich in har-monics.

Air flow - Very economical air flow - character-ized by long phrases.

In addition to the vocal cords acting like a reed, as in the above illustrations, they can also cause the sound of a whistle, flute, and act like a flue (not flute) stop of an organ (See Fig. 22).

In this phenomenon of vibration eddies of air just above a small slit between the vocal cords are set into high frequency vibration. The eddy phenome-non is the basis of the edge tone which the flute and piccolo resonate. Incidentally, do the lips vibrate when you whistle? Would the cords vi-brate in Whistle Register? They have not yet been seen. Do the edges of the flue stop vibrate? They do not!

I believe there is also another phenomenon of vibration involving the vocal cords. As winds flow past an object, small eddies are set up behind it. This also occurs in fluids and can be experienced by drawing your hand quickly through water with the fingers loosely spread. You will find that your fingers tend to flutter, vibrating from side to side across the track of your hand. They may strike each other, wave at each other, or merely set up eddies. We may con-jecture from our fluttering fingers observation that a vocal cord on either side is given a slight push as each eddy is formed. I will conjecture that this alternating vibration in the voice can make a transition to the vocal cords striking each other in the reed form of vibration in Figs. 19, 20, and 21. I believe these actions are involved with the crescendo and the diminuendo of the classical messa di voce called by Corri (1810, p. 14) "the soul of music." Garcia inferred this was the mechanism for mezzo voce (1872, footnote p. 7.).

I must say that Fiberscopic observations of the vocal cords and the complex laryngeal components in singing are so captivating that one is almost forced to forgive investigators for believing that the vocal cords are all there is to singing. But Nature invokes Newton's third Law of Motion. To every action there is an equal and opposite reaction. That is how we travel in outer space. The law is also involved with the inner spaces of Man's throat. This involves the vibration of air and the feedback of alternating high and low pressures upon the vocal cords from the front of the mouth. It is interesting to hear the sound when one tries to sing with helium in the lungs. The sound is very high and nasal. Think of what kind of a sound there would be if the throat were a vacuum (even though it does look like the throat is a vacuum).

VOCAL CORD THEORY

Ever since Garcia invented the laryngoscope, investigators have been overly interested in the vocal cords. As far as he was concerned the instrument had served its purpose within a year of its discovery and the presentation of his observations to the Royal Society of London in 1855. The vocal cords were established as being the generator of voiced sound. He considered further observation and study to be merely satisfying the curiosity of those who wanted to see for themselves that which he had already established (Mackinlay, 1908, p. 205).

I suspect that because of the awesome Fiberscopic revelations of the larynx in action in both speech and singing many may be lured into believing that the vocal cords are the sole generators of sound. Although these and stroboscopic observations have seemingly confirmed the vocal cord theory of sound generation, there is more to phonation than that. Manén has felt there is a vacuum created by a click above the vocal cords which begins the vibration. This means there is a vacuum or low pressure area. This thought deserves consideration. There is a low pressure area there part of the time and a high pressure area there part of the time in singing. In high speed pictures of the vocal cords, why do the cords look as though they are being blown downwards in part of their cycle?

Garcia knew there was more than just vocal cord theory since he gave the modification of vowels in both his books. The medical profession has led us to believe that the vocal cords are the sum total involved. Many believe that acoustics are involved. Manén and others are correct when they raise a big question about the total importance of the vocal cords. Of course we cannot sing without them (although we can speak without them by means of an artificial

larynx or by whispering).   The visible throat and larynx are the only parts of
the vocal apparatus with which throat doctors deal.   I am afraid that we must
resolve to accept their continued blindness to this aspect of the vocal instrument - they make a big part of their living treating the results of the misuse
of source and system.   For sure we do not wish to have them learn more
about it by teaching singing - there has been enough of that in the history of
vocal pedagogy.

The resonating system is quite complex since it involves the interplay of two
tunnels - that through the mouth and the other through the nose.   The use of
these tunnels is guided by the sophisticated ear of the teacher of singing.   They
deal daily with live performance and go to hear performances of live music,
most researchers and throat specialists do not.   I must say that I appreciate
and am grateful for what throat doctors can do for us.   I am not thankful for
their blind spot concerning the bad effects of the poor relationship between
source and system.

The magic of the vocal tract is involved with the way it can adjust itself for
pitch height.   See the adjustment of the jaw as shown in the illustration by
Manén (1974 p. 30):

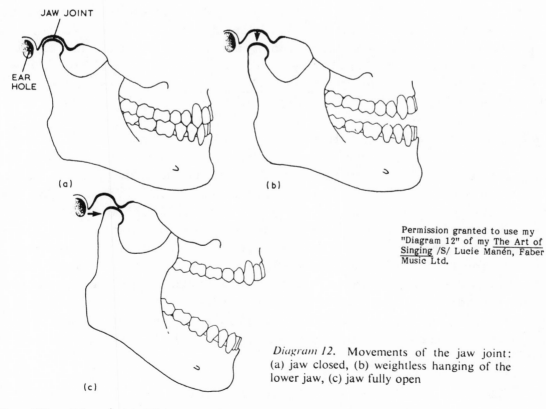

Permission granted to use my
"Diagram 12" of my The Art of
Singing /S/ Lucie Manén, Faber
Music Ltd.

Diagram 12. Movements of the jaw joint:
(a) jaw closed, (b) weightless hanging of the
lower jaw, (c) jaw fully open

Fig. 23.   Manén's Illustrations of Jaw Openings

There is still more to phonation than I have stated. Vennard (1967 #288), who stands as a prime researcher of the larynx, has made the succinct observation:

> "There is good evidence that when we are learning the
> shaping of the cavities above the larynx, we are training
> the vocal cords at the same time."

I believe this is the reason why the Chromatic Vowel Chart, derived by means of a Vowel Resonator, works. His observations and research were turned to the acoustics of singing at the end of his career.

The following questions have arisen concerning various registers:

Q. 1: What should I do when the throat catches or makes harsh, husky sounds on or above the upper passaggio ?

A. This may be due to some lingering heaviness in the vocal cords due to allergies, some swelling in the cords from oversinging, or singing without warming up properly. If it occurs very often, it is probably due to the type of vocal cord action and the airflow used. The vocal cords may be slapping each other too vigorously. Use the falsetto /U/ with the mouth having an opening of a pencil sharpener. This may be followed by falsetto /UH/ behind the palm of the hand. Several of these beginning on Note #23 in Male voices and Note #35 Female voices should assist in establishing the proper vibration and in activating a better use of the musculatures involved. This may be followed by singing Blue vowels on those notes and by alternating Blue - Green - Blue vowels of the Chromatic Vowel Chart in the same mechanism.

Q. 2: What happens when the middle of the voice sounds breathy?

A. The vocal cords need to strike each other more in each cycle. This may be accomplished by beating rather vigorously an imaginary timpani with the fists and arms from the elbows while singing /AH/ and /EH/ in middle voice for a period of a 30 second tempo. This coordinates rib action and the muscles of the chest with the laryngeal and postural muscles for beginning the tones between Notes #7 and #15 for Male voices and between Notes #23 and #28 for Female voices. The same action an octave higher than these locations will cause the voice to have a harsh and grating sound. The /A/ and /EH/ attacks are from Garcia's Art of Singing (any edition) and the idea of the hands is borrowed from Dr. Friedrich Brodnitz, the noted physical therapist.

Q. 3: How do the above actions affect the vowel color?

A.   They dilute the vowel color where more breath is used and intensify the the vowel color where more laryngeal action is used.

Q. 4: How many timbres are there for the Male voice above Note #21?

A.   There is one - the <u>sombre</u> timbre or covered voice. Pavarotti in a television interview said that a <u>real</u> tenor covers on fa (f^1). I would add that a baritone covers on e or e♭, a bass-baritone on d, and a bass on c#.

Q. 5: How can I cover?

A.   Sing the <u>Green</u> vowels beginning in the lower loop at Note #21 and continue in the green going up. The tenor will sing the high c most effectively on the [æ] vowel as in the American pronunciation of <u>fantastic</u>.

Q. 6: How many timbres in the Female voice at Note #35 and above?

A.   Marchesi said that a soprano should go into Head Voice at f^2, so sing on the <u>Green</u> vowels from Note #34 on up. The <u>Yellow</u> vowels may be used if there is sufficient Whistle quality blended into them. Otherwise the voice may sound like a scream, which should be used only where intended.

Q. 7: Can I be understood if I sing that way?

A.   Probably just as well. If you are not that is the composer's problem for having written wrong words on high notes. If you want the voice to be healthy sing in the Head Voice. Marchesi's singers sang so long that they did not have time to learn how to teach. Your career will be shorter if you spread on the high notes.

Q. 8: What is the acoustical significance of the Chiba and Kajiama air-flow, glottal action diagrams?

A.   The phenomena are that 1) the voice can only amplify those frequencies which are in the glottal source and, 2) it cannot completely filter out the frequencies which it does not need. Sharp explosions are for the middle and lower notes of voices. Since the higher notes of sopranos have only four or less harmonics the soft explosions are better for those notes.

Q. 9: But what if I want to express some violent emotion in my upper voice which I can gain only by violent glottal explosion?

A.   Go ahead. There is no enforceable law against vocal suicide. But not too long, too high, or for too long. Even too much perfect singing would be vocal abuse.

In conclusion, vocal timbres involve both resonance and vocal action and their actions are controllable for musical and emotional expression.

CHAPTER X. LARYNX POSITION

Much has been said about larynx position in the teaching of singing and much misdirection has occurred. I will cite the statement of Manuel Garcia who was the first person to observe the vocal cords in singing. He is also our best linkage to Bel Canto. He knew the Bel Canto composers; he was in Naples at the time they were creating many of their masterworks. Rossini wrote the role of Almaviva in the Barber of Seville for his father. His sister, Malibran, was a reigning queen of Bel Canto and he had much to do with the formation of her voice. His sister, Pauline Viardot was the Mezzo Soprano for whom Berlioz adapted the role of Orpheus in Orpheus and Euridice. He did a great deal of investigation of the singing voice and gave a report to the French Academy under the title of MEMOIRE ON THE HUMAN VOICE in April 1841. I will quote from Paschke's translation of Part I of Garcia's A Complete Treatise on The Art of Singing (1984 p. liv.).

> "...the larynx, serving as the base of the vocal tube,
> must necessarily raise or lower itself to permit this
> tube to shorten and lengthen itself, and to vary its shape,
> its diameter, and the tension of its walls."

He points out that the larynx behaves differently when the clear and sombre timbres are sung. In clear timbre the larynx begins the chest register a little lower than rest then ascends and is carried forward as the pitch ascends. At the top of a register, just before a "thin and strangled sound" occurs, it drops slightly and again follows the ascending pitch. And in the highest registers of Male and Female voices, the head lifts to "facilitate the elevation of the larynx." This certainly can be seen in live television opera.

He states that in the sombre timbre the larynx is held low and "the voice gives all the 'volume' of which it is capable." However he notes that:

> "As for the head tones, the larynx almost always produces
> them while rising rapidly. One could not prevent these
> movements; trying to do so to swell the voice would be
> dangerous and often useless effort."

If a singer or teacher has a visual monitoring device, either by mirrors or television camera where a profile can be seen, it can be observed that the throat is following the above actions when singing the diagonals of the Chromatic Vowel Chart or with the Vowel Resonator. Nothing is new, just perceived differently.

Garcia explained the positioning of the larynx quite clearly before he observed the action with the laryngoscope. Much is being said today about keeping the larynx down while singing. This is a partial truth, not an absolute truth. Birgit Nilsson (Hines 1982 p. 199) said:

> "There was a voice teacher who very much wanted to give me lessons. He said, 'When you sing a high note the Adam's apple goes up. It should go down with high notes.' He started to push it with his thumb. My Adam's apple ached for fourteen days. That was the worst thing I ever experienced. It goes automatically. It cannot go deeper for the high note."

Miss Nilsson, who made her debut in 1948 and is still singing, must know something about survival in the art. How can any teacher say, "Keep the Adam's apple down and be successful" when Miss Nilsson has been so successful in her vocal approach. The answer is that teachers have successes with different types of voices - or should I say genders.

When I observe singers on television, I notice that the baritones and basses seem to be using the sombre position of singing and that the sopranos and tenors, singing their higher notes, throw the head back and open the mouth quite wide for the high pitch of the vocal tract, the resonator. For the high voices, the holding of the head down for the upper notes is counter-productive.

Luchsinger and Arnold (1965 p. 67) found that -

> "supraglottic resonance is an integral part of the shaping of vocal registers and the determination of vocal timbre."

They also state (p. 77) that the antagonistic action between the elevator muscles and the downward tracheal pull upon the [rising] larynx contribute to shortening the vocal cords. This can be "read" in close-ups of singers on television. They further observed that this is accompanied by increased activity of the vocal-cord tensors. In addition, they have noticed in young persons that the wings of the thyroid cartilage come as much as 1 centimeter closer together during the phonation of high tones. When teachers seek relaxation in singing, are they searching for relaxation, flacidity, or a balance of muscular action? I hope it is the latter.

Resonance tracking is involved with the above observations. In sombre timbre the lips will usually be forward a great deal of the time. In clear timbre, there will be more of a tendency to sing on the "smile." And in the gymnastics of runs by the prima donnas there will be a great deal of play by the lips in the fast runs and arpeggios. In the singing voice, the vibrators and the resonators are very dependent upon each other, whether one knows it or not.

The diagonals on the Chromatic Vowel Chart are quite symbolic in this respect. As voices go up the scale, there is a tendency for the larynx to rise as the diagonals rise. If there is a change from one register to another, in ascending, the larynx will lower so that the singer can proceed higher. The opposite is true in descending.

Basically what the singer wishes to have is great gymnastic ability of the throat which is, at the same time, acoustically maximal - that means that he/she wishes to have the most for the least amount of energy. Forced resonance is a lot of work and is fatiguing; sympathetic resonance is efficient and allows an artist to sing for a considerable length of time without fatigue. That statement must be followed with a plea for adequate rest after a performance and during the time of rehearsals. The singing voice, being 100 - 1000 times as loud as a conversational voice will need more rest than an actor's voice. Of necessity, his voice must be of a good quality; less so that of the actor. A word of warning from my experience in Europe, if the Intendent of the Theater is from the spoken stage, beware and be protective of yourself in rehearsals - some of them schedule singers like actors and expect 9 hour days which, incidentally, are not allowed by the Unions of the German language houses.

I have used the term "dimple falsetto" in Overtones of Bel Canto. The thyroid cartilage sits on top of the cricoid (or ring) cartilage. The thyroid cartilage is fastened to the cricoid cartilage by an elastic hinge in the back. The cricothyroid muscle is made up of two parts. The vertical one pulls the two cartilages together at the front. It is frequently overlooked that there is also an oblique part of the muscle which, when shortened, pulls the tyroid cartilage forward on the cricoid cartilage and causes a dimple to form underneath the Adam's apple or thyroid cartilage. The use of this muscle helps stretch the vocal ligaments to give the higher pitches in the Male falsetto and the Female Whistle voice. For those teachers who say "relax, relax," they will not be able to use this musculature because it comes about through the assistance of the extrinsic muscles which pull upon the larynx.

There is another interesting factor that is concerned with larynx position - the intrinsic muscles of the larynx. The clearest description, related to singing, is found in Husler and Rodd-Marling (1965, p. 98). They describe the laryngeal process involved with the three primary vowels [u], [i] and [a]. They continue to say...

> "Practicing the vowels that lie between u, i, and ah serves
> to exercise functions in the vocal organ consisting of
> various combinations of these three types. (Vowels as
> written down, are not, of course, unchanging magnitudes.
> In every language they vary, if only slightly, but in each
> case their formation is due to a different combination of
> forces between the Stretchers and Tensors, the inner
> and outer muscles of the larynx.)"

"As mentioned before, the singer has to overcome the functional <u>one-sidedness</u> of these three basic types of vowels until, as singers say, 'each vowel has something in common with all the others' or 'until all vowels are identically placed.'"

Husler and Rodd-Marling also have something very interesting to say concerning the comparison of elocution and singing.

"When working on the specially "schooled" voice of the elocutionist, the picture perceived by the voice trainer is, as it were, that of a vocal organ much reduced in size; the Closers and Tensors of the vocal folds are exceptionally well-ennervated, the action of the Suspensory mechanism, and the expiratory muscles, extremely weak."

Surely this is the reason that actors of the spoken stage cannot sing well, actors of the lyric stage cannot speak well, and singing/speaking actors of the operetta have difficulty in doing both well. They are different species of vocal use.

With that statement, I will remind the reader once again that the functional co-ordination of the muscular parts of the vocal organ is one thing for speaking and quite another in singing. Every teacher knows that singers are influenced by their speech habits. If there is too much use of "the Closers and Tensors" a condition, called "laryngeal squeeze" by Dr. Van Lawrence, exists (as I have seen on his Fiberscope). It requires the assistance of a Vocal Therapist. Several singing teachers are assisting in this valuable work.

Is there any relationship between the Caruso Scale, the Garcia scale, and the pulls upon the laryngeal muscles as described by Husler and Rodd-Marling? I believe that there is. In addition I have found that the /U/ for covering in both Male and Female voices is limited to certain notes and that above that Front and Neutral Vowels are more effective. They give the frontal and upward pull on the tongue necessary for the extreme high notes.

Did anyone say that the training of the singing voice is simple? No wonder it is the King/Queen of instruments, the possessors of which are befriended by the royalty by birth, by wealth, and by talent. Now let us put things together!

CHAPTER XI. HISTORICAL REGISTERS, PASSAGGIOS, AND VOWEL SCALES

Some teachers say there are no registers and passaggios. I wish things were that simple. I believe it is a result of the European Kämmersinger Syndrome in which teaching is a "retirement" for opera and Lieder singers. No doubt, they can coach mature and natural voices similar to their own - but it takes years to learn the craft of teaching singing. The National Association of Teachers of Singing has done much to establish the teaching of singing as a profession in the United States although there is unfortunately a growing tendency towards the Kämmersinger Syndrome. Consequently there is an increasing amount of singing on natural talent without sufficient technical foundation.

Most teachers will acknowledge that the Male and Female voices can carry their Chest Voice to the passaggio in the area of e^1 above middle c. And a passaggio exists in both Male and Female voices in this area when they are trained for singing over a heavy orchestral accompaniment or an extended range, as in Mozart. Carrying Chest Voice higher than this in either Male or Female voices is injurious to the voice and a transition of registers is required. Folk singing and "pop" singing are matters which will not be addressed at this time. The endeavor to be different and to get into print (publish or perish) has caused many deviations from the truths which were discovered long ago. I repeat, some teachers have gone so far as to say that registers do not exist. The result is that the voices taught are confined to a very limited range, volume, and/or make excruciating sounds which cannot be described as beautiful in the sound and style of bel canto.

Marchesi taught only female voices, believing she did not understand the male voices sufficiently well to teach them. Her singers had such long careers that none had time left in which to learn the craft of teaching singing! It would be well for all teachers who are beginning to teach, regardless of age and length of career to read Marchesi's work, and the new translation and comparison of Garcia's first and eighth editions of The Art of Singing by Paschke (1984). This is the historical and definitive statement of great singing according to the Laws of Nature. Without this knowledge of Natural Laws the singer is a bit like an astronaut being rocketed into space without Mission Control having a knowledge of Newton's Laws of Universal Gravitation. He does not wish to become a star that way; neither should a singer attempt to become a star unless his technique is based on the Laws of Nature. No teacher should have the effrontery to brag about his ignorance of these great laws - although many find denial to be the easiest way out!

Registers are involved with the position and actions of the throat in singing. Recently, registers have been thought of as being primarily the result of the action of the vocal cords. Too few have thought of the effect of the acoustical load upon the vocal cords, causing changes in their action. This is a cause and effect situation which needs much further examination. I have found little evidence of concern with this phenomenon in the research of today. I believe that the pressures of air from the pulsations caused by the vocal cords are reflected back upon them and have a great deal to do with their oscillation. When in harmonic phase with the swing of the vocal cords, they assist the vibrator. When out of phase with the vibration, the vocal cords are disrupted. Whether my conjecture is correct is unimportant; the effect is easily heard and proven with the Vowel Resonator. Garcia's schematic of registers for all voices is found in the Cramer edition (1872, p. 6.) as follows:

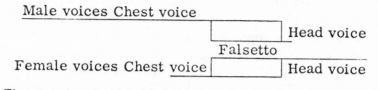

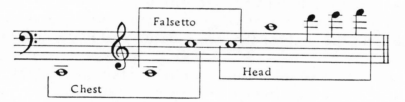

The general scale of the three registers is as follows:

Two or three notes are given as the possible limits of each register because the organs being elastic, naturally admit of fluctuation.

Fig. 24. Garcia's Register Schematics of Voices

The register schematic of the Female voice is different from that of the Male voice. Garcia was acoustically and physiologically correct in his definition of registers. The only way a man can have a Head Register is for him to be a castrato, to be a Counter Tenor singing soprano notes, or to reinforce the notes of the Female Head Voice at the octave. The vowels for all of these resonations are shown on the Chromatic Vowel Chart.

Tosi, 1743, p. 23, writing of the castrato voice, said there were two registers, but with the advent of Male singers and the larger opera houses, beginning with San Carlo, a method of amplification of vocal sound had to be used. This is the period of bel canto composer, who were commissioned by Barbaia. They were employed to write operas and to coach the singers, and, as a consequence, they wrote the music to fit the voice. Rossini wrote the part of Almaviva in "The Barber of Seville" for Garcia's father, and we are largely indebted to him for the classical thought of three registers. The pitch of San Carlo was one note lower than Roman pitch (Pleasants, 1966, p. 185), and the parts of Don Basilio and Figaro were both written for basses. With contemporary pitch of A-440, Figaro has become a high baritone and much of Don Basilio's music is transposed down a whole step. The Vowel Chart was written for the 440 pitch.

One of the earliest vowel scales was that which Garcia described for the Ah vowel in Male voices (1872, p. 12.). To correlate the Chromatic Vowel Chart with Garcia's description, I have used note numbers on the Chart instead of note names. When the arrow is placed on f# the notes will be those stated for tenor by Garcia; when placed on eb they will be those for bass-baritone. This passaggio of the voice from Chest Voice to the register immediately above it is of vital concern to all Female singers with the possible exception of some Coloratura and Lyric Sopranos.

> [When singing the /A/ vowel - Male singers] "should begin to gently round at Note #16 for the actual clear quality would be too thin. The reader will remark that the word rounding, and not closing is here used: this applies to the Notes #19, #20, #21. From #22 the two qualities agree, but the closed timbre [cover] should not be practiced until a pupil has mastered the bright timbre which is difficult to attain in this part of the vocal scale. If this caution be neglected, there is the risk of the voice being veiled or muffled."

> "The bright timbre alone can make the voice light and penetrating, but though it may communicate its character to the entire compass, it is especially in this tenth of the chest voice, viz Notes #6 - #21, that its effects are pleasing. But voices should, without exception, abandon it upon reaching Note #22; nor should tenors and other male voices use it above Note #23 in the chest register as it renders the tone disagreeable [spread]. Generally, tenors, will take up the falsetto [Mixed Voice in my terminology] at Note #19 and continue it upwards as far as Notes #28 and #29. Between Notes #19 and #23 these voices experience great difficulty in firmly ennunciating sounds, the timbre of which should be neither too shrill nor too muffled.... However accomplished a singer may be, the sounds on Notes #24, #25, #26, #27, #28 in the clear timbre will always appear shrill, even when heard in a very large room, and will resemble a boy-chorister's voice. Therefore they should never be used except in closed timbre."
> [In present terminology, the voice should be "covered" by the use of Mixed Voice.]

Garcia's statement means that Notes #25, #26, #27, and #28 should always be sung in the sombre timbre (Mixed Voice) in Male voices.

I will say that the Garcia Vowel Scale was his procedure for establishing the Italian form of cover in the Male voice and that it is also a way of establishing the transition from Chest to the register above it in both Male and Female voices. Men should practice this Vowel Scale daily and Women should daily practice this scale between Notes #13 and #28. Garcia's Vowel Scale for tenor would appear as follows when notated in the bass clef:

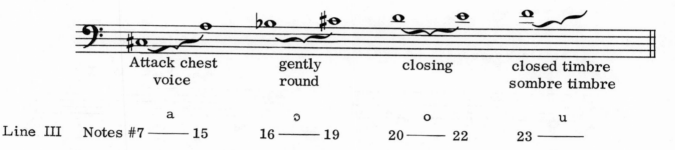

Line III   Notes #7 ——— 15   16 ——— 19   20 ——— 22   23 ———

Fig. 25. Garcia's Vowel Scale Values

Caruso's vowel scale had a half open /A/ from c# to a, /O/ from b to e, and /U/ from f# and above. This was in Italian by an Italian - that language does not differentiate between [u] and [U]. His Vowel Scale would appear thus when notated in the bass clef (Fucito 1929, p. 150):

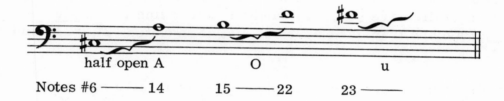

half open A   O   u

Notes #6 ——— 14   15 ——— 22   23 ———

Fig. 26. Caruso's Vowel Scale

Furthermore, the Chromatic Vowel Chart for Caruso would be placed on f#[1].

Schoen-Rene (1941, p. 195) said that when she was talking with Caruso in 1903 he was anxious to "pay his respects to the great master Garcia, who was then ninety-eight years old. He had not realized that the old master whom he admired greatly was still living." Was Caruso trained on Garcia's vowel scale? Perhaps he derived his vowel scale independently of Garcia. Or perhaps it came from Naples where both received their early training!

Both scales utilize Back Vowels only. In my experience I have found that it is best to use all series of vowels through the passaggio and that the Front and Neutral Vowels be used for the extreme high notes. The only exceptions I have found are in the Scandinavian languages which have a more central position of the Back Vowels. For instance the Scandinavian /U/ is written phonetically as [u].

Fischer-Dieskau has stated (Sugg, 1973) that his two teachers were students of Julius Stockhausen and that his own principles of singing could be found in Stockhausen's Method of Singing (1884) and Garcia's Treatise on the Art of

<u>Singing</u>. Stockhausen, p. 17, quotes Garcia's <u>Nouveau traite sommaire</u>, "Great difficulty is evidenced in drawing the tones in two registers at once, which occurs for females and tenors in this extent" [also baritones, Heldenbaritones, and some basses].

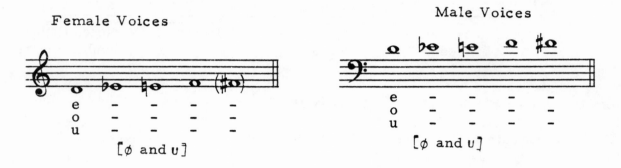

Fig. 27. Julius Stockhausen's <u>passaggi</u> for Male and Female Voices

Garcia stated, "The pupil must commence the note piano in Falsetto [Mixed Voice for Men and Women], and in the sombre quality." The sombre quality vowels in Italian are [e], [o], and [u] according to his <u>Memoire on the Human Voice</u>, Paschke translation 1984 p. lix. See Notes #21, #22, and #23 on the Chart.

Garcia's transition through the <u>passaggio</u> is related to a radio broadcast statement by Giovanni Martinelli who sang for 33 years as leading tenor at the Metropolitan Opera. When asked to what he attributed his vocal longevity he replied:

> "First to learn well how to sing, do not spread the voice, and particularly between the middle and the high register, keep the voice collected at e, f, f#. This is the place where most singers, especially tenors, run into trouble. Be sure of the good support of deep breath and it is a must, a must I repeat, do not attempt any role unsuitable to your voice."

Luciano Pavarotti made a similar statement on Mizar record PF3. I am indebted to Barbara Doscher for the translation.

> "A tenor normally starts to cover his notes or better to 'focus' on F, F# and G and it is usually a forced and unnatural sound which a young man finds hard to believe in, but it is a sound which technically and anatomically speaking produces in the voice a rest for the vocal cords, which will then be ready when the voice goes higher, to vibrate with greater elasticity and therefore enables the notes to be taken which are B flat, B and C, the most difficult for a tenor."

Dorothy Kirsten, the American Puccini Soprano, said in a conversation that all of the bodies of the tenors with whom she sang shook when they sang their high notes. The "deep support" is part and parcel of the high notes of tenors and baritones. The compression and intensity give the exciting sound.

The statements by Martinelli and Pavarotti are related to the transition of the Female voice through the same passaggio described by Marilyn Horne (Musical America, May 1970, p. 13.):

> "I think the voice has a shape wider at the top and bottom and narrower in the middle. The middle is where the danger area is, around Eb, E, and F. I almost never carry the chest sound above F and because of this I can get from one register to another without difficulty."

Her statement transcribed phonetically would appear for Female and Male voices, with slight adjustment, as follows:

Female voices.

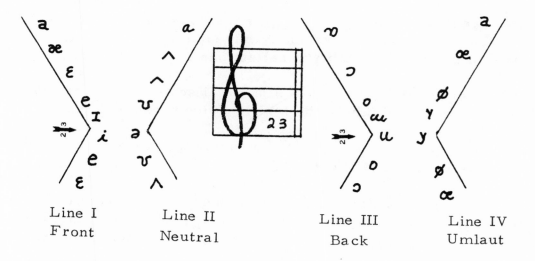

Line I	Line II	Line III	Line IV
Front	Neutral	Back	Umlaut

Fig. 28a. Both Female and Male Voices are narrow at f^1.

Male voices narrow at the same spot, concert pitch. They can be
described as wide at the bottom, narrow at the top of the passaggio,
then opening.

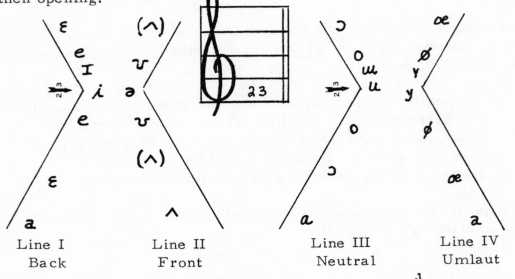

| Line I | Line II | Line III | Line IV |
| Back | Front | Neutral | Umlaut |

Fig. 28b. Both Female and Male Voices are narrow at f^1.

The resonance shifts in the passaggio, Notes #20 - #24 pertain to all voices
which use Chest voice and the register immediately above it. These vowels
are notated in the sombre quality vocalizations in Chapter XX.

Garcia had less to say in the nature of a vowel scale for Female voice. If the
notes were too weak and thin in the Middle Voice between d^1 and a^1

"...this may be corrected by using the close timbre with
the vowel A, half O (aw)...."

He said, "the most essential feature of the head voice is roundness." He believed the first notes of the head voice were eb^2, e^2, and f^2 and that it should
not be practiced above sol [g^2] because the high notes should be economized.

It can be seen he merely suggested a vowel scale for Female voices.

However, Enrico Delle Sedie (1885) made a definite statement about a Vowel
Scale which I have reviewed and given in its complete original form in the
May/June 1982 NATS Bulletin. He was the Renato in the first London perform-
ance of Ballo in Maschera and was the teacher of the lyric Rossini tenor,
Alessandro Bonci, who was at the Metropolitan Opera during the time of Caruso.
Another artist trained on this scale was Gerhard Hüsch. I will paraphrase Delle
Sedie's "Phonic order" in a scalular notation. I give his English versions of
the /A/ vowel modifications:

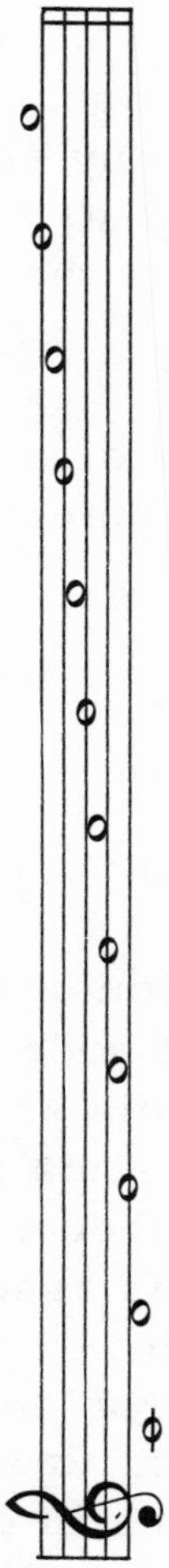

e mute covered as in the word. . . . . Her

e mute as in the word . . . . Nature

eu grave as in the French word . . . . Feu

eu closed as in the French word. . . . Jeune

ô grave as in the word. . . . . Pôle

o closed as in the word . . . . Or

â grave as in the word. . . . . Wâs

ā open as in the word. . . . . Bār

α grave as in the word . . . . Wâs

ᾱ closed as in the word . . . . Cᾱto

α a little closed as in the word . . . . Fαther

ᾱ open as in the word. . . . . Bᾱr

Fig. 29. Delle Sedie's Phonic Order

It is astounding that this scale has been in print and use for a Century! It is a pity that it was not written in the International Phonetic Alphabet. One can only guess at the vowel values in the absence of a teacher from that line. However, they can be used as a hunting license for finding the placement of the voice through the use of vowel colors. It does allow for the lower and upper passaggi in Female voices and the upper passaggio in Male voices. Again it proves that nothing is new, just differently perceived!

Herbert Witherspoon was influenced by the vowel pitch work of Aikin (1925, p. 92) who also had a vowel scale. Witherspoon, a bass at the "Met" during the time of Caruso, a noted teacher of singing, and later General Director of that company for a short period of time, believed the A had three values (1925, p. 92.):

AH as in "on" or "hot" in the lower range.
AH as in "Father" in the normal middle range.
AH as in "Un" in the upper range.

Witherspoon was a student of G. B. Lamperti, and Giovanni Sbriglia among others.

There is also the passaggio to the Female Head Voice which is described by Marchesi on p. 232 of this text. This has been overlooked by many singers and teachers resulting in the screams and cries which Garcia mentioned - that is one of the prices of attempting too large a tone in the middle of the Female voice.

Is it because of secrecy or just plain lack of study that the above scales and passaggi are virtually unknown today? We are told that we are entering an informational Century. Perhaps that will help!

QUESTIONS AND ANSWERS

Q. Does closing at the passaggios have anything to do with vocal health?

A. Yes. Dr. Friederich Brodnitz at the 1964 National Convention of the National Association of Teachers of Singing spoke on the incidence of nodes in singers. There is a great frequency associated with problems around the f^1 area of Male voices and the f^2 area of Female voices. Statistics showed that there were many problems with baritones attempting to become tenors, and mezzo-sopranos attempting to become sopranos. This is associated with the kind of vibration which occurs at this area. If the lower type of vibration is driven up, or openness carried too high, then problems are bound to occur. Nicolai Gedda told me that his first teacher, Carl Martin Ohmann, cautioned him against exaggerating the c, d, e notes in the middle of his voice. Those would be Noted #18 to #22 on the Chromatic Vowel Chart. He points out how some of the lower voices of today have "dried out" because they have abused these notes. The same thing can be said of Female voices, roughly an octave higher.

Q. What should I do when the throat catches or makes harsh, husky sounds on or above the upper passaggio?

A. This may be due to some lingering heaviness in the vocal cords caused by allergies, some swelling in the cords from oversinging, or singing without warming up properly. If it occurs very often, it is probably due to the type of vocal cord action and the airflow used. The vocal cords may be slapping each other too vigorously (See Fig. 52). Use the falsetto /u/ with the mouth having an opening of a pencil sharpener. This may be followed by falsetto /uh/ behind the palm of the hand. I have called this the open mouth hum symbolized by an [m] in a circle, viz. Ⓜ. Sing downward arpeggios or sighs in this manner. Several of these beginning on Note #23 in Male voices and Note #35 Female voices should assist in establishing the proper vibration and in activating a better use of the musculatures involved. This may be followed by singing Blue vowels on those notes and by alternating Blue - Green - Blue vowels of the Chromatic Vowel Chart in the same laryngeal mechanism.

Q. What happens when the middle of the voice sounds breathy?

A. The vocal cords need to strike each other more in each cycle (See Fig. 52). This may be accomplished by beating rather vigorously an imaginary timpani with the fists and arms from the elbows while singing /A/ /EH/ /A/ /EH/ in middle voice for a period of 30 seconds or so at a walking tempo. This coordinates rib action and the muscles of the chest with the laryngeal and postural muscles for beginning the tones between Notes #7 and #15 for Male voices and between Notes #23 and #28 for Female voices. It involves both the phonatory and breathing muscles in a very spontaneous way. The same action an octave higher than these locations will cause the voice to have a harsh and grating sound. The /A/ and /EH/ attacks are from Garcia's Art of Singing (any edition) and the idea of the beating hands is borrowed from Dr. Frederich Brodnitz, the noted physical therapist.

Q. What about the relationships of glottal action/air flow and consonants?

A. Probably the best rule is to keep the consonants soft; at no time should the consonant closure be more firm than the closures of the glottis. The vocal cords are in danger of being stopped in their vibration when hard [b], [d], and [g] are sounded. Either soften them towards [m], [n], and /ng/ or make an articulatory movement which would resemble the gesture of the intended consonant. This is not so great a problem with Male voices. This is one reason that Italian and Spanish are better for singing than German and English. French is more difficult because nasalization and denasalization differentiate meaning.

Q. But what if I want to express some violent emotion or be dramatic in the passaggio and upper voice which I can gain only by violent glottal explosion?

A. Go ahead. There is no enforceable law against vocal suicide. But not too long, or too high for too long. Even too much perfect singing would be abuse.

Q. What is the acoustical significance of the Chiba air-flow, glottal action diagrams?

A. The phenomena are that 1) the voice can only amplify those frequencies which are in the glottal source, and 2) it cannot completely filter out the frequencies which it does not need. Sharp explosions are for the middle and lower notes of voices. Since the higher notes of sopranos have only four or less harmonics the soft explosions are better for those notes.

Q. How many timbres should there be in the Male voice above Note #21?

A. There is one - the sombre timbre or covered voice. Pavarotti in a television interview said that a real tenor covers on fa (f^1). I would add that a baritone covers on e^1 or $e\flat^1$, a bass-baritone on d^1, and a bass on $c\#^1$ or c^1. The covering note on the Chromatic Vowel Chart is Note #22.

Q. How can I cover?

A. Sing the Green vowels beginning in the lower loop at Note #21 and continue in the green going up. The tenor will sing the high c most effectively on the æ vowel as in the American pronunciation of fantastic.

Q. How many timbres should there be in the Female voice at Note #35 and above?

A. Marchesi said that a soprano should go into Head Voice at f^2, so sing on the Green vowels from Note #34 on up. The Yellow vowels may be used if there is sufficient Whistle quality blended into them. Otherwise the voice may sound like a scream which should be used only where intended.

Q. How do the above actions affect the vowel color?

A. They dilute the vowel color where more breath flow is used, and, intensify the vowel color when more laryngeal action is used.

Q. Can I be understood if I sing that way?

A. Probably just as well. If you are not that is the composer's problem for having written wrong words on high notes. If you want the voice to be healthy sing in the Head Voice. Marchesi's singers sang so long that they did not have time to learn how to teach. You will have a shorter career if you choose to spread on the high notes.

Q. What if a singer is required to be dramatic in the passaggio?

A. How long do you wish to sing? Great singers have vocal difficulties too! Schumann-Heink, one of the great mezzo-sopranos was injured in "Elektra" in which Strauss's orchestration was of dense, writhing sound, covering the singers (Emmons, NATS Bulletin, May/June, 1984). It took that voice a considerable length of time to get over it. Any voice can be damaged by singing beyond its resources. Then the option is to not sing or to sing less demanding roles.

Q. But is there a spot for "character" singers who have shorter ranges by nature or by usage?

A. Yes. Those who are less vocally gifted by nature or leading singers who have "graduated" downwards may choose character roles. It is best to find the individuality of a voice and then train it for what it is capable of giving.

Q. How does one raise the vowel pitch?

A. By going up a diagonal the pitch is raised in ascending, or by jumping up to another diagonal in descending.

Q. How does one lower the vowel pitch?

A. Lower the vowel pitch by going down a diagonal in descending, or by jumping down to another diagonal in ascending. In short - to raise the pitch of the resonator go up; to lower the pitch of the resonator, go down.

Q. Why do some observers state that the Front vowels are single resonance vowels?

A. Because they believe it! I do not. When working with the Vowel Resonator, I will admit that it is more difficult to find the lower resonance in the Front vowels but when the lower resonance is found on a pitch, the tone sung immediately afterwards has a fuller, rounder tone. It is coupled - both resonances singing together. When a Front vowel is uncoupled, only the upper resonance is heard. When listening to my throat with a RadioEar - Headphone hook-up, I have heard the Front series uncoupled. To couple an [i], [e], /eh/, or [æ] alternate it with the Neutral vowel on the same pitch. An adjustment of the throat may be felt and observed. That is the reason that the Front and Neutral vowels are grouped at the top of the chart on Vowel Lines I and II, and the Back and Umlaut vowels are grouped at the bottom of the chart on Vowel Lines III and IV. The Passaggio Lines I and II are based upon coupling vowels.

Q. Should vowels ever be sung uncoupled?

A. The [i] and [e] can be sung both coupled and uncoupled. Both colors of the vowels should be available to the artist - at least in the middle of the voice. Let us hope there is the artistic and physical sensitivity to know when to use them.

Q. What about imitating other singers?

A. If a person is listening functionally as to cover, vowel coloring, and coupling, it may be fine. However, G. B. Lamperti (1905 p. 5) said that the teacher's task is the individualization of singer's voices. When a person imitates another singer's voice he/she is attempting to clone his/her voice. They say that Caruso wiped out a generation of tenors and that Leonard Warren wiped out a generation of baritones.

Q. Is not mimicry a fine talent for a singer?

A. Yes. It is a wonderful asset for characterization but it should be within the limitations of the vocal instrument. Each voice has its own innate quality which should always be respected.

Q. What happens to a Coloratura soprano voice when the singer takes as a model the voice of a heavy Lyric soprano?

A. There will be vocal problems, too much pressure which causes excess glottal closure and a hardening of the voice at the f^2 area passaggio. Trouble eventually shows up in the high voice.

Q. Is this a frequent occurrence?

A. Yes. Because singers frequently learn their songs, arias, and roles from records in which the artists are ten to twenty years more mature. Young voices should not sound old but old voices should sound young.

CHAPTER XII

VOCALISES FOR FEMALE VOICES WITH CHROMATIC VOWEL CHART

Indicated always by F encircled, Ⓕ.

Arrow Placement.   Place the Chart on the piano behind the black notes with the arrow located at:

f^1 for contralto.
$f\#^1$ for lyrico-spinto soprano or mezzo soprano.
g^1 for lyric soprano or dramatic soprano.
$a\flat^1$ for high lyric or coloratura soprano.

If you know the terminology of "lifts," Note #29 has been considered as a "lift" by Witherspoon (1925, p. 90).   Note #22 has also been referred to as a "lift" by others.   Place the Chart so it will fit your voice.

Before there can be resonation, there must first be vibration from the larynx. It is advisable to establish the types of vibration discussed in Chapter IX.

VOCALISE ONE

Ⓕ   Beginning on Note #35, sing "little oo" in Whistle Register on a downward glide to a /AH/ on the lowest note, which may be either two octaves or a twelfth below.   The "little oo" is first gained by a pencil sharpener sized opening of the lips and with a thought of nasality.   Later the sound can be gained by a certain opening in the back of the throat as heard by children on the playground.   This was referred to by Nathan (1836) as "the voice of a child."   Proceed by half steps up the scale to Note #43, always on [u] and disregarding the vowel values on the Chromatic Vowel Chart.   You are establishing the vocal cord action for Female Head voice which will allow you to retain it into advanced years according to Lilli Lehmann (1914).

VOCALISE TWO

(F) Beginning on Note #35, glide downward from "little oo" to an /AH/ a double octave or a twelfth below and then glissando back to the "little oo" on the high note. Again, go up by half steps as far as is comfortable according to the nature of the voice. <u>The voice cannot resonate a sound which is not in the glottal source.</u>

VOCALISE THREE

(F) Beginning on Note #35, glide downward on the "open mouth hum" (m). The open mouth hum is gained by placing the <u>palm of the hand</u> tightly over the mouth while singing the /UH/ vowel with the mouth open. The "open mouth hum" causes the soft palate to relax its closure and gives strong vibration in the turbinates. Proceed by half steps up the scale to Note #43, or as far as comfortable according to the nature of the voice. This also is related to the glottal action and rounding for high notes.

VOCALISE FOUR

(F) Beginning on the vowels "ah" and "eh" as in the words, "alma, sempre," attack the vowels on one note at Note #15 on Lines III and I. Proceed note by note to #21 ♪ ♪ ♪ . (The range from Garcia, 1872, p. 11.) α ε α These attacks "will bring out all the ring of the voice. The notes must be kept full and equal in force. This is the best manner of developing the voice. At first, the exercise must not exceed two or three minutes in duration," Garcia (1894, p. 14.) (The Ah values of Line I may be used for unblended chest voice. The Caruso Scale is transitional to Female

Middle Voice and Male Upper Voice.)

(F)   With your <u>Chromatic Vowel Chart</u> on the piano, play pitches immediately above the heavy underline. Sing those vowels, going back and forth between [ə] and [i] on Lines I and II and [u] and [y] on Lines III and IV.

(F)   Sing the underlined vowels, going back and forth between [ʊ] and [e], and [ʌ and ɛ], etc. on Lines II and I.

VOCALISE FIVE

<u>Diagonals</u>. On Line III of the <u>Vowel Chart</u> are several <u>diagonals</u> which are in reality modifications of the [u] to [𝑣] series of vowels.

(F)   On Line III sing 4-tone scales or short arpeggios on the vowels directly over the notes you are singing. Start on the <u>Blue</u> vowel over Note #16.

(F)   Sing from the lowest <u>Green</u> vowel up the scale to the highest <u>Green</u> vowel on the different diagonals within the range of your voice. The Italians preferred to teach on the open vowels.

VOCALISE SIX

(F)   <u>Columns</u>. For example, sing the pitch of Note #24 and pronounce up and down the <u>column</u> of vowels in Line III directly above the note you are singing except the vowels in <u>Red</u>, which are spread. You are pronouncing vowels on the harmonically related tones of the note you are singing.

(F)   Sing the vertical columns in Line III between Notes #13 and #28 avoiding the vowels in <u>Red</u>.

VOCALISE SEVEN

(F) The singer should constantly alternate vocalises between Lines I, II, III, and IV to activate the muscles used in forming the different vowel series. Too much vocalizing on Line III will make the voice hollow sounding and dark. Too much vocalizing on Line I will cause the voice to sound reedy and shrill. By alternating between the series the vowel musculatures and acoustics are balanced.

VOCALISE EIGHT

(F) On Line II sing 4-tone scales or short arpeggios on the vowel diagonals over the notes you are singing, starting with the <u>Blue</u> vowel on Note #16.

(F) Sing from the lowest <u>Green</u> vowel up the scale to the highest <u>Green</u> vowel on the different diagonals in the singing range of your voice, avoiding the <u>Red</u> vowels. Use [ʌ] instead of /a/ where a passaggio is difficult. The voice is placed, or focused when there is a feeling that the entire air column from lips to lower trachea is in greatest vibration. There is also a good vibrato. Give preference to singing notes in the middle voice such as Notes #18 to #33.

VOCALISE NINE

(F) On Line I sing such a Note as #25, pronouncing up and down the columns on the same pitch with [j] on the first vowel only. For example [ɛ - a - ɛ]. When the amount of resonation does not seem to be enough, slightly move the tongue and jaw until the greatest vibration is felt. A singer can always find [a] by preceding it with [j]. The [j] can frequently be heard at the beginning of runs by coloratura sopranos. G. B. Lamperti (Brown p. 97) said, "The larynx moves up and down to assist in modifying resonance (vowels) and not to aid vibration (pitch of tone.) This seems to be true except on Vowel Row 67 (Female Head Voice) in which the larynx raises. Garcia said: (1841, p. lv in Paschke's 1984 translation of the Memoire):

"As for the head tones, the larynx almost always produces them while rising rapidly. One could not prevent
these movements; trying to do so to swell the note would
be dangerous and often useless effort."

VOCALISE TEN

(F) Starting on such a Note as #30, sing the Line III diagonals from **right** to left. Begin the exercise with [w] to find the [ɒ or ɑ] vowels.

[wɑ] followed by indicated modifications on the Chromatic Vowel Chart. Do not sing vowels further down the vowel diagonals than [o]. Tosi (1723) said that training should be on the open vowels [ɔ, ɛ, a] and that in the better schools, fast vocalization on [o] and [e] was forbidden. In all schools of singing, [i] and [u] were forbidden. I believe that the close vowels should be practiced, but with moderation.

(F) Sing the same exercises with the [a]. Sing [a] without modification.

126

VOCALISE ELEVEN

(F) Sing alternately the vowels in Vowel Series I, II, III, and IV which are heavily underlined on the notes over which they are written as high as Note #33.

VOCALISE TWELVE

(F) Sing the Blue and Green vowels within the singing range of your voice - do not overdo the high notes.

VOCALISE THIRTEEN

(F) Sing scales on the 1.5 diagonal on the Front, Neutral, Back, and Umlaut Vowels (Lines I, II, III, and IV).

VOCALISE FOURTEEN

(F) On Line II, sing and pronounce the Blue and Green vowels on the vertical columns of the diagonals over the same pitch between Notes #17 and #33. The Neutral vowels reinforce the same lower harmonics as the vowels in Lines I, III, and IV.

VOCALISE FIFTEEN

(F) On Note #17 alternately sing the Green vowels, Line I, with the Green vowels on Line II, on the same note. Proceed as high as Note #33.

VOCALISE SIXTEEN

(F) On Note #17 alternately sing the Green vowel, on Line III with the Green vowels on Line IV, on the same note. Proceed as high as Note #33.

VOCALISE SEVENTEEN

(F) Sing 5-tone scales on the Caruso Vowel Scale, starting on Note #15 in order to make a transition into the Vowel Register. This can also be used to blend the Chest Register to the Middle Voice.

(F) Sing alternately the vowels on Passaggio Lines I and II to make the harmonic transition between the different registers. This lesson should be very valuable to operatic singers who need the use of the lower extension of the voice and the dynamic color which it gives to the rest of the voice.

VOCALISE EIGHTEEN

(F) (Garcia Special Exercise.) On Line I, Notes #20 and #21 go back and forth on the upper and lower Green vowels.

(F) On Line II, Notes #20 and #21, sing back and forth on the upper and lower green vowels.

(F) Do the same on Lines III and IV.

N. B. This is very much the same as Garcia's Special Exercise "intended to unite the chest and falsetto registers." [The term falsetto, as he used it was handed down from the earlier Italian teachers of singing. Hence, the women's middle voice he called falsetto. The exercise was in his books of all editions from his first one in 1841 until his last in 1894, p. 21.]

BLENDING THE REGISTERS.

Q. How are the chest and medium registers to be blended?

A. By passing repeatedly from the chest to the medium, and *vice versâ.** This passage will take place on the following exercises :—

Exercises for blending the Chest and Medium Registers.

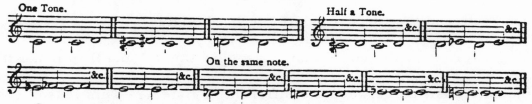

Some notes, common to both registers, are preserved to facilitate the transit and meet the requirements of particular passages.

At the first succession of notes must be short, and sung very slowly. Later on a long succession may reach ♩ = 100 of metronome. Care must be taken not to aspirate the medium.

---

* Although the term mixed tone (*voix mixte*) is not used by the author it is obvious that these exercises for blending the lower registers were intended for the express purpose of developing and strengthening this particular tone which if helped by correct breathing and well-rounded vowels will form itself in a perfectly easy and natural manner —(*Note H K.*)

Fig. 30. Garcia's Exercises for Blending the Registers

[H. K. are the initials of Hermann Klein who assisted him in writing the 1894 edition of Hints on Singing.]

Many singers have great problems with intonation in arias, songs and declamation on the above pitches. The only way to overcome this problem is to train first on the close vowels on these notes or on Notes #18 - #23 on the Passaggio Lines and the Caruso Scale on the Vowel Chart. Later the singer can alternate between the close vowels and the open vowels on these notes, however, close vowels will tend to always be more stable. It would seem logical that one can sing the same vowel on every note, but such is not the case. The nature of resonance is such that vowels change their color semi-tone by semi-tone; see the diagonals of all vowel series.

VOCALISE NINETEEN

(F) <u>Lip Slurs.</u> Sing [ɔ] on Notes #20 and #32, slurring between the notes. Do the same with other like vowels on the diagonals. Except for minor adjustments your resonator remains the same. It is like a brass instrumentalist practicing lip slurs without changing the pitch of the resonator. You will notice the intervals between the vowels vary - this is because of the harmonic relationships involved.

(F) <u>Lip Slurs.</u> Sing [ɔ] on Notes #13, #20, #25, and #32, slurring between the notes. Do likewise with the other vowels. <u>This is one of the best exercises for memorizing vowel colors in your voice</u> and for finding vowel colors for the placement of high notes.

(F) Slur from a vowel on a diagonal to another vowel on a different diagonal. Now you are "lip slurring" with a changing resonator. This will assist in giving you a singing line (cantilena).

<u>Scoring for Songs and Arias.</u> Score the exposed notes of a song before singing so that you will know what vowel colors to sing. Or sing a song and when you come to a note which is unresonant, stop, place your finger on the note, concert pitch, which you are singing and read the Chromatic Vowel Chart directly above that note. Select the vowel which you are singing and notice the modification. When you feel there is a resonant feeling in the throat, notate the symbol over that note in your song and sing it with that concept and sensation whenever you perform it. This is the simple procedure for scoring vowel resonances in songs and arias. In case of doubt, check the vowel with the Vowel Resonator.

<u>The Chromatic Vowel Chart can be used in Voice Class and Choirs.</u> Voices of the same classification can be vocalized together in voice class or choir sections (when the arrow is properly placed for that classification.) The teacher calls which Line is being used and then gives the Note number on which the vocalise begins. When each person in the class has a <u>Chromatic Vowel Chart</u> the students will know the vowel colors they should sing. Singers will find there is less fatigue when the voice is placed. <u>Sympathetic</u> vibration is less work than <u>forced vibration.</u>

Exercises. In the previous exercises Chromatic-vowel-colors were utilized.
One of Novikova's basic principles was to alternate between diatonic exercises
and arpeggios. She also alternated between slow and fast exercises. The slow
exercises use more resonance; the fast moving passages use less. The same
phenomena occur in singing Andante-Allegro arias and songs. Her vocalization
was usually on /a/. She did not ask for the vowel to change on upper notes but
allowed it to do so. I prefer to ask for the close vowels in the area of Notes
#32, #33, #34, and #35 to be assured that Female voices find and use their
Head Voice.

Practice Procedures. Record the notes of a song or aria slowly on a flute stop,
or with a Vowel Resonator and Realistic hookup, practice resonation of the song
or aria before singing it. Go slowly! Learn to "place" your voice before
singing instead of correcting your misplacement after singing.

Which Dynamics Should Be Used in Practice?

Tosi, in one of the first treatises on singing, said:

> "Let the Master instruct him [male soprano] in the
> Forte and Piano, but so as to use him more in the first
> than the second, it being easier to make one sing soft
> than loud. Experience shews that the Piano is not to be
> trusted to, since it is prejudicial though pleasing; and if
> any one has a Mind to lose his Voice, let him try it."
> Francesco Tosi (1723).

Is there any more reason for trusting soft vocalization today than in 1723? We
are under a continuing spell cast by a microphone. How many have heard
orators without the aid of a microphone? Charles Wesley, a small man in
stature, preached to an audience of 30,000 in England. Who can do it today?
How many have heard great singers in excellent auditoriums? Those are the
sounds which should be kept in mind for the training of singing. The singer's
amplification is within his/her own body - success will depend on how well one
attains and sustains it.

There are many who are teaching dull voice sounds today. One problem is that
our models are mature and, in many cases, are tired singers. Youth in voices
is to be cherished. We need to return to the principles which the Bel Canto
teachers of the past discovered. This is also at odds with the teaching of many
choral conductors who want dark, hollow sounds which have fewer overtones.
In that way they can hide the individuality of voices. The duty of the teacher of
singing is to individualize each voice - let voices be what Nature intended them
to be.

CHAPTER XIII

VOCALISES FOR MALE VOICES WITH CHROMATIC VOWEL RESONANCE CHART
Indicated always by M encircled, Ⓜ.
(Please read the Directions for using the Chromatic Vowel Chart, p. 90.)

<u>Arrow Placement</u>. Place the Chart on the piano behind the black notes with the arrow located at:

$f\#^1$ or g^1 for tenor
$e\natural^1$ or f^1 for baritone
$e\flat^1$ for bass-baritone
$c\#^1$ or $d\natural^1$ for bass.

If you know the terminology of "lifts," Note #17 has been considered as a "lift" by Witherspoon (1925, p. 90). Note #22 has also been referred to as a "lift" or "break by others. Place the arrow of the Chart 1/2 step above the "lift" around e^1 or f^1 in your voice so that the correct vowel colors are indicated for your voice.

Before there can be resonation, there must first be vibration from the larynx. It is advisable to establish the types of vibration discussed in Chapter IX.

VOCALISE ONE

Ⓜ Beginning on Note #23, sing "little oo" in the Falsetto Register on a downward glide to /AH/ on the lowest note, which may be either two octaves or a twelfth below. The "little oo" is first gained by a pencil sharpener sized opening of the lips and with a thought of nasality. Later the sound can be gained by a certain opening in the back of the throat. Proceed by half steps up the scale to Note #30, always on [u] and <u>disregarding</u> the vowel values on the Chromatic Vowel Chart. You are establishing the vocal cord action for Male Mixed Voice or "covered voice."

VOCALISE TWO

(M) Beginning on Note #23, glide downward to an /AH/ a double octave or a twelfth below and then glissando back to the "little oo" on the high note. Again, go up by half steps as far as is comfortable according to the nature of the voice. <u>The voice cannot resonate a sound which is not in the glottal source</u>.

VOCALISE THREE

(M) Beginning on Note #23, glide downward on the "open mouth hum" (m). The open mouth hum is gained by placing the <u>palm of the hand</u> tightly over the mouth while singing the /UH/ vowel with the mouth open. The "open mouth hum" causes the soft palate to relax its closure and gives strong vibration in the turbinates. Proceed by half steps up the scale to Note #30, or as far as comfortable according to the nature of the voice. This also is related to the vocal cord action and rounding for high notes.

VOCALISE FOUR

(M) Beginning on the vowels "ah" and "eh" as in the words "alma sempre," attack the vowels on Note #7. Proceed by half-steps to Note #15 ♪ ♪ ♪. These attacks "will bring out all the ring of the voice. The
a ε a
notes must be kept full and equal in force. This is the best manner of developing the voice. At first, the exercise must not exceed two or three minutes in duration" (Garcia 1894, p. 14).

(M) Following this, alternate the <u>Green</u> vowels on Line I and II on Note #16. Continue as high as Note #21.

VOCALISE FIVE

Diagonals. On Line III of the Vowel-Color Chart I have written several vowel scales which are in reality modifications of the [u] to [ɑ] series of vowels.

Ⓜ On Line III sing 4-tone scales or short arpeggios on the vowel scales over the notes you are singing. Start on Note #6. The Italians preferred to teach on the open vowels.

Ⓜ Sing from the lowest Green vowel up the scale to the highest Green vowel on the different diagonals within the comfortable range of your voice.

Ⓜ When you come to Vowel Scale ② begin on [o] over Note #15 and continue the modification sequence to around Note #22. Sing Vowel Scale ①.5 upward from Note #16. Sing Vowel Scale ① upward from Note #23 in Falsetto.

VOCALISE SIX

Ⓜ Columns. Sing, for example, the pitch of Note #10 and pronounce down and up the columns of vowels in Line III directly above the note you are singing. You are changing the strength of overtones of the sound you are singing. (At first, do not sing the vowels which are over the dotted line.) These vowels may be sung after the others are established.

Ⓜ Sing the vertical columns in Line III between Notes #6 and #22.

VOCALISE SEVEN

Ⓜ Sing 1353123454321 scale patterns and short arpeggios starting on Note #8 with the starting note and upper note always being on Green vowels. Alternate between Lines I and II. This can be carried as high as Note #22.

VOCALISE EIGHT

(M) Do the same on Lines III and IV. If exercises are done excessively on Lines I and II the voice will tend to become overly bright because of the higher overtones of the front vowels. If the voice is vocalized too much on Lines III and IV it will tend to become hooty and dark. The best procedure is a rotation of vowel series in vocalization. Balanced vocalization with resonant pronunciation is a secret of voice building.

(M) Do the same on Line III and Line II.

VOCALISE NINE

(M) On Line IV sing 4-tone scales or short arpeggios on the same vowel scales over the notes you are singing, starting on the Green vowels over Note #8.

(M) Sing from the lowest Green vowel up the scale to the highest Green vowel of the different diagonals within the comfortable range of the voice.

(M) When you come to Vowel Scale (2) Upper Voice begin on [ʊ] over Note #14 and continue the various modifications to Note #21. Garcia had a rule which said, when transposed to the Vowel Chart, that the Notes #22 to #28 should be sung in the sombre timbre, (1972 p. 12.). Sing three note scales Falsetto and supported Falsetto upward from Note #16 on Vowel Scale (1.) 5.

VOCALISE TEN

(M) Sing scales and arpeggios on the Caruso Vowel Scale from Note #7 upward to a comfortable height in your voice. Sing this modification daily on scales and arpeggios. See the Caruso modification, p. 138.

VOCALISE ELEVEN

Ⓜ In Line II, sing and pronounce the vertical columns over the sung pitch between Notes #3 and #21. The Neutral columns have the same mode of vibration as the columns in Lines I, III, and IV.

VOCALISE TWELVE

Ⓜ <u>Lip slurs</u>. Alternately sing [ɛ] on Notes #8 and #13, slurring between the notes. Do the same with other like-vowels on the diagonals of Line I. Except for minor adjustments, your resonator remains the same. It is like a brass instrumentalist practicing lip slurs without changing the resonator. You will notice the intervals between vowels vary because the diagonals are separated by different intervals (due to the harmonic series). <u>Memorize the vowel colors in your voice</u> in relationship to sung pitch.

VOCALISE THIRTEEN

Ⓜ <u>Lip slurs</u>. On Line II alternately sing [ɔ] on Notes #8, #13, and #20 slurring between the notes. Proceed likewise with other vowels within the range of your singing voice.

Ⓜ Do the same exercises on the diagonals of Line IV.

VOCALISE FOURTEEN

Ⓜ <u>Messa di Voce</u>. In Upper Voice Vowel Scale②sing softly, then crescendo and diminuendo. Always use favorable vowel colors in <u>Messa di Voce</u>.

Ⓜ Practice crescendo and diminuendo while changing favorable vowels and while changing notes as in the beginning of a song or in a final cadence.

VOCALISE FIFTEEN

Practice the Garcia and Stockhausen patterns p. 111 and 112.

VOCALISE SIXTEEN

Vowel Substitution. There are optical illusions in which non-existent things are seen and there are aural illusions in which vowels can be substituted and the listener hears the written vowel. This is especially true for Male voices on Note #22. The close /O/ sound is dangerous because it is back and gives heaviness to the voice. I have seen Alfredo Kraus in a Master Class in which he had Male voices use the Nasal open AW [õ] for Oh in the Passaggio in the area of Note #22. To be specific it was in the Germont aria of La Traviata - "Dio mi guido [õ], Dio mi guido [õ]." Where is the baritone who has not strangled on these phrases because of the weight of voice when sung with true vowel values? This is vowel substitution!

Mr. Kraus also used Nasal [ʌ] as in fun for AH as well as for [ʊ] in full, and nasal [æ] as in fantastic for [e]. It will be noticed on the Chromatic Vowel Chart that Gold nasalized vowels are substituted for Green vowels on that note. The nasalization is related to the "mask resonance" exercise of De Rezske and gives a feeling of resonance in the area which would be covered by an eye shade - the area of the eyes and the bridge of the nose. Why would mask resonance be taught by De Reszke's teacher, Giovanni Sbriglia, who was a Neopolitan tenor (Coffin, NATS Bulletin, Nov/Dec 1983)? The answer is simple. French meanings differ with nasalization and denasalization; Italian, English, and German do

not.

You may find this technique valuable to you in the passaggio area of

your voice.

* * * * *

Scoring for Songs and Arias. Score the exposed notes of a song before singing so that you will know what color to sing. Or sing a song and when you come to a note which is unresonant, stop, place your finger on the note, concert pitch, which you are singing and read the Chromatic Vowel Chart directly agove that note. Select the vowel which you are singing and notice the modification. When you sense there is a resonant feeling in the throat, notate the symbol over that note in your song and sing it with that concept and sensation whenever you sing it later on. This is the simple procedure for scoring vowel resonances in songs and arias. When there are several vowel colors that work, use the one nearest to your artistic intent for the word and phrase.

Use a Realistic Concertmate - Vowel Resonator hook-up to practice the resonation of a song or aria before singing it. Go slowly! Learn to place your voice before singing instead of correcting your misplacement after singing.

Chromatic Vowel Charts can be used in Voice Classes and Choirs. Voices of the same classification can be vocalized together in voice classes or choir sections (when the arrow is properly placed for that classification). The teacher calls which Line is being used and then gives the Note number on which the vocalise begins. When each person in the class has a Vowel Chart the students will know the vowel-colors they should sing. Singers will find there is less fatigue when the voice is placed.

Exercises. The exercises shown in the previous pages have been quite simple. Favorable vowel-colors are utilized in the following exercises of Paola Novikova. One of her basic principles was to alternate between diatonic exercises and arpeggios. She also alternated between slow and fast exercises. The slow exercises will use more resonance; the fast ones will use less. The same phenomenon occurs in singing Andante-Allegro songs and arias. Her vocalization was usually on [a]. She did not ask for the vowel to change on upper notes but allowed it to do so.

CHAPTER XIV

AGILITY AND DICTION

<u>Scales and Arpeggios.</u> It is necessary that all voices have agility for highly exciting passages as well as for vocal health. The exercise books of the Garcias indicate that great feats of coloratura were trained at that time. The voice simply lasts longer when a balanced "diet" of agility and sustained tones is taught. Exercises on long notes and dark vowels will make the voice overly heavy. However, exercises of nothing but agility will reduce the power of the voice. Of prime importance in agility is the use of the Italian "ah" [a]. That vowel can be used from Note #6 to the neighborhood of Note #18 in Male voices. The [a] vowel has the right combinations of overtones to run; the [ɑ] and [ɒ] vowels are slow moving because of their weight and darkness. How often do Heldentenors sing bravura passages? Sing the agility passages/exercises beginning with [ja], or dentalized [da] or [la]. These consonants will all establish the Italian [a]. Vowel modification is less necessary on this vowel since it is a mixed vowel and has a lower resonance which tends to do its own changing.

However, male voices should mix it with a form of <u>oh</u> between Notes #18 and #22, and a form of <u>oo</u> on Notes #23 and above. These zones of vowels were used by Caruso. Fucito (1929), p. 150, stated of Caruso, "...his great industry, which he always applied intelligently contributed its large share to make him the foremost vocal artist of his time. And to no phase did he devote more attention than to the equalization of the voice." How did he do it? Among the many exercises used by Caruso there is a reappearing pattern of half open <u>ah</u> on the low notes, <u>oh</u> between c# and f, and <u>oo</u> between f# and bb, such as in the following shortened exercises:

Fig. 31. Caruso Exercises

There are many other such exercises. The Caruso Vowel Scale could also be called the Garcia Vowel Scale which is described in his <u>Art of Singing</u>, Part I. It is the harmonic transition to the actual pitch of vowels which begins on Note #23 (at the arrow). A fascinating aspect of vocal technique is that Female voices must use the same vowels on the Caruso scale to make the transition from Chest Voice to the Vowel Register of their voices. They will build an even passaggio by practicing on that scale.

Two of the queens of song of this generation are descendants of the Garcia school of singing. Beverly Sills was a student of Estelle Liebling, a student of Marchesi, who was a student of Garcia. Marilyn Horne, a student of William Vennard, stated in The New York Times, January 17, 1971, "Not only do I believe in three registers, but I'm sure that everybody who sings in the same category of voice has the same transition points between the registers. That's Manuel Garcia, and I'm a disciple of Garcia: I've pored over those books." Garcia said that the chest voice was the basis of the male voice as it was the female. So I repeat that female voices should practice the vowel sequences of the Caruso Vowel Scale from their lowest notes to and above Note #23 when studying agility. There will also be a resultant increase in power.

Garcia's father studied with the famous tenor Ansani in Naples in 1816. Five years later (1821) he published a book of exercises. A few of his exercises will interest you. Portamento came early. Does anyone criticize a singer for portamenti today? Yes, but it is an essential part of vocal technique.

After the portamenti came the divisions.   Manuel Garcia I (1821)

Then there was preparation for the trill.

simile jusqu'a l'octave

Fig. 32. Exercises of the Senior Garcia

His son, Manuel Garcia II, the teacher of Jenny Lind, stated that he extended his father's principles and so we have the following agility exercises, about half of which are his father's.

Manuel Garcia II (about 1855)

Fig. 33. Exercises of Garcia, son

No singer can expect to survive long without agility. I have shown how agility can be developed - on the bright [a]. I have told how one can acquire the fuller tone - on the darker vowels. The Garcia <u>Hints</u> <u>on</u> <u>Singing</u> should be at the finger tips of every serious singer and is one of the few classic books on singing remaining in print.

What did Garcia's father know about vowels? The following is one of two exercises with words. How did he know that c^1 and c^2 had <u>oh</u> values? Through one of the most phenomenal organs of man - the ear.

Garcia I, 1821

Fig. 34. Exercises of the Senior Garcia.

Modification of Consonants. Just as vowels must be modified so that they will amplify rather than diminish the vibrations of sung pitch, consonants must also be modified. Characteristic of any wind instrument is the fact that there must be a standing wave in it - a continuing vibration. This is as true of the voice as it is of the brass and woodwind instruments.

142

There are certain consonants that tend to destroy the standing waves which can be established by the Vowel-Color studies of sung pitch. The explosives [p, t, k] are antivocal. They should be modified to the soft [p, t, k] of the Italian so that, according to a traditional story, a candle held in front of the mouth would not be blown out. Also the consonants [d, n, t, l] should be dentalized with the tongue thinly and widely placed on the upper front teeth to draw the tongue upward out of the throat to give a more frontal vibration to the vowels which follow them. This gives a gentle transition from the consonant to the vowel and allows the standing wave to occur earlier at the beginning of a phrase and to remain standing during the continuants [n and l]. This is a basis of legato and phrasing. It is like tonguing with a light [d] on the trombone in fast passages. The tone will be a continuing one rather than a disrupted one. This is the basis of flow or spin in a singing voice.

I use the IPA symbol [̪] to indicate dentalization, e.g., d̪, n̪, t̪, and l̪. Dentalization of l̪ removes a constriction from the base of the tongue which is a characteristic of the American singer. Phonetically there are two l's - a clear "l" and a dull "l." The dentalization will give the clear "l." Let us note that the Lampertis taught continually on la's. They were noted for the number of great artists they trained, the length of their careers, and the brightness of their tones. Of course, they were teaching the Italian Ah [a] and the clear "l." They are inseparable. Here are a few examples from F. Lamperti's book (1890), G. Schirmer, p. 35.

Fig. 35. Lamperti Exercises

There is another consonant modification the American singer must make. He must substitute the flipped or rolled [r] for the bunched or inverted [ɹ] as in the code word "Roger." What other nationality can pronounce this carnivorous semi-vowel? It is murder! It actually devours voices, for X-Rays have indicated a constriction at the base of the tongue and at the front of the tongue. Look at the underlined r's and notice the emotional color of the words. [ɹ] is throaty. It is twice as bad as we have heretofore believed. The great teacher, Sbriglia, who taught the DeReszkes, used an exercise of "TeRoo." You can correctly guess that the [t] was unexploded and the [r] rolled. I use the additive ˇ to indicate an r is rolled, e.g., ř. Americans will sing much better if they dentalize [d, n, t, and l] and roll their r's.

Fig. 36. CHART OF CONSONANTS

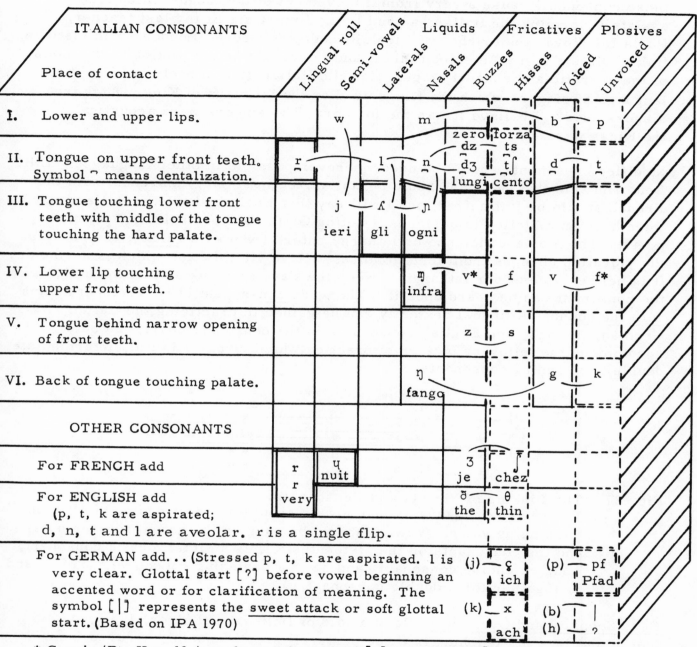

* Garcia (Pt. II p. 13.) preferred the buzzed [v] and plosive [f].
* Consonants within solid lines are voiced and should be practiced daily for vocal line.
* Consonants within dotted lines are unvoiced. [p, t, k] should be unaspirated.
* Underlined consonants have different formations in Italian than in English.
* Boxed consonants do not exist in English and should be correctly established.
* ⌒ of space markings indicate consonant contrasts which should be practiced frequently.

Coffin, Feb/Mar 1976

In singing Italian, the singers must watch that the tip of the tongue touches the lower front teeth in the consonants [ʎ] as in Gigli, and [ɲ] in "ogni." Both of these consonants cause a very frontal movement of the tongue which also assists in forming the Italian [a] and [ε]. I must credit my last teacher, Paola Novikova, the teacher of Nicolai Gedda and George London, with instilling Italian diction in my American throat and mind. Italianate diction is the basis of the operatic and concert stage. How did Italian diction evolve? Was it the language of singers which the Kings used or the language of Kings which the singers used? I believe it was the former. The singers were acoustical, the Kings were not.

Modified consonants should be used wherever possible in other languages. Lilli Lehmann said that German should be Italianized in singing; Marchesi said that French should be Italianized; and I will say that English should be Italianized when harmonic diction is desired. Quoting G. B. Lamperti (1931, Brown), p. 45, "The moment violence or lethargy enters [who said relax], the sound of the vibration changes from tone to noise." Have vital diction which is harmonic. It is neither violent nor lethargic. Keep the wave standing so that the action of the consonant can be heard upon it. The word con-sonant is correct - it means with the sound. A lingual dexterity can be gained in practicing the Italian, German, French, and English consonants in the consonant chart. I would recommend the following pattern of practice which involves initial, intermediate, double, and ending consonants.

Fig. 37. The Linking of Vowels and Consonants.
The various consonants and vowels should be practiced on pitches of the singing voice. Vowels should be sung on the dotted quarter notes and the consonants on the sixteenths. 1. is an intervocalic consonant, 2. is an ending consonant, and 3. is a beginning consonant. Tie 2. and 3. together for a double consonant.

Head Sonority and Overtones. It was said of DeReszke (Leiser, 1934), p. 267 that he outlined his teaching in three parts: 1) breath control, secured from the diphragm; 2) resonance; and 3) head sonority and overtones. The Chromatic Vowel Chart deals primarily with the second and third parts of his teaching program. How does one obtain head sonority and its overtones? Use the open mouth hum [h]ⓜ. For example place the palm of the hand tightly over the open mouth and sing. The soft palate will usually tend to blow open. If it does not, the voice will be stopped because there is no exit for the moving air. Repeat until there is a continuation of tone with the hand over the mouth. I call this the open mouth hum because of G. B. Lamperti (Brown, 1931), p. 104 who said, "Singing is humming with the mouth open." This is a method of gaining participation of the nasal cavities. As a symbol, I use a small [h] followed by an encircled small "m." Go directly from ʰ(m) into any vowel and allow a slight bit of vibration to remain in the nasal passages. This opening of the nasal port may be difficult to see on X-Rays but it is surely there. Without it [e], [ɪ], and [i] will not have strong resonance. This is the way the vowels in <u>Blue</u> on the Chromatic Vowel Chart are brought into resonance.

<u>French Nasals.</u> The French nasals are usually indicated as being [ɛ̃, œ̃, ɑ̃, ɔ̃]. Nasality does not change the wavelength of the resonance of vowels. Differentiation of Nasal Vowels is accomplished by the weakening of the lower resonance according to Delattre. Nasal modifications are indicated as follows:

ɛ̃ can be nasalized ɛ or æ ;

œ̃ can be nasalized œ or ʌ ;

ɑ̃ can be nasalized ɑ or ʊ ; and

ɔ̃ can be nasalized ɔ or ɤ .

The study of nasalized vowels will assist in adding head sonority and overtones. It will soften the hard ring of mouth resonance.

<u>The Singer's Diction.</u> I will allow Herbert Witherspoon to give the final word on diction. He was an internationally famous bass and teacher of singing who later was General Manager of the Metropolitan Opera Company until his death in 1935. His vocal training was with G. B. Lamperti and Sbriglia, among others, and he was an outstanding teacher of singing in New York and Chicago. He wrote (1925, p. 30):

> "The modification of the vowels, and the perfect action
> of the vocal organs for tone, does not injure or make
> indistinct our pronunciation, or harm our enunciation
> and emission. On the contrary, the obedience to the
> natural laws of singing, which causes the slight modifica-
> tion, is alone possible if we accept this doctrine, and the
> result will be far more natural and spontaneous and true
> to laws of pronunciation than if we force the vowels to
> sound their "medium-normal" form."

Without the writing of Witherspoon and my study with one of his associate teachers, Graham Reed, the Chromatic Vowel Chart would not have been formed.

The Chromatic Vowel Chart is the result of a study of inner space and its Nature. We have been observers of the exploration of outer space, of the moon and of the planets. Scientists have theorized about the nature of these celestial bodies, the poets have written an enormous literature of their nature, and the comic strips have also told us about them and planetary travel. Not until man <u>saw</u> through distant cameras have we really known what actually exists. As a result, many theories have been found to be of small value - others of great value.

In the study of inner space I have observed the nature of resonance in the air chambers of the throat by <u>sound</u> (Vowel Resonator and Throat Microphone) and <u>sight</u> (Oscilloscope, Fiberscope, Sonograph and motion picture X - ray). Some theories of singing have held up quite well - others will need modification in light of these findings. You have knowledge of these resonance phenomena which you can use although you may not fully understand them.

CHAPTER XV

SINGING WITH VOWEL THINKING

A singer in the midst of performance has little time to think of his technique.
We can say that his art is very much like an automatic camera which will
regulate the technique of taking a picture, yet at the same time has a manual
override. This allows the photographer to change from automatic to manual
when he has time to think, if he wishes. The situation is much the same in
singing performance. How can it be automated? This involves the thinking of
vowel color and the feeling of vibration in the throat since in most halls and
opera houses, the sound simply does not come back. (La Scala has a reverberation time of 1.2 seconds with a capacity audience.) Following are exercises
of various kinds in which the lower vowel resonance R^1, or R^1 and R^2 will feed
back upon the vibrating vocal cords and give amplification. They are exercises
in which there is a continuous standing wave in the vocal tract.

The Trumpet Principle Phonetic System. Witherspoon (1925, p. 82) called his
procedures a "phonetic system." He stated, "It enables us to exaggerate or
lessen activity on any part of the vocal mechanism; we can practically 'massage'
any part; we can cure many stubborn cases of vocal fault, degeneracy, and even
disease...." The amplifying phonetic system of this text is based on a Trumpet
Principle; please allow me to state it again:

> "A trumpet [voice] produces musical tones when the
> vibration of the players lips [the singer's vocal cords]
> interact with standing waves in the instrument [the vocal
> tract]. These waves are generated when acoustic energy
> is sent back by the instrument's bell [the opening at the
> lips and teeth]." Benade (1973, p. 24) Bracketed words
> are mine.

I have notated the amplifying resonances of the singing voice by means of a
phonetic system. A phonetic is a symbol which describes a specific vowel
sound. Just as ♩♩ are specific pitches, so is [ɔ] a specific vowel color
which resonates 𝄞 on those pitches (with the slight variation indicated for
the various voice classifications). This is built entirely on the lower pitch of
the vowels and the relationship of the harmonics of the sung pitch to them. It
was an oddity that a singer and teacher of singing who was taught by the
Witherspoon Phonetic System should have been associated with Pierre Delattre,
"the first linguist to have completely produced intelligible artificial speech by
synthesis involving the right combination of pure tones, frequency changes,
timing in changes, and relative frequencies among the pure tones." Boulder
Daily Camera, July 1, 1973.

Prior to my investigations with Delattre I asked him if there was any interplay between the resonance of the vowels and the vocal cords in singing. He thought there was not very much - "You can sing any note on any form of cavity in the mouth, the frequency of the fundamental is commanded by only the speed of the vocal cords." I stated, "I think there is some. There are certain notes in the voice which can not be sung effectively on certain vowels," (taken from a tape of 12/2/68). Because of the death of Delattre in 1969 our physiological-musical studies of sung vowels and consonants were not concluded, otherwise a part of this work would have had his co-authorship. I have proceeded as best I could from his writings and a study of the vocal tract with an artificial vibrator. My guess is that together we would have arrived at the same conclusions, only much earlier. My final observations are that the compressions and rarefactions of air of the vocal tract (resonator) in such a way that the Trumpet Principle exists. In many slides made from our X - Ray motion pictures of singing the forms of the throat were so extreme for high notes that the vowels could not be identified. They were so similar visually that one vowel could not be distinguished from another. It seems that unless limited by extreme conformations of the throat for high or low pitch, any note can be sung on any form of the cavities of the vocal tract but some forms will have constructive interaction with the vocal cords (aid and amplify their air pressures) and others will have a diminishing acoustical interaction (distort and diminish their air pressures). In good singing it is to the singer's advantage to sing with constructive interaction where the air compression of the vocal cords and the air compression of the vocal tract augment each other. This is the acoustical basis of voice building and tone placing. The following exercises are notations of this relationship.

The numbering of exercises. The numbering of exercises such as ⑯ refers to the beginning note number on the Chromatic Vowel Chart when properly placed at the piano. Simply begin the exercise on Note #16. This allows the singer to move in various intervals instead of the usual diatonic progression of exercises up or down. The singer should deliberately jump from exercise to exercise - it is more in the manner of contemporary music. However, do nothing to excess! No matter how right a singer is in his vocalization - too much is bad.

Crossovers. The exercises are built upon the phonetic principle of crossing over between the various vowel series. The tongue hump is continually crossing the Velopharyngeal Axis (See Fig. 54, p. 260. The vowels notated are resonance peaks while the voice is moving and will assist in forming proper throat spaces - in other words the vowel modifications are already written for fast passages. All languages vary between vowel series. Italian varies between Front and Back series (many Italian singers mix in some of the Neutral and Umlaut sounds).

continued on page 150.

THE PHONETIC SOUNDS OF SINGING

The IPA of all sounds and consonants in Italian, German, French and English.

a	mine - maɪn. Italian Ah between æ and ɑ.	o	boat, without diphthong
ɑ	Bright Ah - Cheeks up, corners of lips back and chin down, shout.	ɤ	Open O, between o and ɔ
ɒ	Dark Ah - father	ɔ	awe. Dark aw.
ã	dans, French nasal	ɔ̃	Fr. non. Nasalized ɔ or o
æ	fast	ʊ	(My symbol) Bright aw
b	back		Between ɔ and ɑ, joy.
ç	ich, German. human, Eng.	œ	Fr. coeur, ε with rounded lips
d	do	ø	Ger. schön, e with rounded lips
d̪	dentalized d, Don - don	p	pet
ε	ebb	pf	Kopf, Ger.
ε̃	plain, Fr. Nasalized ε or æ	r	red
e	first sound in may, meɪ	ř	rolled r, rosa It. ˇ indicates roll
ə	puckered le, Fr.	r	One flip of r, British.
f	fit	s	see
g	gave	ʃ	show
h	hot	t	tell
hw	white	t̪	dentalized t, moto It.
i	eat	θ	thin
ɪ	it	ð	this
j	yes	u	pool
dʒ	just	ɯ	bright u, with lips unpuckered between u and ʊ
k	keep	ʊ	pull
l	low	ʌ	fun, accented neutral vowel
l̪	dentalized l, lingua	v	voice
ʎ	gli, It. Tip of tongue touching gum line of lower front teeth.	w	win
m	my	y	i with lips rounded. Fr. du, Ger. fühl
ɱ	infra, It. Lower lip pressing against upper front teeth.	ʏ	ɪ with lips rounded, Ger. Hütte
n	now	z	zeal
n̪	dentalized n, Nina, It.	ʒ	pleasure
ŋ	It. ogni with tongue touching lower gum line of front teeth	x	Ger. ach, soft palate fricative.

Fig. 38. The Phonetic Sounds of Singing.

The American singer, usually monolingual, is called upon to sing Italian, German, French, and English in a very short period of training time. His study can be facilitated by learning to use all of the sounds of singing - the various colors of vowels and the various gradations of American consonants. Singers need to be trained in the use of the non-explosive consonants of the Italian language to reduce disruption of vocal cord vibration.

German uses the Front, Back, Neutral, and Umlaut series. English uses the Front, Back, and Neutral series, and French uses the Front, Back, Neutral and Umlaut series plus the nasalization of open vowels. The Vowel-Pitch exercises should be sung for several minutes each day for linguistic agility. As the singer progresses he may add various consonants to this study. The term vocalize comes from the Italian word vocale. However, most written vocalises are limited in the number of vowels used. For clarity I have called the next chapter Resonating Vowel-Pitch Studies. They may be sung with or without the use of a Vowel Resonator, however, the use of the Vowel Resonator will give better assurance when the tone is right.

Narrower in the Middle. I have shown that Female voices are narrower (more close) around f^1 and that Male voices are also narrower (more close) around f^1. The exercises in sombre timbre are designed to give those resonances.

CHAPTER XVI

RESONATING VOWEL-PITCH STUDIES - <u>FEMALE VOICES</u>

<u>Vocalize</u>! Begin your daily practice by vocalizing your acoustical alphabet on the diagonals and columns of the Chromatic Vowel Chart.

Sing on the vowel scales for vowel modification in diatonic movement. Sing on the vertical columns over each note for vowels which will amplify the <u>harmonic</u> indicated by the number at the end of the diagonal; singing that vowel-color on that pitch will give the best tone of the voice. The tuning is fineline - no leeway for approximation. Resonate the vowels on the dotted diagonals of the Chart after the others are established. They have an interharmonic or difference tone relationship (see p. xx). The heavy lines indicate the vowels which are <u>exactly</u> in tune with the sung pitch. There is one resonance wave for every vocal cord vibration. <u>Adjust the Chart up or down for your voice classification.</u>

Place $_2\big\Downarrow_3$ on f above middle c for use at the piano for contralto, on f# for mezzo or dramatic soprano, g for lyric soprano, and ab for coloratura soprano.

The Chromatic Vowel Chart is for the lower resonance of Front, Neutral, Back, and Umlaut Vowels. Practice the Vowel diagonals and vertical columns of the Chart daily.

<u>Numbering of Resonation Exercises</u>. The first number refers to the pitch on which an exercise begins when the Chromatic Vowel Chart is located properly on the piano for the singer's voice classification.

<u>Manner of Practice</u>. Start in the middle of the voice moving downwards or upwards and from page to page in a random order. This alternates the vowel series and results in activating and strengthening all musculatures with none being overworked. The voice is more of an elastic strength instrument than one of set strength. The voice is always in movement of vibrato, pitch, dynamic, etc. It should be trained according to its Nature. Sounds of beauty cannot come from a pained thraot - keep the voice elastic!

NOTHING TO EXCESS

Fig. 39. FEMALE VOWEL CHART

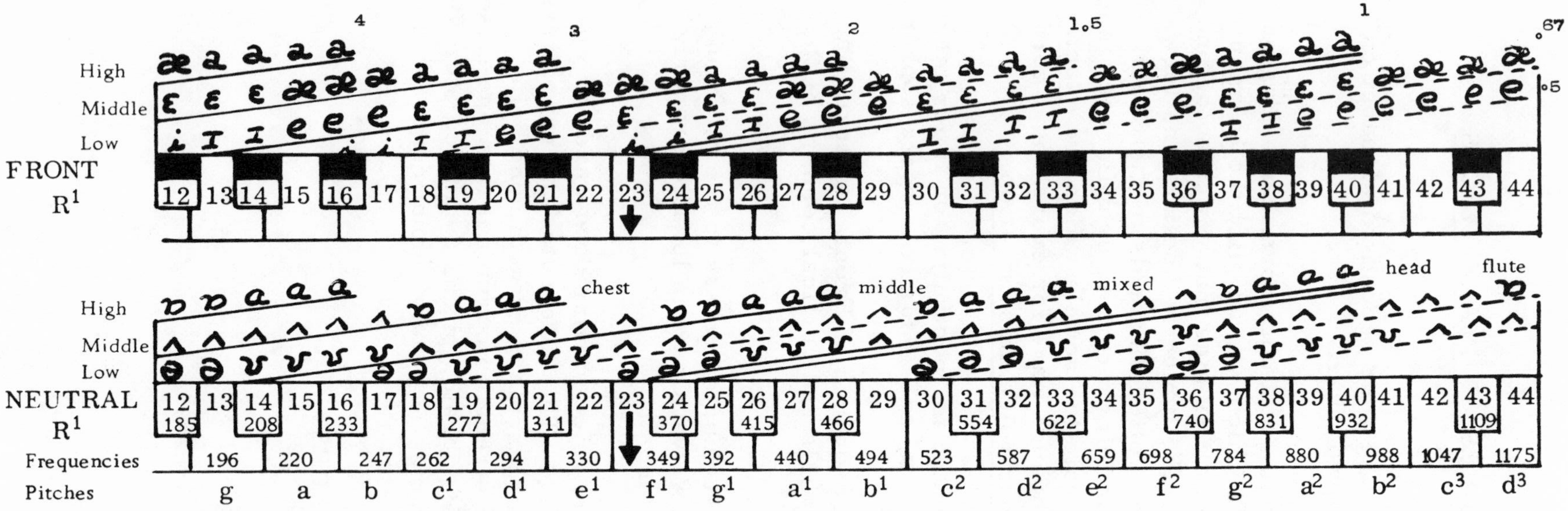

DIRECTIONS: 1) Sing and pronounce the vertical columns over single notes in your voice. Crossover frequently between the vowel series; and 2) Sing roulades on all of the diagonals, alternating the series.

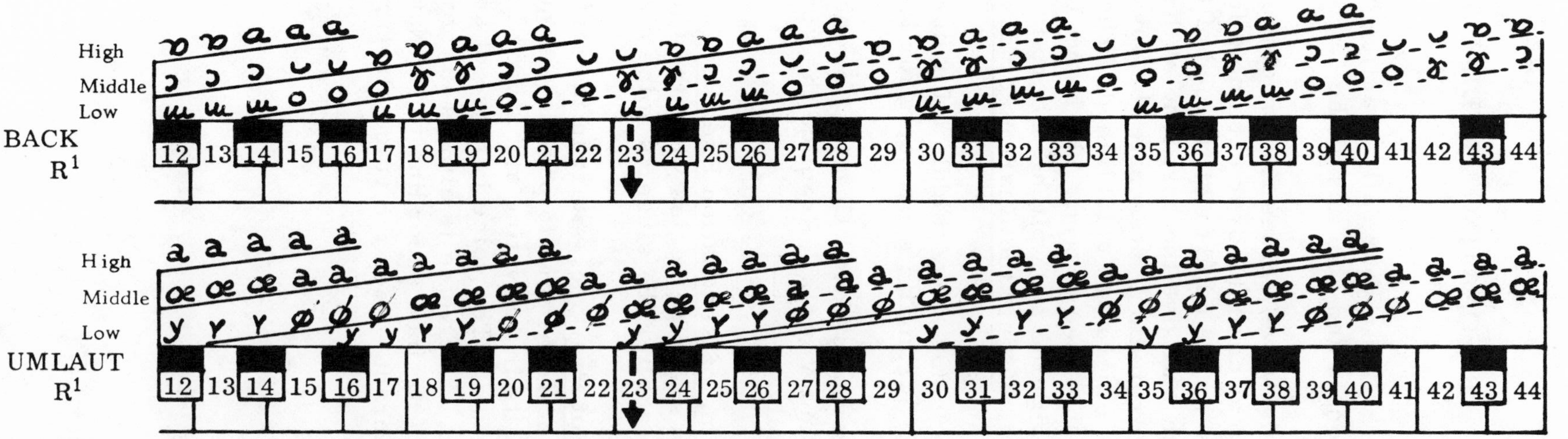

REGISTERS OF THE FEMALE VOICE. "This is the Alpha and Omega of the formation and development of the female voice, the touchstone of all singing methods, old and new... The three registers of the female voice are the Chest, the Medium, and the Head... To equalize and blend the Chest and Medium registers, the pupil must slightly close the last two notes of the former in ascending, and open them in descending... The same instructions...apply also to those of the Medium and Head." Mathilde Marchesi (Opus 31), G. Schirmer. To close in ascending, move to the next lower diagonal; to open in descending, move to the next higher diagonal. Register changes are resonance shifts.

FEMALE VOICES: HARMONIC CROSSOVERS: BACK VOWELS AND FRONT VOWELS.

Portamento study. Sing in random order with slight transposition for your voice classification. When sung in the sequence in which they are written the pivot vowel goes from close to open, when sung backwards the pivot vowel goes from open to close. When the arrow is placed on your note at the piano you can find your correct pitch for any vocalise by starting on the reference note number. In portamento all of the vibrations should be sounded between notes.

Glide from note to note with alternating favorable vowels. These studies may be sung Mezzo voce, Sotto voce, Messa di voce. On the high and low notes blow the tone a bit to assist the vocalization. (Begin near the middle of the page.)

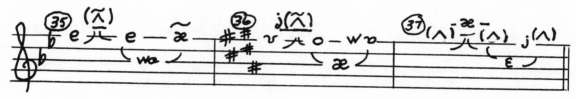

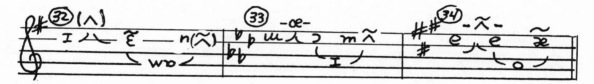

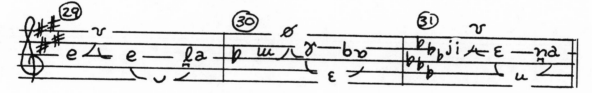

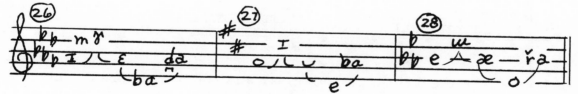

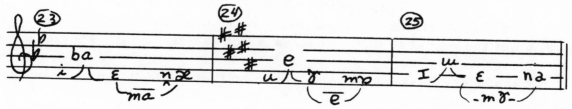

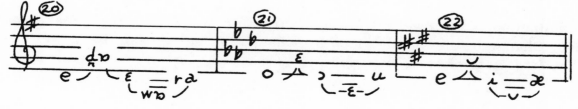

FEMALE VOICES: HARMONIC CROSSOVERS: BACK TO FRONT VOWELS;
            BACK TO UMLAUT VOWELS.

Alternate the harmonic a, ε, ɔ vowels for establishing the bright colors of the
voice. Tosi (1723, p. 29) in writing of the soprano voice recommended study
upon the three open vowels, a, ε, ɔ, so that the singer "may not confound one
with the other, and that from hence he may easier come to the use of words."
Fill in all the vibrations between the notes.

To find a dark Ah [ɒ or ɑ] preceed it with a [w] as in woe.
To find an Italian Ah [a] preceed it with [j] as in yes.

Exercises 30-37 are written in both clear and sombre timbres - the others are
in clear timbre only. Use exercises 23-25 to establish the lower notes of your
voice. The throat will feel wide in the direction of the shoulders because of
the action of the omo-hyoideus muscles which fasten into the shoulder blades.

Practice these exercises with portamento so that there is a continuous tone
from the beginning to end. Use variable breath flow.

The coincidence of vowel pitch and a harmonic of the sung pitch makes good
tone. Change of the mouth shape for change of color. Use the Vowel Resonator
on the first note of each exercise.

FEMALE VOICES: <u>HARMONIC CROSSOVERS: FRONT TO BACK VOWELS.</u>
<u>CLEAR TIMBRE.</u>

Roulades, timbre studies. The progression of the underlined high notes is from sombre to half clear to clear timbre. Sing in reverse to go from clear to half clear to sombre timbre. Vary between "sighing" voice (cords waving at each other) and "sharp" voice (cords striking each other).

<u>Forward Sounds.</u> "A forward position of the tongue is a proof of its freedom, hence all the exercises such as ah and lah for producing its forward action, if rightly studied, must result in the desired freedom." Shakespeare (1921, p. 23).

(Alternate with exercises on other pages.)

The consonant assists in establishing the loudest resonance in the vowels which follow them. The short attacks trigger the 3, 000 Hz of the voice.

FEMALE VOICES: HARMONIC CROSSOVERS: BACK, FRONT, AND NEUTRAL
VOWELS. CLEAR TIMBRE.

Roulades, timbre studies. Alternate phonetics with a progression from the
clear towards the sombre timbre of the underlined vowels.

Your understanding is by pronunciation (forming of resonators); your understanding
is through the sensations of tone.

(Alternate with exercises on other pages.)

When a harmonic of the sung pitch coincides with the pitch of the vowel pipe
(echo chamber), there is amplification of resonance and a physiological feeling
of well being. In the vernacular, the person is "singing where it is. " If the
vibrations of sung pitch and of vowel do not coincide harmonically the resonance is lessened and the singer feels a physiological interference in the
voice. This is "singing where it isn't. "

FEMALE VOICES: HARMONIC CROSSOVERS: BACK TO FRONT; BACK TO
UMLAUT VOWELS. SOMBRE TIMBRE.

The underlined vowels have a progression from sombre to clear timbre. The
upper line is Italianate, the lower line gives more compression and a more
Nordic sound.

(Alternate with exercises on other pages.)

The sombre timbre progression through the "narrow area" of the voice gives
the dramatic character referred to by Garcia (1840 - Paschke 1984 translation
p. xxxvii). This has been referred to as mixed voice and is a phenomenon
which occurs in both male and female voices between   concert
pitch. Alternate with exercises in clear timbre.

"A most important point to observe in teaching, especially women, is the
development of the medium notes; these, generally weak by nature, are rendered more defective still, in the case of sopranos, by the mania for forcing
high notes, and vice versa the low notes in the case of contraltos. " F. Lamperti
(1820, p. 12.) Build the middle voice with harmonic crossovers. These will
bring about automatic coupling.

FEMALE VOICES: HARMONIC CROSSOVERS: FRONT TO BACK; FRONT TO UMLAUT VOWELS.

Roulades, timbre studies. The Umlaut series gives a more enclosed physical appearance and a more close acoustical sound than the Front series.

The singing voice is born from the overtones of regular vibrations of the vocal cords. Brown (Lamperti), p. 19.

(Alternate with exercises on other pages.)

"Only through the sense of touch in the mucous membrane lining nose, pharynx, mouth and throat, does the mind control the vibration of the singing voice." Lamperti (Brown, p. 35.)

Marchesi (G. Schirmer) "To equalize and blend the Chest with the Medium register the pupil must slightly close the last two notes of the former in ascending, and open them in descending," p. xv. These exercises are harmonic notations of the roundings which will bring about easy transitions.

FEMALE VOICES: HARMONIC CROSSOVERS WITH ARPEGGIOS: FRONT AND BACK VOWELS - ITALIAN.

Everything is written for optimum resonance which will, at the same time, allow the voice to go smoothly <u>over</u> the f¹ area of the voice in <u>Clear</u> <u>Timbre</u> and <u>into and through</u> this region of the voice in <u>Sombre</u> <u>Timbre</u>.

(Begin near the middle of the page. Alternate with exercises on other pages.)

Clear Timbre   Sombre Timbre

<u>Clear Timbre</u>. "The vowels (a), (ɛ), (ɔ), ouvertes à l'italienne, are modifications of the clear timbre which bring about this conformation of the organ." From the (1970) Paschke tr. of Garcia's <u>Memoire</u> of (1840, p. 43). This chapter is partially built on the alternate phonetic principle used by Witherspoon (1925 p. 97).

FEMALE VOICES: HARMONIC CROSSOVERS WITH ARPEGGIOS: NEUTRAL AND FRONT VOWELS - ENGLISH

These exercises will give instrumental resonance to the Front vowels which have a high second formant (R^2). The Front vowels are in all languages of singing.

(Begin near the middle of the page. Alternate with exercises on other pages.)

Clear Timbre   **Sombre Timbre**

Sombre Timbre. "The vowels (e), (o), _fermées à l'italienne_, and the vowel (u) are modifications of the sombre timbre which impart these dispositions to the organ. Note the vowel (i), not having any character of its own, can receive the two timbres equally." Paschke's (1970) tr of Garcia's _Memoire_ (1840, p. 44).

FEMALE VOICES: HARMONIC CROSSOVERS WITH ARPEGGIOS: UMLAUT
AND BACK VOWELS - GERMAN AND FRENCH

Although the Umlaut vowels occur in only the German and French languages,
they are used in dark colorings of the Italian and English languages. They
should be practiced for a balanced vocalization as well as linguistic virtuosity.

(Begin near the middle of the page.   Alternate with exercises on other pages.)

Clear Timbre   Sombre Timbre

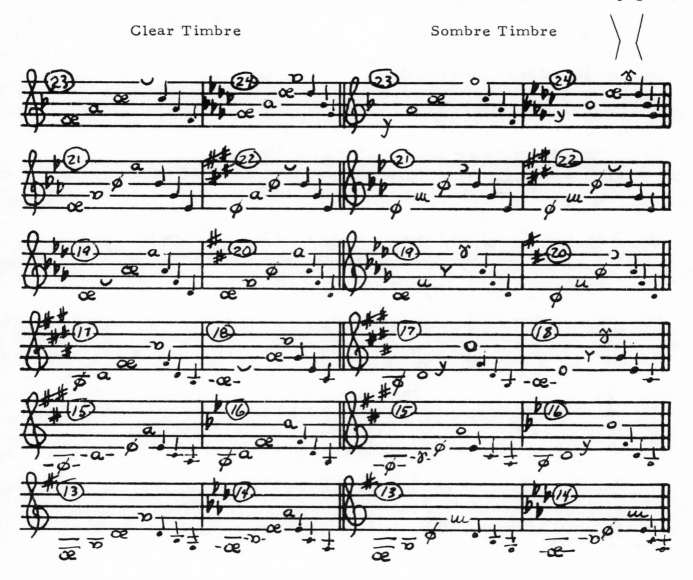

Sing all arpeggios as though there were one long tone with varying colors and
pitches. Sing at various dynamics. Start on the upper note going down and
lower note going up in the various exercises.

Sing with various connections - portamento, legato, marcato, and staccato.

FEMALE VOICES: HARMONIC CROSSOVERS, NEUTRAL TO FRONT VOWELS

Agility exercises of the ninth <u>over</u> the passaggio. Progression on the roulade is from open to close on the underlined vowels. Alternate with exercises on page xxx.

"Pronunciation, forming of the tone with the vowel sounds should be made a vital part of the teaching of the beginner. Never forget that tone and vowel sound are one." Witherspoon (1925, p. 75). Later he was General Manager of the Metropolitan Opera Company until his early death in 1935. <u>I believe that this process should be utilized by all singers, beginners or professionals, since the same acoustical laws exist for all.</u>

(Alternate with exercises on other pages.)

"Phonetic vibrations felt at lips, nose, head, throat and chest, carry distinct messages to every part of the body. These messages are recorded in the singer's consciousness until habitual reaction takes the place of effort and thought." G.B. Lamperti in Brown (1931, p. 17).

"Be vowel conscious and not sound conscious. Every phrase is a compilation of vowel sounds." Paola Novikova.

FEMALE VOICES: HARMONIC CROSSOVERS, FRONT TO NEUTRAL VOWELS

"The Head Voice (which Lamperti says begins on d♭^{2}) will 'speak' more readily if aided by a slight extra pressure, and it is allowable to draw a little breath through the nose. As we said before, the resonance must be felt on the top of the head where the parietal bone joins the frontal bone." G. B. Lamperti/Brown (1931, p. 15). Beginning with d♭^{2} there is only one harmonic available for the lower resonance of vowels.

(Alternate with exercises on other pages.)

"Consciously or unconsciously used, technique remains a necessity to art and to the artist himself, as without it there is no art. Is it not a magnificent task to secure for one's self a privileged position in the world of art by acquiring conscious ability? By gaining for one's self a beautiful voice or, if such a one naturally exists, by preserving it to the end of one's life?" Lilli Lehmann (1914, p. 287). She practiced what she preached - she sang into her 70's.

PRONOUNCE - HEAR - FEEL - UNDERSTAND

CHAPTER XVII

RESONATING VOWEL-PITCH STUDIES - <u>MALE VOICES</u>

<u>Vocalize!</u> Sing on the vowel scales for vowel modification in diatonic movement. Sing on the vertical columns over each note for vowels which will amplify the <u>harmonic</u> indicated by the number at the end of the diagonal; singing that vowel-color on that pitch will give the best tone of the voice. The tuning is fineline - no leeway for approximation. Do not resonate the vowels on the dotted lines until the other vowels are established. The heavy line indicates the actual pitch of the vowels most of which are resonated by your overtones. <u>Place the vowel correctly for your voice classification.</u>

Place $_2\downarrow_3$ on f above middle c for use
at the   piano for high baritone, on
f# or g for tenor, e♮ for baritone, e♭
for bass-baritone, or d♮ for bass.

Lines I and II are the lower Resonances of Front and Neutral Vowels. Practice the Vowel Scales and columns daily.

Lines III and IV are the lower Resonances of Back and Umlaut Vowels. Practice the Vowel Scales and columns daily.

Follow by random vocalises on the following pages for Male Voices.

<u>Numbering of Resonance Exercises.</u> The first number refers to the pitch on which an exercise begins when the Chromatic Vowel Chart is located properly on the piano for the singer's voice classification.

<u>Manner of Practice.</u> Start in the middle of the voice moving downwards or upwards and from page to page in a random order. This alternates the vowel series and results in activating and strengthening all musculatures with none being overworked. The voice is more of an elastic strength instrument than one of set strength. The voice is always in movement of vibrato, pitch, dynamic, etc. It should be trained according to its Nature. Sounds of beauty cannot come from a pained throat - keep the voice elastic!

NOTHING TO EXCESS

165

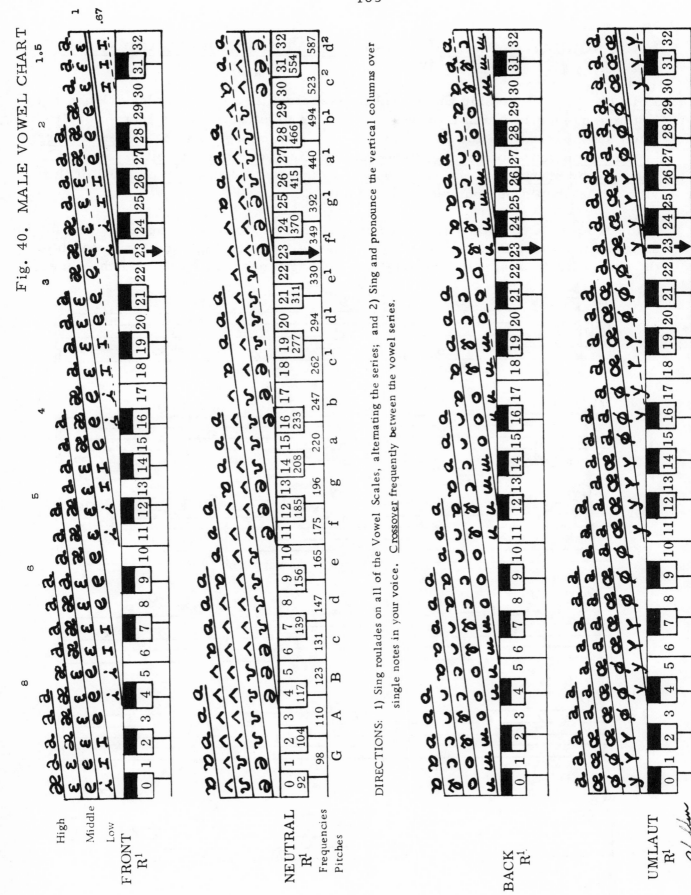

Fig. 40. MALE VOWEL CHART

DIRECTIONS: 1) Sing roulades on all of the Vowel Scales, alternating the series; and 2) Sing and pronounce the vertical columns over single notes in your voice. Crossover frequently between the vowel series.

MALE VOICES: HARMONIC CROSSOVERS: BACK VOWELS AND FRONT VOWELS

Portamento Study. Sing these timbre exercises in random order. When sung in the sequence in which they are written the pivot vowel goes from close to open, when sung backwards the pivot vowel goes from open to close. When the arrow is placed on your note at the piano you can find your correct pitch for any vocalise by starting on the reference note number. In portamento all of the vibrations should be sounded between notes.

Glide from note to note with alternating favorable vowels. These studies may be sung Mezzo voce, Sotto voce, Messa di voce. On the high and low notes blow the tone a bit to assist the vocalization. (Begin near the middle of the page.)

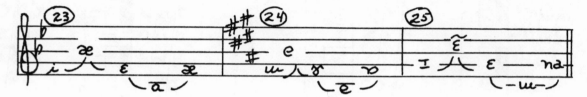

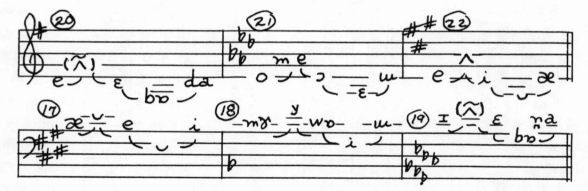

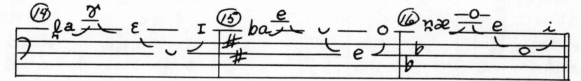

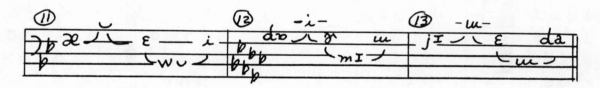

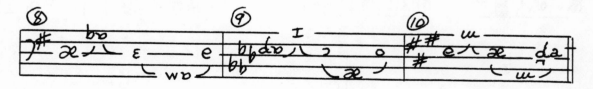

MALE VOICES: HARMONIC CROSSOVERS: BACK TO FRONT VOWELS

Thin the edges of the vocal cords for open vowels on low notes in order to give an explosion spectrum which is in the area of their resonance.

To find a dark Ah [ɒ or ɑ] preceed it with a [w] as in woe.
To find a bright, Italian Ah [a] preceed it with a [j] as in yes.

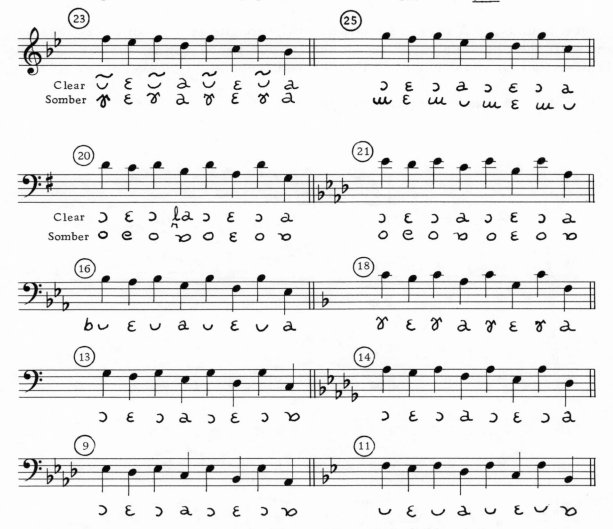

Exercises 21-25 are written in both clear and sombre timbres - the others are in clear timbre only. Use exercises 11-13 to establish the lower notes of your voice. The throat will feel wide in the direction of the shoulders because of the action of the omo-hyoideus muscles which fasten into the shoulders.

Practice these exercises with portamento so that there is a continuous tone from the beginning to end. Use variable breath flow.

MALE VOICES: HARMONIC CROSSOVERS: BACK TO FRONT VOWELS.
                        CLEAR TIMBRE.

Roulades, timbre studies.   The progression of the underlined high notes is from
clear to half clear to sombre timbre.   Sing in reverse to go from sombre to
half sombre to clear timbre.   Vary between sighing voice (cords waving at
each other) and "sharp" voice (cords striking each other).

Frontal Sounds.   "A forward position of the tongue is a proof of its freedom,
hence all the exercises such as ah and lah for producing its forward action, if
rightly studied, must result in the desired freedom."   Shakespeare (1921, p. 23).

(Alternate with exercises on other pages.)

The consonant triggers are used to establish the correct resonance in the
vowels which follow them.   The short attacks trigger the 3,000 Hz of the
voice.

MALE VOICES: HARMONIC CROSSOVERS: FRONT TO BACK VOWELS.
CLEAR TIMBRE.

Roulades, timbre studies.   Alternate phonetics with a progression from open
to close vowels of the underlined vowels.

Your placement is by pronunciation (forming of resonators); your understanding
is through the sensations of tone.

(Alternate with exercises on other pages.)

When a harmonic of the sung pitch coincides with the pitch of the vowel pipe
(echo chamber), there is amplification of resonance and a physiological feeling
of well being.   In the vernacular, the person is "singing where it is. " If the
vibrations of sung pitch and of vowel do not coincide harmonically the resonance is lessened and the singer feels a physiological interference in the voice.
This is "singing where it isn't. "   These are flexible resonations of the throat.
Pain in the throat is unknown in this type of vocalization unless singing is
done for an excessive period of time.

MALE VOICES: HARMONIC CROSSOVERS: BACK TO FRONT - BACK TO
UMLAUT VOWELS.   SOMBRE TIMBRE.

The vocalises above the hash marks have a progression from sombre to clear
on the underlined vowels.   The upper line is Italianate, the lower line gives
more compression and a more Nordic sound.

(Alternate with exercises on other pages.)

The sombre timbre progression through the "narrow area" of the voice gives
the dramatic character referred to by Garcia (1841 - Paschke 1970 translation p. xxx).   This has been referred to as mixed voice and is a phenomenon
which occurs in both male and female voices between ♭ on the Vowel
Chart.   Alternate with exercises in clear timbre.

MALE VOICES: HARMONIC CROSSOVERS: FRONT TO BACK - FRONT TO UMLAUT VOWELS

Roulades, timbre studies. The Umlaut series gives a more enclosed physical appearance and a more close acoustical sound than the Front series.

"The singing voice is born from the overtones of regular vibrations of the vocal cords." Brown (Lamperti), 1931, p. 19.

(Alternate with exercises on other pages.)

"Only through the sense of touch in the mucous membrane lining nose, pharynx, mouth and throat, does the mind control the vibration of the singing voice." Brown (Lamperti), 1931, p. 35.

English vowels are continually in transition, hence like diphthongs. Sung vowels should be sustained in pitch as in the Italian language.

MALE VOICES: HARMONIC CROSSOVERS WITH ARPEGGIOS: FRONT AND BACK VOWELS - ITALIAN

Everything is written for optimum resonance which will, at the same time, allow the voice to go smoothly over the f^1 area of the voice in Clear Timbre and into and through this region of the voice in Sombre Timbre.

(Begin near the middle of the page.   Alternate with exercises on other pages.)

Clear Timbre   Sombre Timbre

Clear Timbre. "The vowels (a), (ɛ), (ɔ), ouvertes à l'italienne, are modifications of the clear timbre which bring about this conformation of the organ." From the (1984) Paschke tr of Garcia's Memoire (p. lix).

MALE VOICES: HARMONIC CROSSOVERS WITH ARPEGGIOS: NEUTRAL
AND FRONT VOWELS - ENGLISH

These exercises will give instrumental resonance to the Front vowels which
resonate in front of the tongue hump. The Front vowels are in all the languages
of singing.

(Begin near the middle of the page. Alternate with exercises on other pages.)

Clear Timbre   Sombre Timbre

Sombre Timbre. "The vowels (e), (o), fermées à l'italienne, and the vowel
(u) are modifications of the sombre timbre which impart these dispositions to
the organ. Note the vowel (i), not having any character of its own, can receive
the two timbres equally." Paschke's (1984) tr of Garcia's Memoire (p. lix).

MALE VOICES: HARMONIC CROSSOVERS WITH ARPEGGIOS: UMLAUT AND BACK VOWELS - GERMAN AND FRENCH

Although the Umlaut vowels occur in only the German and French languages, they are used in dark colorings of the Italian and English languages. They should be practiced for a balanced vocalization as well as linguistic virtuosity.

(Begin near the middle of the page. Alternate with exercises on other pages.)

Clear Timbre   Sombre Timbre

Sing all arpeggios as though there were one long tone with varying colors and pitches. Sing at various dynamics. Start on the upper note going down and lower note going up in the various exercises.

Sing with various connections - portamento, legato, and marcato.

MALE VOICES: HARMONIC CROSSOVERS OF BACK AND FRONT VOWELS

Agility exercises of the ninth through the passaggio.   Below the hash marks
the underlined vowels progress from open to close; above the hash marks
the progression is from close to open.

(Begin near the middle of the page.   Alternate with exercises on other pages.)

"Phonetic vibrations felt at lips, nose, head, throat and chest, carry distinct
messages to every part of the body.   These messages are recorded in the
singer's consciousness until habitual reaction takes the place of effort and
thought." G. B. Lamperti in Brown (1931, p. 17).

"Be vowel conscious and not sound conscious.   Every phrase is a compilation
of vowel sounds." Paola Novikova.

MALE VOICES: HARMONIC CROSSOVERS OF FRONT AND BACK VOWELS

Agility exercises of the ninth through the passaggio.   Below the hash marks
the underlined vowels progress from open to close; above the hash marks the
progression is from close to open.

(Begin near the middle of the page.   Alternate with exercises on other pages.)

"Consciously or unconsciously used, technique remains a necessity to art and
to the artist himself, as without it there is no art. Is it not a magnificent
task to secure for one's self a privileged position in the world of art by acquiring conscious ability? By gaining for one's self a beautiful voice, or if such
a one naturally exists, by preserving it to the end of one's life?" Lilli Lehmann
(1914, p. 287.) She practiced what she preached - she sang into her 70's.

PRONOUNCE - HEAR - FEEL - UNDERSTAND

CHAPTER XVIII

THE BREATH

Breathing has heretofore been considered the most important facet of singing. Without doubt it is of great importance. Lilli Lehmann (1914, p. 280) says:

> "It has become the habit of considering the breath as
> the only cause for a bad or a good tone. This is the
> cause of the eternal breath pressure with which so
> many singers produce their tones and ruin their
> voices....it would be advisable to leave the coaction
> of the diaphragm out of play at first, directing the
> attention to the form only - that is, to the relative
> position of nose, palate, larynx, and tongue, and
> finally after the form has become habit, to the fine,
> subtle, and dirigible coworker, the diaphragm. "
> [Yes, dirigibles were an important part of German
> armament at that time.]

The Chromatic Vowel Chart, Sounds of Singing, and Overtones of Bel Canto are concerned with automating the forms of singing. The voice is made of a hyoid bone, cartilage, ligaments, and several muscles. All are flexible except the bone, yet its movement is significant. No study of the movements involved will ever give good singing unless their product is monitored by the ear, anymore than the deaf can be taught normal speech. They may be taught a fairly normal lip and tongue movement which can be visually read, but the aural sound is "off" to some extent because it has not been adequately monitored.

It is known that the wings of the thyroid cartilage can come as much as 1 centimeter closer together for high notes in young persons (Luchsinger, 1965, p. 76) probably around Notes #30 to #40 on the Chromatic Vowel Chart and that the wings widen for covered singing (Luchsinger, p. 105) around Notes #20 to #27 on the Chromatic Vowel Chart. The size of the vocal tract is simultaneously changed. The one thing we have to go by is the vowel sound. As stated before, the vowels round to allow the upper pitches of the voice to be made. If this does not occur - all of the breath pressure in the world will not yield the tone in good quality. Furthermore, great muscular effort cannot be sustained for a period of time without the muscles "giving in." Hence the reason for the Chromatic Vowel Chart which is comparable to fingering charts for instrumentalists. It was derived by ear, and feel; you can experience it by feel and it can be applied by feel and notation.

Breath is important, extremely important, and must be placed in perspective. Caruso, in Marafioti (1922, p. 158) is quoted as saying:

> "The lungs, in the first place, should be thoroughly
> filled. A tone begun with only half-filled lungs loses
> half its authority and is very apt to be false in pitch. "

The advantage of a full and silent inhalation is that the larynx finds its singing position which is lower than in speech. This occurs because the larynx follows the descent of the diaphragm through a downward pull of the trachea. This action of the larynx must be added to the harmonic pronunciation of this text for great singing.

In addition, the singer should have as a technique the half breath, or mezzo respiro which is

> "used for the continuation of phrases too long for deliv-
> ery within the limits of a single inspiration - the lungs
> are neither completely emptied, nor completely re-
> filled or replenished only, by means of a gentle inhala-
> tion, confined to that portion of the organ which lies
> immediately beneath the claviculae, or collar bones. "
> Rockstro (1894, p. 8) on the analysis of the method of
> Jenny Lind.

Both the full breath and half breath must be within the technique of every singer for the greatest realization of his or her resources.

Jean DeReszke (Leiser, 1934, p. 293) in writing to a student said, "Pour le Meineid de Erda; don't crush the breath, but make your ribs as large as possible and give the tones in their greatest expansion. " Francesco Lamperti (1890) taught the full breath (respiro) and Garcia (1894) also taught it giving the key reason that if the floating ribs were denied their action, the breath was clavicular. They also taught the half-breath (mezzo respiro). In brief, the breath in singing operates fundamentally the same as in any other wind instrument - the energy of vibration and resonation must continually be re- plenished by some means. As a child in a swing must continually be pushed to maintain the same height, so must the vocal cords be energized by the breath to maintain their swing. It is that simple and that subtle. The athletic aspect of the breath is more complex. The importance of a discipline of the breath cannot be overemphasized as long as it is associated with appropriate vowel colors (resonance).

"Voici le clef, je crois. " So, quoting Marguerite in "Faust, " "Here is the key, I believe" - the relationship of the vowels to sung tone (in connection with the breath). How long must a singer think of this relationship? Quoting Cotogni, the first teacher of Jean DeReszke and of Gigli (Herbert-Caesari, 1951, p. 20):

"Remember that always you must mentally shape each
vowel and impart to it the right coulour, timbre, and
expression before actually producing it.... Yes every
vowel and always, for as long as you are a singer and
sing; the habit is soon acquired, and such thinking before doing becomes really quite an easy matter."

You must think of the vowel-sung pitch relationship for as long as you are a
singer, and this will be a long time if you follow the acoustical laws of Nature.

For an in depth study of the breath see Appendix D, p. 237.

CHAPTER XIX

PRACTICING WITH VOWEL RESONATOR

It has been said that no one can learn to sing from a book. It is my belief that many can teach, place and develop singing voices by the use of the Chromatic Vowel Chart with artificially generated pitch - an extension of the Electric Larynx. The phonetic symbols on the Chart are written sounds which will echo the various pitches in the singing scale when the arrow is properly placed for the singer' voice classification. The Chart and these exercises will make many more resonant colors of voice, better intonation, better quality, a more distinguishable diction, and a more robust voice available to a singer for his or her interpretation. There are many books on interpretation. It is the intent of this book to deal primarily with providing the instrument and colors for the interpretative art of singing.

Control of the Voice. Since the earliest writings, singers and teachers of singing have been concerned with the control of the singing voice. Possibly the greatest of them all, according to Henry Pleasants (1966), was Gasparo Pacchierotti (1740-1821) who said, "Mettete ben la voce, Respirato bene, Pronunciate chiaramente Ed il vostro canto sara perfetto." Collected by Philip A. Duey. Francesco Lamperti in his preface (1875) translated this statement as being, "He who knows how to breathe and pronounce well, knows how to sing well [he continues] and this is one of the greatest truths which study and experience have ever suggested to the successful cultivators of the art of singing." Admittedly breath is a control but very few persons speak of pronunciation (resonance) as being the other control. G. B. Lamperti in Brown's Vocal Wisdom (1931) states, "It is strange fact that the throat is controlled by what happens above it, in the acoustics of the head, through word, vibration and resonance." The Chromatic Vowel Chart tells the singer which vowel-colors to use for proper throat space control for each step of the singing voice. The only thing new is that I have, in the process of studying this phenomenon, found a way by which vowel resonances can be heard, felt, notated, and used. The procedure is simple enough so that any one can hear it and feel it, and can apply it during the training of the singing voice as well as during professional performance, stage center, in any opera house or concert hall in the world.

There is a unique advantage to the teacher in using the Vowel Resonator/Realistic or Electric organ combination. The male-voiced teacher can feel and hear what it is like to make vowels like a soprano. He will find that from Note #29 to #40 there is only one (1) harmonic in the vocal tract on which all vowel colors must be echoed. From Notes #17 to #28, there are at most two harmonics on which vowel colors can be engraved with the exception of Note #22 which has one and has, curiously, been known as "the break." On the lower notes of the Chromatic Vowel Chart the female voiced teacher can feel and hear what it is like to make vowels on low notes like a male singer where there are at least four (4) harmonics on which all vowels can be pronounced from Notes #1 to #12; three (3) harmonics on which vowels can be pronounced from Notes #13 to #16; and that there are always at least two (2) harmonics on which the vowels can be pronounced from Notes #17 to #28 with the exception of Note #22. With this knowledge, would any critic or teacher have the gall to criticize a soprano for not having the clarity of diction of a bass, baritone, or even a tenor? We hope voice teachers (and even critics) will avail themselves of this procedure of finding out how the other half lives. How can a female teacher instruct a man on how to "cover," "darken," or "round" the tone without the feel of the lower green vowels over Notes #22 to #28? Garcia said it this way in his <u>Memoire</u> presented to the French Academy in 1840, Paschke Translation (1984, p. lii):

"The tones included between e^1 and b^1 when one gives them some full vigor in the sombre timbre, acquire, in men and women, a dramatic character, which has led to an error in the very appreciation of their nature; in place of recognizing in them the influence of the sombre timbre, joined by intensity, in conditions of effect more favorable than anywhere else, people have seen an exceptional case, and they have designated them by the name mixed tones, or mixed voice, darkened [sombrée]. The A string of the violoncello, although weaker, reproduces rather well the same effect."

Please note that the lower <u>Green</u> vowels on Notes #20 and #26 bring about this condition in either male or female voices, concert pitch. Acoustically speaking, the vowels over a broken line have a pitch exactly a 5th above the sung pitch and when one pronounces them exactly, both the sung pitch and its 2nd harmonic (octave) are reinforced. Said in another way, this pronunciation seems to cause the voice to sing in two registers at once!!! No wonder it is called <u>mixed</u>. This 1.5 series is quite unstable and the pitch will wander either to the sharp or flat side depending on which side of the 5th the singer pronounces the vowel. If the singer resonates that vowel on the Vowel Resonator he will find a resonating vowel color and when singing the pitch a 5th below the vowel, dead center, will have good resonance, focus, and good intonation. This reinforces both the sung pitch and the octave. If the singer resonates the vowel at the 8ve, the 8ve will be reinforced and the sung pitch will not be reinforced but it will be heard as a phantom fundamental (See difference tone, p. 69.).

Incidentally, Garcia was quite concerned about the above terminology of <u>mixed</u> as late as his 1872 edition, Paschke, translation of Part II of "A Complete Treatise on the Art of Singing," p. 161, (1972).

> "The designation of voix mixte and mezzo petto are
> equally improper [to the Italian terms voce di petto
> and voce di mezzo petto], for they would make us
> suppose that these clear and high pitched tones are
> produced by the two mechanisms of the chest and
> falsetto [he also used this Italian term for women's
> middle voice] registers at the same time. Now
> physiologically, the simultaneous conjunction of two
> different mechanisms serving to produce the same
> note, or two notes in unison, is an unacceptable idea."

It is no more unacceptable than the tone produced by a bassoon player on a reed
without the horn in which two tones are produced at the same time. It is called
a "crow" and gives a tone of many harmonics described as a wide spectrum. If
that is unbelievable, quickly find a bassoon player and have him give a demonstration. This tone is considered to be good on the bassoon.

We are at a time in history when the subject of acoustics is not taught in some
of the better Schools of Physics and is not taught in some Schools of Music.
Acoustical phonetics is usually not involved with the singing voice. Even the
Bell Telephone Laboratories have made little study of the singing voice; and
very seldom is the acoustical basis of phonetics taught to those who use them
in the pronunciation of French, German, Italian, and English. Is there a reason
why some of the findings of this study happen to be unusual? Also, in some
Schools of Music the traditions of the great singing masters are not studied in
vocal pedagogy classes. Does there happen to be a reason why the relationships
between their precepts and the nature of sounds in the singing voice are largely
unknown? With a Vowel Resonator hookup any teacher or singer can quickly gain
an enormous knowledge, through his senses, of the uses of pitch-vowel-register
relationships. Yes, we are in an age of discovery which should lead us again to
the great singing of the past.

Why not a Stradivarius? People speak with pride of owning a Stradivarius, a
Steinway, a Baldwin, a Selmer or some elite kind of a musical instrument which
has been constructed by specialists in sound. Is it not just as important to take
natural materials of voice and construct them into a superb musical instrument?
The artist's craft of creating and maintaining an harmonic vocal instrument of
living members is just as distinguished as that of creating an harmonic instrument of inanimate members. Somewhere along the way a lack of perspective
has arisen in the evaluation of this creative process.

Lilli Lehmann (1914), p. 104, said of maintaining a singing voice,

> "Therefore, the motto must be always, practice, and
> again, practice to keep one's powers uninjured; practice
> brings freshness to the voice, strengthens the muscles
> and is for the singer, far more interesting than any
> musical composition."

Isn't that an <u>odd</u> twist? How often today do singers want to perform <u>now</u> and not take time to form their instruments? Unfortunately, they cannot buy a vocal Stradivarius to play upon - they must form it as they play upon it. How exciting if they follow a procedure based on the acoustical laws of sounding the vocal instrument!

CHAPTER XX

RESONANCE LESSONS FOR FEMALE VOICES

This chapter is concerned with making the phenomena of multiple vowel resonances even more apparent to you. Some very knowledgeable investigators have
written that [i] and some of the other Front vowels are one resonance vowels.
Exercises ONE through FIVE are given to dispel that theory and to show how
those vowel resonances can be used. When used as one resonance vowels, the
voice sounds very tight and tends to sharp.

To do this, it is necessary to use a Vowel Resonator with an instrument which
plays simultaneously many pitches of a Flute quality. We will see them in such
a way that the various resonances will become apparent to you. We will see
this approach in Lessons ONE through FIVE. If you do not have such equipment
and cannot make a casette of such sounds, you should skip to exercise six.

LESSON ONE

(Exercises with Vowel Resonator and Organ or Cassettes.)
The Resonances of Vowels between [u] and [ɑ].

(F) Place the arrow over the correct note for your voice classification.

1. (With an Organ) Hold down ALL organ notes between Notes #23-#40

   while holding a Vowel Resonator in front of the mouth with cords

   closed.

2. Pronounce WOW in very slow motion [u-ɑ-u]. Your vocal tract will

   resonate a glissando from Note #23 up to #40 and back down to #23 if

   the vocal cords are together as when grunting. Go slowly to hear the

   individual notes come into and go out of resonance. Notice the vowel-

   colors of the various notes. VOWELS ARE DEFINED BY PITCH OF

   LOUDEST RESONANCE.

3. Foreign vowels - all vowels must be developed for a good vowel scale.

Stop on Notes #25-#26 to hear the lateral oo [ɯ] which we do not use in spoken English. This vowel is a modification between [u and o].

Stop on Notes #30 and #31 to hear the lateral Oh [ɤ] which Americans do not use in spoken English. This vowel is a modification between [o and ɔ].

Stop on Notes #34 and #35 to hear the lateral Aw [ʊ] which Americans do not use in spoken English. This vowel is between [ɔ and ɒ].

Stop on Notes #38, #39 and #40 to hear the lateral Ah [ɑ] which is a brighter vowel than we use in spoken English.

4. All of the above vowels are used in Italian speech. The throat is opened differently for them than in our Back Vowels [u, o, ɔ, ɒ]. The throat is opened as though it were being widened 3 inches below the lower molars (in the direction of the shoulders). The opening is highly involved with the omohyoid muscle which attaches to the tongue bone, goes through a loop 2 inches or so lower, and then attaches to the shoulder blade. When it is said that someone has an Italian throat, he is probably speaking of this opening. This is not gutteral; in gutteral singing the tongue is depressed in such a way that the spaces above the larynx are almost closed and the resonances shut off. The Lateral vowels are involved with opening, and resonance is increased on the pitches indicated. Thus the Vowel Resonator can be used in training the spacing muscles which form the vibrating air columns of the vocal tract. If these muscles are inactive or weak, daily practice will soon give them strength and agility. I believe this is a key to the singing voice which can be used consciously or subconsciously for proper opening of the throat and mouth. It also helps in the proper playing of the tongue.

LESSON TWO
(Exercises with Vowel Resonator and Organ or Cassette.)
The Low Resonances of Vowels between [a and i] going down.

1. Hold down all of the organ notes which are under the underlined Notes #23-#40.

2. Pronounce [ja-i-a] very slowly. Your vocal tract will resonate a glissando from Notes #40-#23-#40. Go slowly enough to hear the individual notes come into resonance and go out of resonance. Hear the resonance that goes down when going [a to i]. When the tongue pulls forward to make the small cavity of [i], a large cavity is created in the throat. Hence the pitch goes down. See Delattre's diagrams of speech (p. 274). The spaces vary similarly for [e, ε, æ, and a].

3. Foreign vowels. Sustain resonance on Notes #30 to #33 to get the feel and sound of the lower speech resonance of [ε]. Feel for the greatest vibration. This vowel is also involved with the omohyoid spacing muscles. Pronounce [jε] to find the resonance easily.

4. Stop on Notes #34 to #40 to pronounce the lower resonance of [a]. Pronounce [ja], with the teeth no more than a finger's width apart. This can be called the tongue Ah, the front Ah, or the Italian [a] since it also has a high resonance.

LESSON THREE
(Exercises with Vowel Resonator and Organ or Cassette.)
The High Resonance of Vowels between [a and i] going up.

(F) 1. Hold down all of the organ notes which are between Notes #41-#59 which are on the organ.

2. Pronounce [ja-i-a] very slowly. Your vocal tract will echo a glissando from Notes #41-#59-#41. Go slowly enough to hear the individual vowel pitches come <u>into</u> resonance and go <u>out</u> of resonance.

3. Foreign vowels - good vowel scales must be developed for good singing scales.

   a. Stop and hold the resonance on Notes #41 to #44 to hear the Italian Ah [a] so named by Helmholtz, (1885), p. 106 and Garcia (1894), p. 17. Pronounce Yah, Yah [ja, ja] to find this resonance. The mouth opening should be about the width of a finger.

   b. Stop on Notes #49-#52 to hear the sustained [ε] which is not used in some parts of our country - witness "Tennessee" [t ɪ n ɪ s i] rather than [t ε n ə s i]. Pronounce [jε, jε] to find this resonance.

   c. Stop on Notes #55 and #56 for German [e] as in "geben" [g <u>e</u>: b ə n]. Americans think it is almost an [i] which <u>is</u> on Notes #58 and #59; it <u>is</u> very close to [i].

LESSON FOUR
(Exercises with Vowel Resonator and Organ or Cassette.)

Ⓕ   Do not sing in this lesson. Pronounce the heavily underlined vowels starting on Note #32 going above and below the line and find the resonances of the indicated underlined vowels. Continue as high as Note #40 and as low as Note #23.

   Preceed the vowels below the line with [w] as in <u>wo</u>e [wo].

   Preceed the vowels above the line with [j] as in <u>yes</u> [jεs].

LESSON FIVE
(Exercises with Vowel Resonator and Organ or Cassette.)

Ⓕ   Do not sing in this lesson. In Line III, pronounce the vowels in the vertical columns over Note #22 which are not in parenthesis. Proceed as high as Note #28 and as low as Note #13. (I have "tempered" the vowel

scale on Notes #23 and #24 since [ʊ] and [ɒ] are on the same harmonic.

The same can be said of Notes #17 and #29. Learn to resonate the cor-

rect vowel on them. If you can resonate them you can sing them!)

The following exercises require only one pitch so the Vowel Resonator can be

used with a Concertmate or similar instrument.

LESSON SIX
(Exercises with Vowel Resonator and Organ or Concertmate.)
Play and Pronounce, then Sing.

Ⓕ   Pronounce the vowels in Lines II and IV beginning on Note #25. Proceed

as high as Note #33 and as low as Note #13. Listen for the resonance.

Stay on it for a few seconds after you have found it, then sing the vowel.

LESSON SEVEN
(Exercises with Vowel Resonator and Organ or Concertmate.)
Play and Pronounce, then Sing.

Ⓕ   On Vowel Row ①, Line III, play Notes #27 pronouncing [o] and #32

pronouncing [ɔ]. As soon as you hear them resonate, sing Notes #27,

#29, #31, #32 and back on the pattern - 1 2 3 4 3 2 1 modifying the vowels

[o to ɔ to o]. Feel the resonance on the intermediate notes. This is

called [resonance tracking].

Ⓕ   Play and sing in like manner with vowel modifications of Vowel Row ①

to around Note #35.

Ⓕ   Play and sing in like manner with vowel modifications of Vowel Row ①

as low as Note #23. You have been pronouncing and singing on the actual

pitches of these vowels.

(F)   <u>Play</u> and <u>sing</u> all the underlined vowels on the notes over which they stand between Notes #23 and #40. G. B. Lamperti (1931), p. 28, said, "To know the result before we act is the golden rule of singing." Sing on the feel.

LESSON EIGHT
(Exercises with Vowel Resonator and Organ or Concertmate.)
<u>Play and Pronounce, then Sing</u>.

(F)   <u>Play</u> Notes #15 and #20 <u>pronounce</u> [o] and [ɔ], Harmonic Diagonal ②, Line III. As soon as you hear them resonate, sing Notes #15, #17, #19, #20 and back on the pattern - 1 2 3 4 5 4 3 2 1. Feel the resonance on the intermediate notes.

(F)   Proceed up the scale as far as Harmonic Diagonal ② extends.

(F)   Do the same with the other Harmonic Diagonals.

LESSON NINE
(Exercises with Vowel Resonator and Organ or Concertmate.)
<u>Play and Pronounce, then Sing</u>.

(F)   <u>Pronounce</u> up and then <u>sing</u> down the vertical columns of Line III over the various notes below Note #28. When you pronounce the vowels over a note with the Vowel Resonator, you <u>hear</u> the harmonics of the pitch you are playing on the organ. You will eventually become aware of the harmonic changes as you pronounce the various vowels on sung pitches. The lesson is one that should be repeated daily to retain the feel of the harmonics in your subconscious controls of <u>hearing</u> and <u>feeling</u> of vibration. The spacings of the throat can be finely tuned by your <u>sense of vowel-colors</u>.

Ⓕ Pronounce up and sing down the vertical columns of Line IV.

LESSON TEN
(Exercises with Vowel Resonator and Organ or Concertmate.)
Play and Pronounce, then Sing.

Ⓕ Pronounce and sing on the notes with one harmonic in the vocal tract.
From Note #30 to #40 there is only one harmonic which resonates in the
vocal tract. Alternate between the Green vowels of Line I and II for
each note to find their strongest resonances for vocal beauty and vowel
differentiation. Alberta Masiello stated on the Metropolitan Opera
intermission broadcast of March 10, 1973 that "Above E♭ in the women's
voices, English always sounds like nonsense syllables." There is only
one harmonic of the vocal tract between Note #29 and #40 on which all
vowels are engraved. Italian, with only seven vowels, has a better
chance of being understood; English and German having so many vowels
are very, very difficult to differentiate. They frequently sound horrible
and/or somewhat like nonsense syllables.

LESSON ELEVEN
(Exercises with Vowel Resonator and Organ or Concertmate.)

Ⓕ The three Ahs [ɒ, α, a].

1. Hold down alternately the Notes #36 and #37. Pronounce WAH slowly
   until you find the maximum resonance. You will find the corners of
   the mouth are rather neutral, the jaw is down and probably the head
   is back. There is something else which occurs and Helmholtz has
   described it, (1885) p. 115, thusly,

"Besides this a contraction of the skin on both sides of the larynx which takes place at the commencement of the tone of the voice, shews that the omohyoideus muscle, which runs obliquely down from the tongue-bone backwards to the shoulder-blade, is also stretched. Without its co-operation the muscles arising from the under jaw and breastbone would draw the larynx too far forwards."

This down and backward action is seen in the caricature of Duprez singing in "William Tell" about 1840. This [ɑ] is useful for a dramatic sound. Because of its heaviness it does not run well. The head is usually slightly raised for this sound. If the chin is jutted forward there is a tendency for the larynx to be drawn away from the backbone. The voice can "break" if the omohyoid muscles do not pull the larynx down and backwards. On the other hand, if the head is lowered these muscles have difficulty in contracting.

2. Hold down alternately Notes #38, #39 and #40. Pronounce WAH slowly until there is the most resonance. You will find the corners of the mouth are back, the jaw is down, and the sides of the neck pulled back towards the shoulders. You will notice that the vowel will resonate better if the head is slightly back. This is one of the dramatic Ah's for female voices and does not run well since it has so much weight. Also, it is slow in articulation and cannot be used in patter songs either on its actual pitch of harmonically related lower pitches as seen in the various vowel rows on the diagonals.

3. On Notes #34 to #40 pronounce YAH [ja] with the teeth a finger's width apart. You have found the Italian Ah which is of great value in runs and arpeggios. This can be called the bel canto Ah. Mancini

(1777, p. 93) said, "Every pupil must shape his mouth for singing, just as he shapes it when he smiles. The upper teeth show a little, and are slightly separated from the lower ones." You will notice that the larynx has pulled up a bit to shorten the vowel pipe. I repeat, this is the Italian Ah [a] and runs extremely well. It is a lyric Ah whereas [ɒ] and [ɑ] are dramatic vowels.

Our text Phonetic Readings of Songs and Arias, Coffin, Errolle, Singer, and Delattre (1982), indicates that there are two Ah's in German - the long Ah which we have notated [a:] is in reality [ɒ], or [ɑ]. We notated it [a:] because singing must be Italianized to maintain a good vocal line by means of continuing high overtones. [ɒ and ɑ] will tend to drop "out of line." In French the two ah's are notated [a] and [ɑ]. In English we have the dark Ah (which tends to drop out of line because of lack of overtone) and the bright Ah (which tends to lack depth because of poor tuning of the throat cavity). A career of any extent must be based upon good harmonic diction, otherwise the cords will be disrupted. It is best that vowel differentiation be taught at the same time as vowel resonation since today's opera directors are intent upon the projection of the text which will communicate the dramatic situations on the stage. Some singers can make their living singing [ʌ] or [œ] on every note. They sound the same in any language. With great vocal gifts they may do very well, but a less opulent voice had better opt for a resonant vocalization in which there is better vowel differentiation. Outstanding diction does not just occur. It is constructed over a period of time. The sooner the singer understands its construction, the sooner she can become a singing actor, which means that the action is communicated through her vocalization and pronunciation. Whether we like it or not, today's audiences demand it. It is the duty of a singer to give the audience what is possible. If she gives what is impossible, she soon finds out that has given her voice and that she has burned out at an early age.

Some have said that words are enemies of singing and the less words in a text the better chance there is of singing. F. Lamperti in the Preface of his book (1890) ascribed the beginning of the decline of singing to Bellini who was the first to place a syllable on each note the artist sang (1890). Things are even more involved now. We have many more languages with which to deal and many more oblique intervals. Singing must be at a more highly intellectualized level than ever before. The singer must know what to do and how to do what she knows. The use of modified vowel-colors in relation to sung pitch will help her immeasurably in building and maintaining the voice for the performance of opera, oratorio, art songs, and show tunes.

<u>Add your own exercises</u>.   You may have guessed that there can be no complete book of exercises related to the harmonics of the human voice.   The harmonics have been a part of the singing voice since the creation of man and will be as long as he has vocal cords and a mouth and throat.   I hope that I have started you on your way to one of the greatest explorations you will ever have.   You can discover and you can find just as the singers and teachers of singing who have gone before you.   However, you are better off than they; you have a compass (Vowel Resonator) and "map" (Chromatic Vowel Chart) by which you can navigate, come fair weather or foul.

<u>Scoring for Songs and Arias</u>.   One of the basic rules for the professional singer is - <u>Do not learn music with the voice</u>.   The reason being that there is a right way to sing vowels for good placement.   In learning a new song with the voice, it is inevitable that wrong placement is ingrained while singing the music.

By means of the Chromatic Vowel Chart, score your song with the resonating vowel-colors <u>before</u> singing.   In case of doubt, pronounce the vowel on the note with the assistance of a Vowel Resonator and then sing it.   This will show you the correct opening of the throat.   That vowel color can be notated over the word in the song or aria.   You can do much to improve your singing without using the voice.   Practice is more fruitful if you know the result before you sing.

CHAPTER XXI

RESONANCE LESSONS FOR MALE VOICES

This chapter is concerned with making the phenomena of multiple vowel resonances even more apparent to you. Some very knowledgeable investigators have written that [i] and some of the other Front vowels are <u>one</u> resonance vowels. Exercises ONE through THREE are given to dispel that theory and to show how those vowel resonances can be used. When used as one resonance vowels, the voice sounds very tight and tends to sharp.

To do this, it is necessary to use a Vowel Resonator with an instrument which plays simultaneously many pitches of a Flute quality. We will see them in such a way that the various resonances will become apparent to you. We will see this approach in Lessons ONE through THREE. If you do not have such equipment and cannot make a cassette of such sounds, you should skip to exercise FOUR.

LESSON ONE
(Exercises with Vowel Resonator and Organ or Concertmate.)
The Resonances of Vowels between (u and ɑ).

<u>Place the arrow over the correct note for your voice classification.</u>

(M) 1. Hold down <u>ALL</u> organ notes which are beneath the underlined Notes #23-#40 while holding the Vowel Resonator in front of the mouth. Place the vocal cords together by imagining you are grunting.

2. Pronounce WOW in very slow motion [u-ɑ-u]. Your vocal tract will echo a glissando from Note #23 to #40 to #23 if the vocal cords are together. Go slowly enough to hear the individual notes come into resonance and go out of resonance. Notice the vowel-colors of the various notes. Do the same with a whole tone scale, and also a diminished 7th chord from Notes #23-#40, so you can better hear the various notes progressing into resonance.

3. Foreign vowels - all vowels must be developed for a good vowel scale, for male voices. These resonances lie at about the same region as those for female voices.

Stop on Notes #25-#26 to hear the lateral oo [ɯ] which we do not use in spoken English. This vowel is between [u and o].

Stop on Notes #30 and #31 to hear the lateral oh [ɤ] which we do not use in spoken English. This vowel is between [o and ɔ].

Stop on Notes #34 and #35 to hear the lateral Aw [ʊ] which we do not use in spoken English. This vowel is between [ɔ and ɒ].

Stop on Notes #38, #39 and #40 to hear the lateral Ah [ɑ] which is a brighter vowel than we use in spoken English.

4. All of the above vowels exist in Italian speech. The throat is opened differently for them than in our Back Vowels [u, o, ɔ, ɒ]. The throat is opened as though it were being widened, 3 inches below the lower molars (in the direction of the shoulders). The opening is highly involved with the omohyoid muscle which attaches to the tongue bone, goes through a loop 2 inches or so lower, and then attaches to the shoulder blade. When someone says a singer has an Italian throat, he is probably speaking of this opening of the throat. This is not gutteral; in gutteral singing the tongue is depressed in such a way that the spaces above the larynx are too closed and the resonance lessened. The Lateral vowels are involved with opening, and resonance is increased on the pitches indicated. Thus the use of a Vowel Resonator is involved with training the spacing muscles

of the vocal tract. If they are weak, daily practice will soon strengthen them. I believe this is a key to the singing voice and like any key must be used consciously or subconsciously to open this closed door which is an acoustical one.

VOWELS ARE DEFINED BY PITCH OF LOUDEST RESONANCE. LEARN THE VOWEL-COLORS, FEEL THE DIFFERING VIBRATIONS.

LESSON TWO
(Exercises with Vowel Resonator and Organ or Concertmate.)
The Low Resonances of Vowels between [a and i] going down.

Ⓜ

1. Hold down all of the organ notes which are under the red Notes #23-#40.

2. Pronounce [ja-i-a] very slowly. Your vocal tract will echo a glissando from Notes #40-#23-#40. Go slowly enough to hear the individual notes come into resonance and go out of resonance. Hear the resonance that goes down when going [a to i]. When the tongue pulls forward to make the small cavity of [i], a large cavity is created in the throat. Hence the pitch goes down. See Delattre's diagrams of speech (p. 274). The spaces vary similarly for [e, ε, æ, and a]. This is the low pitch range of high vowels in Male voices.

3. Foreign vowels. Sustain resonance on Notes #30 to #33 to get the feel and sound of the lower speech resonance of [ε]. Feel for the greatest vibration. This vowel is also involved with the omohyoid spacing muscles. Pronounce [jε] to find the resonance easily.

4. Stop on Notes #34 to #40 to pronounce the lower resonance of [a]. Pronounce [ja], with the teeth no more than a finger's width apart.

This can be called the tongue Ah, the front Ah, or the Italian [a] since it also has a high resonance.

LESSON THREE
(Exercises with Vowel Resonator and Organ or Concertmate.)
The High Resonance of Vowels between [a and i] going up.

Ⓜ 1. Depress all of the organ notes which are between Notes #41-#59 which are on the organ. This is the pitch range of high vowels in Male Voices.

2. Pronounce [ja-i-a] very slowly. Your vocal tract will echo a glissando from Notes #41-#59-#41. Go slowly enough to hear the individual vowel pitches come into resonance and go out of resonance.

3. Foreign vowels - all vowels must be developed for a good vocal scale.

   a. Stop and hold the resonance on Notes #41 to #44 to hear the Italian Ah [a] so named by Helmholtz, (1885), p. 106 and Garcia (1894), p. 17. This vowel must be used in agility passages where AH is indicated in all languages. Pronounce Yah, Yah [ja, ja]. The mouth opening should be about the width of a finger.

   b. Stop on Notes #49-#52 to hear the sustained [ɛ] which is not used in some parts of our country - witness "Tennessee" [t ɪ n ɪ s i] rather than [t ɛ n ə s i]. Pronounce [jɛ, jɛ] to find the resonance.

   c. Stop on Notes #55 and #56 for German [e] as in "geben" [g e: b ə n]. Americans think it is almost an [i] which is on Notes #58 and #59; it is very close to [i].

The following exercises require only one pitch so the Vowel Resonator can be used with a Concertmate or similar instrument.

LESSON FOUR
(Exercises with Vowel Resonator and Organ or Concertmate.)

Ⓜ Do not sing in this lesson. Pronounce the vowels in <u>Red</u> starting on

Note #32 going above and below the line and find the resonances of the

indicated <u>Red</u> vowels. Continue as high as Note #40 and as low as Note

#23.

    Preceed the vowels below the line with [w] as in <u>woe</u> [wo].

    Preceed the vowels above the line with [j] as in <u>yes</u> [jɛ s].

LESSON FIVE
(Exercises with Vowel Resonator and Organ or Concertmate.)

Ⓜ Do not sing in this lesson. In Line I, Note #9, pronounce the vertical

column of vowels which are not in parenthesis. Proceed as high as

Note #28 and as low as Note #1. I have tempered the vowel scale on

Notes #17 and #12 since [ʊ] and [ɒ] are on the same harmonic. Note #17

has been called the "lift of the breath" for Male Voices by Witherspoon,

(1925, p. 90).

Ⓜ Do the same in Line II. Proceed as high as Note #26 and as low as

Note #1.

LESSON SIX
(Exercises with Vowel Resonator and Organ or Concertmate.)
<u>Play and Pronounce, then Sing.</u>

Ⓜ <u>Play</u> Notes #8 and #13 <u>pronouncing</u> [ɔ] and [ɒ], Vowel Scale ④, Line III.

As soon as you hear them resonate, <u>sing</u> Notes #8, #10, #11, #12 and

back on the pattern - 1 2 3 4 3 2 1. Feel the resonance on the intermed-

iate notes. Proceed to the highest [ɑ] which is not <u>Red</u>.

Ⓜ Play and sing in like manner with vowel modifications of Vowel Scale ③ to Note #21.

Ⓜ Play and sing in like manner with vowel modifications of Vowel Scale ② as high as Note #23. You have been pronouncing and singing on the actual pitches of these vowels.

LESSON SEVEN
(Exercises with Vowel Resonator and Organ or Concertmate.)
Play and Pronounce, then Sing.

Ⓜ Play the Green vowels, Notes #23 to #35, and sing them an octave lower than written. Sing in single note and short scale patterns.

LESSON EIGHT
(Exercises with Vowel Resonator and Organ or Concertmate.)
Play and Pronounce, then Sing.

Ⓜ Pronounce up and then sing down the vertical columns of Line I over Note #6. Proceed note by note up the scale. When you pronounce the vowels over a note with a Vowel Resonator you hear the harmonics of the pitch you are playing on the organ. When you sing you eventually feel and hear them changing as you pronounce the various vowels on that sung pitch. This lesson is one which should be repeated daily to maintain the feel of the harmonics in your subconscious controls of hearing and feeling of vibration. The spacing of the throat should be finely tuned by your sense of vowel-colors.

Ⓜ Pronounce up and sing down the vertical columns of Line I. The same harmonics are at play as in Line III.

LESSON NINE
(Exercises with Vowel Resonator and Organ or Concertmate.)
Play and Pronounce, then Sing.

Ⓜ <u>Pronounce</u> and <u>sing</u> on the notes with two harmonics in the vocal tract

from Notes #17 to #28, if within the comfortable range of your voice.

Sing the three harmonics on Notes #20 and #21. Be sparing in your

practice of high notes.

Ⓜ Alternate between the <u>Green</u> vowels of Line I and II for each note to find

its strongest resonance for vocal beauty and vowel differentiation.

LESSON TEN
(Exercises with Vowel Resonator and Organ or Concertmate.)
Play and Pronounce, then Sing.

Ⓜ The three Ahs [ɒ, ɑ, a] are so important that we should know more

about them.

1. Hold down alternately the Notes #24 and #25. Pronounce WAH

slowly until you find the maximum resonance [ɒ]. You will find the

corners of the mouth are rather neutral, the jaw is down and prob-

ably the head is back. There is something else which occurs and I

will let Helmholtz describe it, p. 115, (1885).

> "Besides this a contraction of the skin on both sides of
> the larynx which takes place at the commencement of
> the tone of the voice, shews that the <u>omohyoideus</u>
> muscle, which runs obliquely down from the tongue-
> bone back-wards to the shoulder-blade, is also
> stretched. Without its co-operation the muscles
> arising from the under jaw and breast-bone would
> draw the larynx too far forwards."

This action is seen in the caricature of Duprez singing in "William

Tell" about 1840. This [ɒ] is useful for a dramatic sound. This can be called the jaw Ah. It does not run well.

2. Hold down alternately Notes #38, #39, and #40. Pronounce WAH
slowly until you get maximum resonance. You will find the corners
of the mouth are back, the jaw is down, and the sides of the neck
pulled towards the shoulders (see above). You will notice that the
vowel will resonate better if the head is slightly back - the movement
of the head is a tuning device! Sung an 8ve lower than this is the
high c di petto of Duprez, and of the tenor's high c's ever since that
time. This is also one of the dramatic Ah's for Female voices and
does not run well since it has so much weight. Also, it is slow in
articulation and cannot be used in patter songs either on its actual
pitch or harmonically related pitches as in the various vowel scales.
In other words, [ɒ] and [α] are slow vowels. Duprez, the first to
sing the dramatic high notes, also had a reputation for dragging the
tempi. (Pleasants, 1966, p. 169.)

3. On Notes #34 to #40 pronounce YAH [ja] with the teeth a finger's
width apart. You have found the Italian Ah which is of great value in
runs and arpeggios. This can be called the bel canto Ah. Mancini
(1777), p. 93 said, "Every pupil must shape his mouth for singing,
just as he shapes it when he smiles. The upper teeth show a little,
and are slightly separated from the lower ones." You will notice
that the larynx has pulled up a bit to shorten the vowel pipe. This,
again, is the Italian Ah [a] and runs extremely well. This is the
lyric Ah where [ɒ] and [α] are dramatic vowels. Both should be

in the technique of all singers. You have just sung on the lower

resonance of the [a] which keeps it from being white. Surely it is

the vowel which makes Italian throats. All of these resonances are

written out so that they can be sung phonetically with reference to

the Chromatic Vowel Chart.

Vocal Music and Words. Our text Phonetic Readings of Songs and Arias,
Coffin, Errolle, Singer, and Delattre (1964), indicates that there are two Ah's
in German - the long Ah which we have notated [a:] is in reality [ɒ] or [ɑ].
We notated it [a:] because singing must be Italianized to maintain a good vocal
line by means of continuing high overtones. [ɒ and ɑ] will tend to drop "out of
line." In French the two ah's are notated [a] and [ɑ]. In English we have the
long Ah which tends to drop out of line because of lack of overtone and the short
Ah which tends to lack depth because of poor coupling of the throat cavity. A
career of any extent must be based upon good musical diction, otherwise the
throat will be disrupted. It is best that vowel differentiation be taught at the
same time as vowel resonation since today's opera directors are so intent upon
the projection of the text which is necessary to communicate dramatic situations
on the stage. Some singers can make their living singing [ʌ] on every note, or
[œ]. They sound the same in any language. With great vocal gifts they may do
very well, but a less opulent voice had better opt for a resonant vocalization in
which there is better vowel differentiation. Outstanding diction does not just
occur. It is constructed over a period of time. The sooner the singer understands its construction the sooner he can become a singing actor which means
that the action is communicated through his vocalization and pronunciation as
well as his body movement. Whether we like it or not, today's audiences demand it. So it is the duty of a singer to give the audience what is possible. If
he gives what is impossible, he soon finds that he has given his voice and that
he has burned out at an early age.

Some have said that words are enemies of singing and the less words in a text
the better chance there is of singing. F. Lamperti in the Preface of his book
ascribed the decline of singing to Bellini who was the first to place a syllable
on each note the artist sang (1890). Things are even more involved now. We
have many more languages with which to deal and many more oblique intervals.
Singing must be at a more highly intellectualized level than ever before. The
singer must know what to do and how to do what he knows. The use of modified
vowel-colors in relation to sung pitch will help him immeasurably in building
and maintaining the voice for the performance of opera, oratorio, art songs,
and show tunes.

Add your own vocalises. You may have guessed that there can be no complete
book of vocalises related to the harmonics of the human voice. The harmonics

have been a part of the singing voice since the creation of man and will be as long as he has vocal cords and a mouth and throat. I hope that I have started you on your way to one of your greatest explorations. You can discover and you can find just as the singers and teachers of singing who have gone before you. However, you are better off than they; you have a "map" by which you can navigate, come fair weather or foul.

Scoring for Songs and Arias. One of the basic rules for the professional singer is - Do not learn music with the voice. The reason being that there is a right way to sing vowels for good placement. In learning a new song with the voice, it is inevitable that wrong placement is learned while singing the music. By means of the Chromatic Vowel Chart, score your song with the resonating vowel-colors before singing. In case of doubt, pronounce the vowel on the note with the assistance of a Vowel Resonator and then sing it. This will show you the correct opening of the throat. Then notate that vowel color over the word in the song or aria. You can do much to improve your singing without using the voice. Practice is more fruitful if you know the result before you sing. The same can certainly be said of performance.

EPILOGUE

To Sing or to Act, that is the Question.   Two arts are involved in the Lyric-Theatre, singing and acting.   How compatible are they?   Tosi (1723, p. 152) said:

> "I do not know if a perfect Singer can at the same time be a perfect Actor; for the Mind being at once divided by two different Operations, he will probably incline more to the one than the other.   It being, however, much more difficult to sing well than to act well, the Merit of the first is beyond the second.   What a Felicity would it be, to possess both in a perfect degree!"

How many reviews have we seen like the following?   We will leave the singer unnamed.   (Opera, 1975, p. 391)

> "_____ scored another of her personal triumphs as a singer-actress.   Hers may not be a beautiful voice and her intonation sometimes suffers from her own exuberance; but the interpretative uses to which she puts it, particularly in the more dramatic passages, leaves the critic defenceless before her complete involvement in the role.   [The critic should be censured on moral grounds. He sanctioned the artist's vocal destruction and the destruction of the voices of his readers who happened to be singers.]

Some critics may have a moral sense.   Irving Kolodin wrote a letter to Richard Tucker concerning his performance in Pagliacci (Opera News, April 12, 1975, p. 29) in which he was

> "...much impressed by the all-out physical energy you bring...and how the audience responds to it....   I could not but feel that such an expenditure of physical energy bears with it a stress that may not be altogether wise...."

Richard Tucker replied:

> "... I have always given of myself to the utmost, whatever the music and its interpretation demanded...."

Tucker died within a year after the letter.   Kolodin concludes his memorial statement:

"Curious that a man who devoted so much thought and effort to the care of his voice did not guard as carefully something even more precious - himself."

THE SOLE PURPOSE OF THIS BOOK HAS BEEN THE TECHNIQUE OF SINGING. THIS INVOLVES THE UNDERSTANDING AND USE OF BREATHING, PHONATION, RESONATION, AND ARTICULATION. I HOPE THAT YOUR TECHNICAL KNOWLEDGE AND SKILLS WILL BECOME SO GREAT THAT YOUR INTERPRETATIVE INSPIRATIONS CAN BE REALIZED, AND THAT NO COACH, NO CONDUCTOR, NOR YOUR SUBCONSCIOUS DESIRES WILL DISOBEY THE PHYSIOLOGICAL AND ACOUSTICAL LAWS OF YOUR THROAT. SURELY YOU WILL BE ABLE TO DISCOVER AND SUSTAIN YOUR GOLDEN AGE OF SINGING AND THOSE OF YOUR STUDENTS.

APPENDIX A - QUESTIONS AND ANSWERS

Q.   On which Vowel Series should the singer vocalize?

A.   Alternate between the Front and Neutral Series. For Umlauts, alternate them with the Back Vowels. There are two reasons:

1.   Dr. Holbrook Curtis (1900), a laryngologist, observed that there were two categories of problems with singers. Some had <u>bowed</u> vocal cords - these had been taught on "oh." He observed that these had to have about twice as many respirations to do phrasing. The others had vocal cords in which there was a <u>bulging</u> in the center of the cords. They had been taught on <u>Ah</u> and <u>E</u>. [I assume this is [a] and [ε] or [a] and [i], all Front Series.] He had a breathy student (with <u>bowed</u> vocal cords) change to the teacher who had used the <u>Ah</u> and <u>E</u> method and he had one with <u>bulged</u> vocal cords change to a teacher who taught on <u>Oh</u>. To his amazement he found both students "cured" after a few lessons (eventually they would have exchanged problems after continued study). My answer is that it is easier for a student to alternate Vowel Series than to change teachers. In the process of singing alternate series there is a continual building of the muscular silo which forms the throat. Furthermore, the pronunciation is always harmonic, hence the vocal cords swing regularly and can have greater amplitude. The voice then becomes larger. That is the physiological reason for alternating Vowel Series.

2.   There is also an acoustical reason. When one sings with a Radioear Bone Vibrator used as a throat microphone and listens through headphones or to a speaker, an observer can easily tell that there are interesting vibrational phenomena occurring in the throat. (If it is legal to look through a microscope or telescope to <u>see</u> what is happening in nature - is it not also legal to <u>hear</u> more acutely those things which occur in the throat?) The listener will observe that the Front Series of Vowels cross back and forth to the Neutral Series of Vowels with a continuous vibration in the throat (the basis of singing line). When a singer alternates [u with i] and [o with e], he will hear a "swish." I believe the "swish" sound is due to the change of resonance in the pipe so that [u] is heard by itself and the high frequency of [i] is heard by itself. I believe that the coupling of these vowels is poor but that the coupling of [ə with i] and [ʊ with e] is excellent. For this reason I would suggest that singers alternate the Front Series with the Neutral Series frequently. It is also my observation that the Back Series should be alternated with the Umlaut Series because of ease of coupling.

Q.   What should the ratio be when alternating series? 50 - 50?

A. That is a matter of taste and physiology. We are dealing with an Art and human flesh. Too much of the Front vowels will tend to make the voice shrieky. Too much of the Neutral Vowels will tend to destroy understandability of diction. The ratio can be varied according to need and taste. In any event, nothing to excess. Twice as much of what is good is too much, especially when muscular activity is involved.

Q. Why do my vocal cords sometimes tickle on a tone sung immediately after I have used the Vowel Resonator to find its form?

A. 1) Take a piece of pipe about 6-1/4 inches long and hold it in the palm of the hand.

2) Play c above middle c through a Vowel Resonator opposite the other end.

3) You will hear sympathetic vibration, and

4) There will be a tickling sensation on the palm of the hand caused by the vibrating air column in the pipe. The same thing occurs in the correct relationship of the vocal tract to sung pitch. The vibrating air column causes the vocal cords to slap each other more than before. Overcome this by allowing a little more air flow through the cords, perhaps started by a very small [h]. Optimum resonance will require a different breath energy. This is the reason that Lilli Lehmann (1914, p. 280) thought it wise to establish vowel forms before studies of the breath:

"It would be advisable to leave the coaction of the diaphragm out of play at first, directing the entire attention to form only - that is, to the relative position of nose, palate, larynx, and tongue, and finally after the form has become habit, to the fine, subtle, and dirigible coworker, the diaphragm."

Q. Why is this important to a singer?

A. One of the diabolical problems of teaching singing is that the teacher cannot hear all of the components of a complex tone with the unaided ear. Instead of hearing all of the harmonics of a complex tone, the listener hears the fundamental - and in many cases the fundamental vibration is non-existant in air. The Vowel Resonator enables us to center the resonator on an overtone of the sung pitch. The sound is a bit like tuning in on a radio station - there is a centering where the station is loudest with the sound falling off on either side.

Q. Why are you concerned with muscular discipline?

A. I will quote Irving Kolodin, Saturday Review, June 24, 1972, in a review of Lily Pon's excellent singing at the age of sixty-eight,

> "What is too seldom remembered about singing is that, basically, it is a form of muscular discipline like any athletic endeavor. Durability is as much a part of the exceptional singer as it is of the exceptional ballplayer, and, at bottom, the name of both games is technique."

I must add that in the case of the singer it is a technique which is harmonic. If the muscular silo echos the wrong vibrating air pressures on the vocal cords, they become as battered as you would be when flying through very rough weather. In the case of an airplane, the pressures are varying above and below the wing. In the case of the vocal cords, the echoing pressures above and below the vocal cords should be in phase with the vocal cords or their vibratory action can be wiped out (break) or distorted (sharped or flatted).

Maintain the equilibrium of muscular activity, AND, keep the vibratory pressures of the vowel in phase with the vibratory pressure of the cords.

Q. Can I practice too much on a vowel series?

A. Yes, anything can be overdone. I suggest singing short scales and arpeggios on alternating vowel series as a way of equalizing the voice and a way of balancing the various musculatures of the voice.

Q. Can a person practice too much on changing vowels on the same note?

A. Yes, that can be overdone also. I am reminded of G. B. Lamperti's statement (1905, p. 33):

> "We warn the students against too much Lied singing at first, the range being too limited and the numerous tone-repetitions [syllables on a single note] calculated to tire the voice; coloratura sopranos, in particular, should take this warning to heart."

This was written in Germany! The voice develops better on runs on the open vowels, around the Green on the Chromatic Vowel Chart scaled for use at the piano. Composers should know that articulation of words is not only difficult but can be harmful.

Q. I notice that the vowel Oh is not on the Charts on Notes #25, #26, #32, or #33 in the upper voice. Why is this?

A. Neither [o or ɤ] are harmonic on these notes. They are notated over a dotted line on the Chromatic Vowel Chart.

Q. I notice that [i] is absent on some notes on the Vowel Chart pp. 152 & 165.

A. Yes. [i] has a tendency to be pinched at times. The great vocal composers avoided melismatic passages on [i] and [u]. I believe this is related to the above condition.

Q. I notice that Italian [a], [ɛ], [ɔ], and [œ] can be sung on most notes.

A. Yes. These were the running vowels which, with slight modifications of R^1, can be sung on most of the notes in the voice.

Q. Do you have any advice about running scales on the harmonic diagonals?

A. Generally practice ascending exercises from the lower middle of each diagonal and descending exercises from the upper right of the diagonal. [Use the 4 series diagonal chart in reference to the note numbers of a correctly placed Chromatic Vowel Chart at the piano with an adjustment of the arrow for your voice classification.]
Pages 151 and 163 for Female Voices. Pages 164 and 176 for Male Voices.

Q. Why do women have trouble singing words above eᵇ?

A. There are fewer harmonics in the throat cavity available for vowel definition. You will notice that vowels occur in singing where the pronouncing mechanism selects a harmonic of R^2. When there are very few harmonics from which to select, very little vowel color is available.

Q. Has this been studied in singers?

A. Yes. By Mackworth-Young (1953) with twenty-seven of the best singers in England at that time with Dennis B. Fry, Head of the Department of Phonetics, University College, London, England.

Q. How do the vowel pitches differ for men and women?

A. Mackworth-Young found that the vowel resonances of men were 1-1/2 steps lower than those of women. As the vocal cavities of the male head enlarge at puberty, the pitch of vowels drops slightly; as male vocal cords lengthen and gain in mass, they tend to drop an octave. The two phenomena are independent. A tenor will have his vowels on the same pitches as a mezzo-soprano, and a high baritone will have vowel resonances on the same pitches as a contralto. Of course, the male voices have an octave extension of Chest voice and the female voices have an octave extension of Head voice. This is in Garcia's terminology which has proven to be valid in my observations. (See p. 109.)

Q. Does the difference of resonance in the various voice classifications appear elsewhere in the literature of vocal pedagogy?

A. Yes. Witherspoon (1925, p. 90) wrote of the phenomenon he called "the lift of the breath" in which he detected that there was an added brilliance to the voice at a spot in the vicinity of b♮ of medium voices varying as high as a minor third above for coloratura or lyric sopranos and lyric tenors, to a third below for the lowest voices.

Q. Has any recent research supported the observation that the sizes of the vowel cavities vary with voice classification?

A. Yes. Husson quotes the Russian scientist Dmitrieff (1959) as having given measurements of the vocal tracts from the vocal cords to the teeth of the various voice classifications. In the Chromatic Vowel Chart, the movement of the arrow takes care of adjusting the "absolute pitch" of this ratio. The female vowel resonances have been found to be 10 to 15% higher than those of men.

The Resonances of Singing. R^1 is the lower resonance of vowels due to harmonic reinforcement in the complete vocal tract. R^2 is the resonance which falls between b^2 and bb^3. It seems to be the harmonic reinforcement of the cavity in front of the tongue hump. R^3 is the resonance which falls between b^3 and f^4. Delattre believed it to be the harmonic reinforcement of a very small cavity formed by the tongue just behind the teeth in [e] and [i].

The fundamental of the sung pitch below 2^3 is unreinforced. Those pitches are heard by the "transitor radio effect." Low pitches are heard by the difference between their overtones. This is comparable to a phenomenon of the violin as reported by the Harvard Dictionary (1967, p. 164).

> "Recent research has brought about the startling result
> that certain well established sounds, e. g., that of the
> G string of the violin, are physically non-existent, being
> produced only aurally as the differential tones of their
> upper partials."

This is true of the singing voice since there is little energy of a sung pitch below its lowest vowel-selected and resonated harmonic.

Difference tones are physiological and psychological phenomena for they do not actually exist in the air. The Harvard Dictionary explains, p. 163:

> "It is the inner ear (cochlea) which owing to its "non-linear"
> organization, produces the aural sensations corresponding
> to the additive and subtractive frequencies [of two tones
> sounded simultaneously]."

No wonder the teaching of singing has been taught <u>empirically</u> - it takes an ear to find the right sound. It is amazing how much of the teaching of singing is psychological - involving the senses. The Vowel Resonator merely helps the singer's and teacher's hearing process so that it can better guide the placement of the voice.

Q. Why is there a non-linear function of the ear?

A. The answer is beyond the limits of this text. The answer would involve the physiological action of the basilar membrane within the cochlea of the ear and the neural impulses from the hair cells.

Q. Is this scientific?

A. It helps explain how we perceive, thus it relates to the physiological and psychological treatment of sound waves which come to our ears. It also helps explain how we <u>hear</u> what actually does not exist. This is most important to teachers of singing since we must train for what ears and minds <u>hear</u>, just as a chef prepares food for the sensation of <u>taste</u> and the painter for the sensation of <u>sight</u>. One does not analyze a cake in a laboratory to see if it is good - simply taste it! To answer your question as to whether resonant singing is <u>scientific</u> - it probably is to a certain extent, but mostly it is empirical since it is formed by the senses of <u>hearing</u> and <u>feeling</u> of the performer for the <u>seeing</u>, <u>hearing</u>, and <u>feeling</u> of the listener.

Q. Does this mean that singing is largely psychological?

A. The terms scientific and psychological have frequently been loosely used. Garcia was considered to be a scientific investigator, but all he did was to tell what he <u>heard</u> and <u>saw</u> in relationship to what he learned about singing and the anatomy of the vocal organs in the previous years of his life. At 10 years of age he studied with Ansani in Naples, at 20 years of age he sang with his father's company which gave the first performance of Italian opera on this continent. At 25 after his appointment to the French army, he served in military hospitals where he studied the exact anatomy of the vocal cords [and]... 'the throttles of all kinds of animals - chickens, sheep, and cows'," (MacKinlay, 1908, p. 100). At 35 he presented his <u>Memoire</u> <u>on the Human Voice</u> to the French Academy, and published Part I of the <u>Art</u> <u>of Singing</u> at 36. When 42, he published Part II of the <u>Art of Singing</u> which was dedicated to the King of Sweden in honor of Jenny Lind, his most famous student. He was 55 years old when his paper, "Observations of the Human Voice," was read to the Royal Academy of London which was made possible by his invention of the laryngoscope nine months earlier. He was 89 years of age when his <u>Hints on Singing</u> was written. This is the book which Marilyn Horne "pored over." He was 97 years of age when he wrote his letter to Charles Lunn (1904, p. 21) in relationship to the "stroke of the glottis." This was brought about by an attack upon Garcia by George Bernard Shaw.

Q. Was Garcia a scientist, artist, psychologist, singer, or teacher of singing?

A. He probably was all - he observed the art of singing from many points of view over a period of 87 years! He was to singing what Michaelangelo and Leonardo da Vinci were to the visual arts. Fortunately his major works have recently been brought into print.

Q. Are the vowels created by the vocal cords?

A. Scripture (1906, p. 115), built artificial vowel models and vibrated the "vocal tract" (the space between the "vocal cords" and lips) by means of a rubber glottis. Through a glass window in the side of the vocal tracts he was able to observe that the artificial glottis vibrated differently for various vowels. Apparently this was a reaction since there were no muscles in the rubber bands. Always the question is one of cause or effect - action or reaction.

The Bell Telephone hi-speed motion pictures indicate that the vocal cords vibrate differently for various vowels. My comment is that the differing vibration of vocal cords is a reaction of the vowel frequency of vibration of air columns upon the cords. What Scripture observed was reaction as well as action. The vowel echo was the cause of the difference of vocal cord vibration. G. B. Lamperti (Brown 1931, p. 67), stated, "It is a strange fact that the throat is controlled by what happens above it in the acoustics of the head, through word, vibration and resonance." All evidence in my sympathetic resonance studies indicates that the vowels are formed by the cavities of the vocal tract which echo wave reactions upon the vocal cords which created the puffs in the first place.

Q. Why do various pitches have more than one vowel resonating on them?

A. The Chromatic Vowel Chart indicates the heavily underlined notes of four different vowels on the same pitch; that Notes #37 - #40 have three vowels resonating on them; that Notes #41 - #52 have two vowels resonating on them; and that the Notes between #53 and #59 have only one vowel resonating on them. The answer is that the various vowel conformations cause differing pressures in the throat which affect the emission of sound from the throat. The ear perceives varying balances of overtones and by this the vowels on the same pitch are differentiated. Can any one improve on Nature and come up with something better than vowel pitch and the harmonic series as being the basics of singing? It would be like finding a substitute for gravity.

Q. Why do artificial wind instruments give tone and the voice gives tone and vowel?

A. A frequency vibrated in a long hard-walled hallway (wooden or brass)
    gives a <u>tone</u>. A frequency vibrated in a short flesh-walled hallway (voice)
    gives <u>tone and vowel</u> because the elasticity of the articulators allows a
    facile selection of various harmonics. These harmonics and harmonic
    combinations give vowel color. I say 'facile' because there may be as
    high as 500 vowel and consonant parts per minute.

    The problem of the singer is to time resonation in such a way that it will
    amplify one or more of the harmonics of the fundamental pitch on each
    vowel that he gives in slow passages or on long or exposed notes. The
    hallway and its floor must be formed by the time the vocal folds give the
    fundamental pitch. It is somewhat like baseball - the bat must be there at
    exactly the same time as the ball arrives - only in singing, the "bat and
    ball," the vibration of the cords and the vibration of the vocal tract, must
    be there at the same time, 26 vowels in about 6 seconds in such an aria
    as the "Largo al factotum." How much time is there for the thought of
    "placement?" None. This is the reason for the instant, flexible "place-
    ment" exercises in this book, so that the ear and feeling of vibration in the
    vocal tract will be a subconscious guide to our singing.

Q. Can the throat have too much space?

A. Yes. Too much space in the throat can lead to vocal trouble. I have
    pointed out that the slide of a trombone affects the pitch from the mouth-
    piece by lowering it. In the voice, the lengthening or shortening of the
    vocal pipe gives vowels. Trying to sing with as much space as possible is
    quite a bit like a trombonist attempting to play all notes in the 7th position.
    Admittedly the singer has an easier time "lipping" the pitch up or down than
    does the trombonist. But still, the situation obtains. The tuning of the
    throat can be brought about by use of the Vowel Scales and Cross-over
    Vocalises.

    The trombone player's arm would become fatigued if held in 7th position
    all of the time. The vocal tract is lengthened downwardly by the depressor
    muscles. If these are always under contraction, the throat can become
    very fatigued. The long time endurance of such a technique is questionable.

Q. Is it possible to reduce vowel modifications to musical notation?

A. Yes. In an indirect way. Vowels have pitch and the use of the many vowels
    in the International Phonetic Alphabet in relationship to pitch allows this to
    be done for ALL voices with a slight variation for the various voice class-
    ifications.

Q. Aren't individual voices different?

A. Yes. There are qualities which distinguish one voice from another, which would include the balance of harmonics in the voice, the nature of the sound from the vocal cords themselves and the individual formation of the consonants and the speed of articulation. These individual qualities cannot be notated but the harmonic relationship of the lower resonance of vowels to sung pitch can be notated for ALL voices.

Q. Can pleasing and unpleasing notes be notated?

A. When there are non-harmonic overtones in the voice (not a multiple of the frequency of the sung pitch, e.g. 2, 3, 4, etc. times the sung pitch) the voice may be unpleasing.

Q. Am I supposed to feel comfortable when I sing?

A. The primary purpose is not to try to feel comfortable in singing; the purpose is to form a musical instrument into "a concord of sweet sounds." Some of the most discordant tones heard are sung with complete happiness by singers. The prime objective is harmony of resonances - the results will be comfortable if not overdone. In fact, astounding things can be done with amazing ease. More breath energy will be used but the singing is easy. Messa di voce, pianissimos, fortissimos, leaps, scales, etc. can become a part of the singer's resources. The number of colors in a voice will increase immeasurably and youth and vitality will become its habitual quality. To answer your question another way - there should never be pain.

Q. Is my throat supposed to feel free?

A. If a singer practices only the vowels of Line III his voice will become hooty and he may eventually feel that his tongue is overly depressed. These are called the Back vowels. If a singer sings only the Front vowels his voice will become overly bright. In speech, we cross over from Front to Back vowels continually so that there is a flexible freedom. The same practice should be observed in singing. Go from Front vowels to Neutral vowels and from Umlaut vowels to Back vowels on the diagonals. The throat does not become fatigued in vowel tuning exercises if balanced musculature action is maintained. However, do nothing to excess. Only if the cords are heavy because of a cold, an allergy, or fatigue from too much singing, too much singing in the same range, or too much singing on the same vowel series, or on non-harmonic resonation will there ever be a feeling of tightness beyond the vowel contraction for a given pitch. Some medications dry the throat to such an extent that phonation becomes difficult.

Q. Why are there fewer vowel-colors in singing than in speech?

A. In speech the number of vowels is infinite since there is no definite pitch of the voice unless it is intoned; however in singing the number of vowels on a particular sung pitch tends to be reduced by the number of harmonics avail able for vowel differentiation. The vowels appear on the coincidence of sung pitch harmonics and vowel pitches. No vowel sounds have resonances below approximately 300 cps (f^1) and none above 3,000 Hz (f^4). This is relative to the placement of the $_2\downarrow_3$ for the various voice classifications. The action of the harmonic series is the reason that non-singing diction teachers or poor singing teachers can create problems with a singer's voice. A singer's diction should be harmonic or the vocal cords will be disrupted and the vocal energy reduced. In singing, be your own microphone; amplify by harmonic diction.

Q. Why do singers lower their heads in singing?

A. They are using the covering mechanism regardless of the vowels being sung. The vowels will be of a dark color.

Q. Why do singers raise their heads in singing?

A. This is a part of the tuning process frequently overlooked. Luchsinger (1965, p. 76): [the underlinings are mine]

> "(3) The tracheal pull draws the larynx downward in a variable manner. The amount of this downward pull depends on the respiratory position, in particular on the movements of the diaphragm. The amount of tracheal pull from above is determined by laryngeal positioning, and thus by the head position. Since the resulting force of tracheal pull is effective in front of the transverse cricothyroid axis, it tends to lower the cricoid arc. In consequence, it counteracts the cricothyroid muscle, shortening the cords.
>
> (4) All muscles that elevate the larynx increase the tracheal pull. In this manner, the laryngeal elevators contribute indirectly to vocal-cord shortening [and to the high frequency of sung pitch.]" Thus the elevation of the head at certain times assists in giving high pitches.

Q. Is posture of importance in great singing?

A. Yes. You will remember that the sombre timbre is assisted by a slight lowering of the chin and the clear timbre is aided by the head held back slightly. It is interesting to thump the throat and to listen to what happens to Ah when the chin ducks (pitch of vowel lowers) and when the head is thrown back as in laughter (the pitch of the vowel rises). It is important to observe the use of this by the great singers when they go for their climax notes on Ah. This posture is extremely important to resonance. The

basses on back rows of choirs have been singing with their heads down for
years; of course their high notes are in the covering region.
The tenors are short, on the front rows of choirs with heads
raised (usually too much). Their high notes have a frequency
above the cover part of the voice. When watching the great singers on
television one should always think about what their sung pitch is in the vowel
scale. It will be amazing <u>how</u> <u>often</u> you will see the singer's head back and
how <u>infrequently</u> you will see singers ducking their heads for high notes. It
is very interesting that there is a muscular inversion used in singing low
notes; they too will sound better if the head is slightly elevated.

Nathaniel Merrill (1969) says that tenor James McCracken, for example,
can "sing leaning back practically upside down, but Jess Thomas does not
feel he can hit a high B-flat unless his legs are under him." So he stages
around the postures the artists use in their singing.

My statement is that tenors who do not use the backward tilt of the head will
usually have a range only to A♭ (Note #25 on the Chromatic Vowel Chart);
other voices will be limited accordingly. Garcia (1841, p. xxxix), states:

> "When the voice reaches the extremes of which it is capable
> in that register, the larynx moves against the jaw by a very
> pronounced rocking motion, which one can verify by touch-
> ing. The notes produced in this last period of the ascension
> of the larynx are thin and strangled [when carried too high];
> at the last limits of the compass, the head tips back a little
> to facilitate the elevation of the larynx."

Q. Is not the full voiced high C of the tenor thin?

A. Critics have described it as being brilliant. It is to singing what the home
run is to baseball. Pleasants quotes Rossini's comparison of the "head
voiced" high C to the full voiced high C (1966, p. 167):

> "...Nourrit sang it in head voice, and that's how it should
> be sung." Rossini had first heard Duprez's high C in his
> (Rossini's) own home, and had expressed his opinion by
> looking to see if any of his precious Venetian glasses had
> been shattered. It struck his Italian ear, he observed,
> "like the squawk of a capon whose throat is being cut."

That was the effect upon Rossini. It is an effect which has brought scores
of audiences to their feet. A singer who has not used this tuning in his
singing is singing with only part of his voice. Be sure and listen with your
eyes the next time you go to the opera, or a concert, or see a performance
on television. Why do the singers have their heads elevated? To them it
has become a reflex, as natural as your raising your head when you laugh.
This reflex is frequently untaught today at the cost of high notes.

Q. Is the singing of contemporary music hard on the throat?

A. It depends on how it is written. If it is anti-vocal, it would tend to destroy the vocal line. Contemporary music is chamber music and does not call upon the singer to sing loudly as is required of the opera singer whose voice is expected to carry across a wide pit which seats many orchestra players. The question is like one asking if wind is bad - a breeze is fine; a tornado is destructive. There are comparable forces in chamber music and operatic singing. Also some contemporary music calls for the use of a microphone by the singer. This allows many more sounds to be heard by an audience such as the weak consonant sounds of speech, whispers, whistles, giggles, the alveolar, lip and velar clicks, hiccups, and loud inhalations.

Q. Are these sounds new?

A. The Art of Singing has always been in transition. F. Lamperti stated that Bellini began the downfall of singing when he placed a word on every note. Wagner was accused of devastating voices when his music required sustained singing which would carry over an enormous orchestra. I am reminded of what Garcia said (Part II, 1872, tr. of Paschke, 1975, p. 160):

> Changes of tone "produced by the alteration of the breathing and by the use of the different timbres, form an inarticulate language, composed of tears, interjections, cries, sighs, etc., which one could properly name the language of the soul. These means can affect still more powerfully than the word, and take birth principally in the lungs and pharynx. The exact knowledge of these kinds of products, should be familiar to every dramatic singer, and will become the principal source of his success.

Singers have always been searching for greater expression - some sounds have not been used before because of their weakness.

Q. Should singers be wary of which contemporary compositions to sing?

A. Yes. Some music is written for specific singers. If your voice classification is the same as that singer there is a possibility that you can sing this music. I heard Paul Hume, the critic, state that persons who have sung contemporary music sooner or later come to the conclusion that they wished they had not. Much of the singing is uncoupled which makes their singing of standard literature for the voice less effective. Perhaps within moderation the singing of contemporary music would be safe but it is best if the voice is established before such attempts are made.

Q. Are there limitations of teaching only resonance?

A. Yes. Singing is a symphony of clear phonation, resonation, breathing, and articulation. All must work together for good singing to occur. Resonance can be studied effectively only when the vocal cords make a clear sound. If the vocal cords make only a whisper, the vocal tract can only resonate a whisper. If the vocal cords issue a husky vibration, the vocal tract can resonate only husky sound - there will not be much energy in the reverberation. When the vocal cords make clear vibrations, then the vocal tract can reverberate a large amount of energy.

Thus, if the cords are in poor shape because of bad use of the speaking voice, cheering, screaming, etc., or if there has been overuse of the singing voice until the cords are thick, the practice of resonance exercises are of little avail. The same is true if the cords are thick because of asthma, allergies, smoking, drinking, drugs, menstral cycle, birth control pills, etc.

Q. Do you have any final statement on vowel tuning?

A. Yes. When working with an Electric Organ and an Oscilloscope one finds out that the centering of vowel resonances is like being on "the razor's edge." When working with artificial sound, without singing, the pronunciation must be exactly right for the waves to stand tall or in some cases even be seen. Also, the resonance with the cheeks up and mouth almost closed is the one preferred by the classic singing schools. When feeling the neck with the fingers when this resonation is found, the larynx is lowered and the neck widened more than in the resonation which is found with rounded lips. This phenomenon was totally unexpected by me. I have compared the resonances many times and the answer is always the same.

Q. What does it take to become a professional singer?

A. First there must be talent, a good looking physique, excellent musicality, rhythm, good memory and a positive attitude. The tone should be live and "turn people on." Professional singers are really athletes with tremendous enthusiasm, vigor, stamina, and sensitivity. They must be sound machines to sing over the din of contemporary instruments in opera and concert. There are secrets of winning at athletics as at singing. The great golfer, Jack Nicklaus says, "The secrets are learning the right fundamentals, working on them, dedication, and confidence in what you can do. There is no substitute for hard work." I have given what I believe are the right fundamentals; I wish you the best in your voyage in song.

APPENDIX B - THE SINGER'S HEALTH

Air Pollution. A problem facing every singer in the world is that the operatic art with few exceptions occurs in heavily industrialized urban areas. This means that there is heavy air pollution with a continual irritation of the mucous membrane of the vocal instrument. With the irritation there is an excessive flow of mucous to carry the impurities away. If a singer constantly clears his throat he causes a secretion of mucous by the vocal folds themselves, in the process of which the cords are further irritated and enlarged. The voice feels heavy and soon the upper notes become more difficult. Singing over this heaviness begets more difficulty and the singer finds himself in an endless spiral which can lead him to a condition in which it is extremely difficult or impossible to sing. I am of the opinion that some very important careers have been shortened by this malpractice. How should one avoid this trap? Hum and swallow. The hum vibrates the mucus from the cords so that it can easily be swallowed. What an easy way in which to avoid a career-shortening habit of bad vocal hygiene!

Allergies-Colds-Medications. Many singers have various allergies that result in nasal and throat congestion which lead to the swelling of the vocal cords. Their mass is changed, their pitch is lowered, and singing can only be accomplished by great effort and a consequent additional enlarging of the cords which requires more effort. The endless spiral should be avoided. If the cords are the least bit swollen, singing should not be attempted. Careers have been shortened by singing at the wrong time. Colds have the same effect.

It is not known by many that certain medications have a drying effect on the cords in which condition they will not function normally. Changes of humidity affect the singer, however medication can be given which can increase the flow of saliva. One of the best aids is to chew on an apple to encourage the saliva to flow prior to rehearsals and performances.

Vocal Hygiene. There is another matter which I should mention, a matter which I have never seen discussed. There are certain accepted niceties in every society; one of our basic ones is shaking hands. It is really difficult to fault the ritual because it is one of friendship and unspoken communication. So far so good. I am in horror of the number of singers who stick their fingers in their mouths! This is another malpractice. They would abhor licking each hand they have shaken, but in reality they have. Even worse is the collection of germs and viruses on piano keyboards. Would any singer be willing to lick a piano keyboard in a practice room? In actuality this is what he is doing when he places his fingers in his mouth after playing the piano. Can you imagine what a culture from the hands would amount to in a few days? I hope the picture I have drawn is vivid enough to keep singers from putting their fingers in their their mouths!

The singer would do well to be defensive in his eating. There are foods that are never "handled" after they are prepared. They should be safe. There are foods which are "handled" in preparation and not cooked afterwards. A person is surely taking a chance in eating them; he has no idea whether the chef, who actually has his hands in the eater's mouth, has been diligent in his cleanliness. Of course, these hygenic ideas are applicable in all countries.

Choral Singing. In many countries, choral singing is closely associated with solo singing. What is its effect? First of all, we must believe that choral directors and singing teachers are practicing their profession to the best of their knowledge. G. B. Lamperti said the art of teaching singing was the ability to individualize voices. The success of a choral director should be in the same direction. There is no reason to have a Stradivarius sound like a cigar-box violin so that both will sound the same. In the case of blending voices the vowels are frequently uncoupled in fine voices to reduce their resonance to the size of the soggy voices.

How devastating to ask all members of a choir to sing the same vowel color - we have seen that vowels are ratios of vowel resonances which vary with voice classification. When a soprano sings [a, α, or ɒ] like a bass she is choked and has no top voice. When a bass attempts to sing [a, α, or ɒ] with the color of a soprano he will severely constrict his throat in such a manner that the tone becomes bad and non-resonant. When such a person as Casals says that every note of the cello has its own timbre, it would certainly seem to be the same of the singing instrument. Choral directors must allow the different voice classifications to make their own colors in the "symphonic" choir. It is my belief that when choral directors learn how to use the individual merits of voices that choral singing will become much more impressive. The great orchestras are built on the great techniques of the individual in the organization - certainly the greatest choirs will operate with this philosophy since the coloring would be more varied and communicative.

How long should a singer sing at a time? The master teachers of singing also stated that four practice sessions of 30 minutes a day were sufficient for the most robust vocal organs. What happens when choirs have one, two, and three-hour rehearsals several days a week? What happens when operas are scheduled on consecutive nights. If the conductors will not protect a singer, it is up to the singer to protect himself by any guise. The wayward conductor will not be able to return to the singer the voice which he has taken, regardless of any price paid, nor can his singing teacher, nor his throat doctor. Nor can the singer restore his own voice if he has given it away.

We cannot overlook the fact that the history of singing began in the Schola Cantorum of the various churches and in the opera houses of Italy. These were group situations. How singing teachers have wandered so far from basic principals is unimaginable, also choral conductors, and operatic conductors. The operatic conductors must also realize that their "strings" are not made of wire - the vocal cords have not yet had that advantage. Also the brass instruments have had a great reinforcement of resonance since the last major opera came into the repertoire, "Der Rosenkavalier." Vocal tracts have not.

APPENDIX C - READINGS CONCERNING REGISTER TECHNIQUES

The range of any voice is a unique characteristic of the voice and apparently is a result of the physiognomy of the vocal cords themselves and the musculatures involved with the tensing of the vocal cords to give low pitch, middle pitch, and high pitch as in the glissando on a brass mouthpiece away from a brass instrument. Not much can be done to change the physiognomy of the vocal cords except obey their will, in which case they will look healthy. If we disobey their will, they will look battered. So, in such a simple way, voice has range. But since the cords are next to a pipe their vibrations will always show certain reactions from the vibrations of the pipe itself. The Italian school of Garcia talked in terms of three registers in all voices except bass and baritone. The registers were petto (chest), falsetto (middle in female voice), and testa (head). Fig. 41 is from the Italian translation (Ricordi) and Fig. 42 is from around the year 1855. Both are shown to clarify the misconceptions which exist concerning the difference between falsetto and head voice. It will be seen that Garcia has located them in relation to absolute pitch! In female voices he has located them with the falsetto register (middle) extending to $c\#^2$ in all classifications. His footnote is that, "three or four notes have been allowed as the limit of each register, because all voices require this latitude." This indicates to me he would move $2|3$ for different voices. He further indicated that head voice (testa) exists above $c\#^2$ and chest voice (petto) is below $e\natural^1$, and has an overlap with the middle voice (falsetto).

It is interesting to note that when the range is high, there is head voice (testa) in the tenor and counter tenor voice. He does not indicate that the head voice (testa) exists in baritones and basses [that their range does not extend to where that mode of vibration exists]. So this can be used as a cue as to whether a high-sounding voice is baritone or tenor. If there is an extension of the high voice to d^2, $e\flat^2$, or e^2, it is tenor. I believe that the voce di testa extension should be trained in the other male voices.

In conclusion, a voice can have an extended upper (or lower) voice but it can never be independent of the harmonics imposed upon it by the vocal pipe to which it is attached. The "trumpet principle" will always be present for good or bad.

Teachers who train short ranges have a tendency to deny the existence of registers. To be more specific, those who do not teach the chest voice in women and the falsetto (and head voice) in men tend to deny the existence of registers.

Quadro della classificazione delle voci.

Fig. 41. Garcia's Registers in Italian

G. Ricordi, printed in Italy, 1949.
Garcia: Trattato Completa
      dell Arte del Canto,
      Part I. By permission
      of Belwin Mills Publish-
      ing Corp. for the United
      States.

Petto means chest in male and female voices.
Falsetto is just above the chest in male voices.
Falsetto means middle voice in female voices.
Testa means head in male and female voices.

So, in the male voice, head voice exists above the falsetto. Only by its
training does the male voice vocalize to its upper limits - e♭² or so in the
tenor, b¹ or b♭¹ in the baritone and bass. This should aid present-day voice
teachers to understand the difference between falsetto and head. Garcia's
definition of head in male voices was much higher than many teachers think
today.

Table of Scales for the different cultivated Voices.

The classical compass for all voices, in the schools of Italy. was from [musical notation], the rest, whether below or above, being left to the 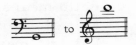 choice of the artist. In the preceding table, three or four notes have been allowed as the limit of each register, because all voices require this latitude.

Fig. 42. Garcia's Table of Registers in English. Curwen ab. 1872.

The harmonic vowel scales of the Chromatic Vowel Chart are the acoustical bases of registers in the human voice. They have been given various names by the writers of the past. Call them what you will - they are for your use in the development of the human voice as a musical instrument.

Registers have always been identified in Italian schools of singing. I will quote several of the teachers and make acoustical comments. Tosi (1723, p. 22) writing of the male soprano voice identified three, as follows:

¶18 - "Let the Master attend with great Care to the Voice of the Scholar, which whether it be di Petto, or di Testa, should always come forth neat and clear, without passing thro' the Nose, or being choked in the Throat, which are two of the most horrible Defects in a Singer, and past all Remedy if once grown into a Habit."

> Note: "Voce di Petto is a full Voice, which comes from the Breast by Strength, and is the most sonorous and expressive. Voce di Testa comes more from the Throat, than from the Breast, and is capable of more volubility. Falsetto is a feigned Voice, which is entirely formed in the Throat, has more Volubility than any, but of no Substance."

¶20 - "Many Masters put their Scholars to sing the Contr'Alto not knowing how to help them to the Falsetto, or to avoid the Trouble of finding it."

¶21 - "A diligent Master, knowing that a Soprano, without the Falsetto, is constrained to sing within the narrow Compass of a few Notes, ought not only to endeavour to help him to it, but also to leave no Means untried, so to unite the feigned and the natural Voice, that they may not be distinguished; for if they do not perfectly unite, the Voice will be of divers Registers, and must consequently lose its Beauty. The Extent of the full natural Voice terminates generally upon the fourth Space, which is D; and there the feigned Voice becomes of Use, as well in going up to the high Notes, as returning to the natural Voice; the Difficulty consists in uniting them. Let the Master therefore consider of what Moment the Correction of this Defect is, which ruins the Scholar if he overlooks it. Among the Women, one hears sometimes a Soprano entirely di Petto, but among the Male Sex it would be a great Rarity, should they preserve it after having past the age of Puberty. Whoever would be curious to discover the feigned Voice of one who has the

"Art to disguise it, let him take Notice, that the Artist
sounds the Vowel i, or e, with more Strength and less
Fatigue than the Vowel α, on the high Notes."

¶22 "The Voce di Testa has a great Volubility, more of the
high than the lower Notes, and has a quick Shake, but
subject to be lost for want of Strength." There is more
energy near 1000 Hz in head voice than in lower registers. Auditoriums are measured at what is called mid-
frequencies, 500-1000 Hz. It is a phenomenon that
these frequencies "ring" auditoriums."

Of special interest is that Tosi spoke of the falsetto going to $c\#^2$ or d^2. Handel's
tuning fork was 422.5 Hz, almost a half step lower than our 440 Hz. Taking the
above statement as being a half step low, Tosi would be saying that the soprano
(male soprano) full voice terminated on b^1 or $c\#^2$. Garcia said that it went to
c^2 in all female voices. (The American Academy of Teachers of Singing has a
Pronouncement "A Recommendation for the Correction of Pitch involving Performances of Singers in Opera, Oratorio, and Choral Music of the Baroque-Classic
Period: 1620 - 1820." The validity of this can easily be checked with the Korg
Tuner described on p. 83. The voice works differently in the low pitch of that
time than it does in our contemporary pitch which is frequently at 445 Hz or
above.)

I now quote a source which is exactly a century later than Tosi. Nathan (1823,
p. 117) was an assistant teacher to Corri, a pupil of Porpora. He describes
registers in the following manner:

"The qualities of the human voice are commonly distinguished
under three heads, according to the natural organs which appear
most particularly concerned in its modulation and tones: - 1st,
where the sound appears to issue almost entirely from the lungs,
it is distinguished as a chest voice, called by the Italians, voce di
petto; also, voce naturale, the natural voice; 2ndly, where the
throat appears the chief organ connected with the production of
sound, it is called a throat voice, termed in Italian, falsetto;
and 3rdly, where the process of breathing seems more than
usually connected with the nostrils, and the sound is accordingly
modulated by their influence, it is termed a head voice, in Italian,
voce di testa. There is a fourth kind of voice, which is but little
appreciated, consequently rarely cultivated - and since I cannot
trace any sponsors, either among the Italian, or English, who
have given a name to this peculiar style, I shall call it the feigned.
I am aware that the falsetto is considered a feigned voice; and
certainly that voice must be feigned which is produced by artificial

constraint, and that does not consequently seem to come forth naturally from the chest; but the quality of the sound that I allude to is not that which is produced in the throat, and already distinguished under the name of <u>falsetto</u>; nor is it the <u>voce di testa</u>. It is a species of ventriloquism, a soft and distant sound produced apparently in the chest, and chiefly in the back of the throat and head - an inward and suppressed quality of tone, that conveys the illusion of being heard at a distance: - It is as a sweet and soft melodious sound, wafted from afar, like unto the magic spell of an echo."

He notes,

"This kind of a voice is in common use with the Hebrews [he was Jewish], and is termed by them 'the voice of a child.' I am decidedly of the opinion that it is partly in consequence of their cultivating this particular tone, that they possess that peculiar sweetness of voice that has even distinguished them from other singers."

I cannot refrain from noting that fifteen years ago the outstanding Italian tenors in the world were Jewish. I must also note that there were two outstanding baritones and a helden-baritone who were also Jewish. They must have had a more ready use of their high voices than did Anglo-Saxons, Teutons, and Latins. It is also interesting to note that the stellar tenor, Nicolai Gedda, had the easy use of the falsetto or head voice heard in the Don Cossack chorus, his father having been a member of that organization. Do we not see that there is a technique of singing which should be blended in with the other registers?

Garcia (ab. 1855, p. 6), defines the Chest, Falsetto (he never used the term middle voice for women but Hermann Klein did in a revision of Garcia's <u>Hints on Singing</u> in 1911), and Head registers. He admits of fluctuation of the limits which I attribute to voice classification. See Fig. 30.

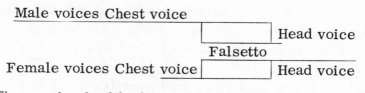

Fig. 43.

The general scale of the three registers is as follows:

Two or three notes are given as the possible limits of each register because the organs being elastic, naturally admit of fluctuation.

He observes the fourth register, explains it and its pedagogical use, p. 7.

"It sometimes happens, that when the female soprano voice attempts to sound the notes si^3 and do^4, it unconsciously rises to re^3 and mi^3, in a thin but pure tone, and with less effort than would be required for trying the notes below. The mechanism of such sounds may be thus explained: - The lips of the glottis are stretched, and perfectly, though gently, touch one another, while the space between the vocal tendons is considerably lessened. In this state of the organ, the least pressure of air will rush through a minute aperture of the glottis, which, however narrow, serves to produce the most rapid beats with extreme facility. The pressure of the air, however, should be very slight, when the aperture of the glottis is to be minute. The process just described, and which is successfully employed by some female voices, is equally capable of application by the male; in which case it will serve to give clearness to the high notes of the bass, and will enable tenor voices to extend the compass of their chest register, and sing the high notes in mezzo voce." [I believe he was describing the <u>whistle</u> register.]

He states that a third of the head register may remain in the tenor voice, and then he indicates its use for other males. Let me say that Vennard called the highest notes of the soprano a <u>whistle</u> register which was brought about by aerodynamic turbulence of air through the vocal cords. I will state that the head voice in men's voices is also aerodynamic and must be used to establish the ringing, vibrant high notes in male voices. Another gain is the <u>sotto voce</u> use of high notes. This added dimension is frequently missing in present day teaching.

I have trained this voice in women and men for over twenty years by using different devices. I first learned of it in the studio of Wilfried Klamroth, the teacher of Dorothy Maynor. He would have sopranos sing an arpeggio of a 10th up from g^1 on "ah" and have them bite the top note, b^2. The sound was a squeaky sound through the nose. I have given it a name, "the Nose Whistle." Sopranos find they can begin on this note with the mouth almost closed. The velocity of air or vibration is so intense in the nose between the eyes that they sometimes get headaches. I tell this to emphasize that this form of vibration is a very <u>real</u> occurrence; it is not imaginary. It extends in range from about g^2

to e♭³ above which the sensation departs from the nose. There is also a Lip Whistle which can be gained with the lips forming an opening the size of a pencil sharpener while phonating a very high pitch. This also can be found in most voices but it sometimes overblows into the region of g³. The "Nose Whistle" can be sung on a descending arpeggio continued into an arpeggio of a regular "ah" which will go up very easily in a beautiful mixed voice. This can be used in both female and male voices (the male an octave lower).

I will also state that in most voices this register can also be gained by what I have called the open mouth hum. Sound a sustained ah with the mouth opened in the shape of a whole note ◗; place the palm of the hand over it, and make an octave jump. My notation of the open mouth hum is ⓜ. My terminology is derived from G. B. Lamperti's statement - "Don't hum - Singing is humming with the mouth open."

The breath must be agile in jumping to the upper note with the air coming out of the nose since none is allowed to come out of the mouth because of the palm being over it. A deep support is immediately felt in the lower back as a result of this technique. This whistle voice can be blended into the other registers and eventually the scale becomes quite smooth. Without thinking, the neutral vowel [ʌ] forms behind the hand. A small [u] or [i] will give the same effect. This is the "pure head tone" of Lilli Lehmann (1914, p. 96). She became quite excited about it:

> "The pure head voice (the third register) is, on account of
> the thinness that it has by nature, the neglected step-child
> of almost all singers, male and female; its step-parents, in
> the worst significance of the word, are most singing teach-
> ers, male and female."

The teachers of singing I know are well intentioned; if there is a failing it exists in the lack of understanding of the phenomenon of Head Voice and how to stimulate that mode of vibration in the singing voice.

I have found that a grunt on the vowel [ʌ̃] as high as Note #21 in Female Voices is valuable for unifying chest voice with the middle. When the [ʌ̃] is sung it has the same sensation as the "Nose Whistle." The use of nasality is not a new concept; it was in fact a favorite device of DeReszke (Leiser, 1934, p. 314).

Now let me quote Mathilde Marchesi (1890) on registers. Her prima donnas dominated the stage between 1892 and 1922; she did not teach male voices.

> "I most emphatically maintain that the female voice possesses
> three registers, and not two, and I strongly impress upon my
> pupils this undeniable fact, which, moreover their own experience

teaches them after a few lessons.

The three registers of the female voice are the Chest, the Medium and the Head. I use the term Medium and not Falsetto (the word used for the middle register by some teachers of singing), firstly, because the word Medium (middle) precisely and logically explains the position that this register occupies in the compass of the voice, and secondly, to avoid all confusion that might be caused by the term Falsetto, which belongs exclusively to men's voices. Falsetto, which signifies Falso (false), that is, in place of the true, is a term that has been used in Italy from the earliest period in the history of the art of singing, to indicate certain piano effects in the high tones of the Tenor voice.

Empiricism, which in these days appears to struggle more than ever against the incessant progress made by all the sciences connected with the phenomena of the voice, as well as against all rules of modern pedagogy, has put in circulation, among other absurdities, the assertion that the female voice possesses only two registers, Chest and Falsetto. This grave error has also been endorsed by several eminent modern physiologists, who have persuaded themselves that they have established this theory, after their observation with the laryngoscope, but who are incapable of making comparative experiments with their own vocal organs.

Nevertheless, the female voice most certainly does possess three registers. But for defining the special nature of the tone of each of them, for determining their respective limits, and for blending the three registers and establishing homogeneity of tone throughout the compass of the voice, theoretical and practical knowledge is needed.

Unfortunately, it is owing to this ignorance of the limits and the treatment of these three registers of the female voice that there are so many imperfectly trained singers, who struggle against the faults and difficulties of a mechanism wrongly used, and so many unequal voices, which possess sets of weak and heterogeneous tones, commonly called breaks. These breaks, however, are only tones wrongly placed and produced.

When commencing to study, the lowest notes of a register, in most voices, have not so much power as the highest notes of the register next below. The theoretical and practical explanation that I give to pupils of this phenomenon soon convinces them that here lie difficulties, inherent to the physical construction of the vocal organs, which are easily conquered when the causes are understood. Therefore, in using the exercises designed for developing, in the Larynx or Glottis, those faculties that are necessary for removing this imperfection of the vocal compass, the homogeneity in the nature of the tone throughout the particular compass of each register, as well as the blending of the three registers, depends, above all, upon the ability of the teacher, the patience and assiduity of the pupil, and the method of practising.

Female voices are divided into Contralto, Mezzo-Soprano, Dramatic Soprano, and Light Soprano (sfogato). The highest note in the chest-register of all female voices varies between the notes

Contralto and Mezzo-Soprano differ from Soprano voices in having generally a chest-register of much greater compass, which extends more or less to the lower tones.

To equalize and blend the Chest and Medium registers, the pupil must slightly close the last two notes of the former in ascending and open them in descending. Every effort expended upon the highest notes of a register increases the difficulty of developing the power of the lower tones in the next register, and therefore of blending the two registers, until eventually it becomes impossible.

When the limits of the register are not fixed, there is always a series of tones that are uncertain, weak, and out of tune, when singing a scale with full voice, or a sustained phrase. According to modern pitch, the highest chest-note of nearly all Contralto and Mezzo-Soprano voices varies from   , Soprano voices from   .

There are Contralto voices which, by reason of a exceptional position of the Larynx, never succeed in developing a Head-voice. These short voices, which consist merely of the Chest and Medium registers, are very rare, and they can aspire only to a career as concert-singers.

The limit of the Medium register in all female voices varies from   ; as a general rule, however,   should be looked upon as the highest note.

As the Head-voice is very rarely used for speaking in ordinary circumstances, the tones of this register are but little developed, and, on commencing the study of singing, they present a great contrast, in intensity and volume, to the highest notes of the Medium register. More time is needed, therefore, for the development of the Head-register than for the other registers.

The same instructions that we have given for the change and blending of the Chest and Medium registers apply also to those of the Medium and Head." (G. Schirmer, ca. 1890.)

Marchesi disliked the two-register theory which came into existence before the publication of her text. She also does not mention the 4th register of Calvé who was her student. Pleasants (1966, p. 51), "It was from Mustafà [the last of the great church castrati], apparently, that Emma Calvé learned the secret of what she used to call her 'fourth voice'." She described this voice, as employed by Mustafà as consisting of "certain curious notes...strange, sexless, superhuman, uncanny. It would appear to have been a greatly refined falsetto." I would call it the Whistle register.

I am reminded of G. B. Lamperti's (1905, p. 15), statement concerning the conditions of obtaining head voice. In an octave jump to c#² in head voice

he stated, "In the last exercise the head-tone will 'speak' more readily if aided by a slightly extra pressure, and it is also allowable to draw a little breath through the nose."

Nathan talked about the nostrils and head voice, so did G. B. Lamperti. It may be gained by the open mouth hum preceding a sung vowel. Lamperti wrote of c#² as the beginning of head voice. Tosi spoke of it after transposition of pitch as being b¹ or c#². Witherspoon wrote of the "lift of the breath" on c# or d for lyric sopranos or tenors, on b for baritones and mezzos, etc. (1925, p. 90).

The above statements all relate to the phenomena occurring at certain spots in the voice when the "ah" vowel is used. The register break could be avoided by rounding a note or two below them according to Marchesi. Why not sing on "aw" all of the time and play things safe. According to Garcia (1894, p. 16), the long scales should be rounded as they go up and the reverse process in descending as in the following quotations:

Q. "But does not this method introduce a real inequality in the vowel sound?"

A. "It does; and the apparent equality of the notes in the scale will be the result of actual but well-graduated inequality of the vowel sound. Without this manoeuvre the round vowels, which are suitable to the higher notes, would extinguish the ringing of the middle and lower notes, and the open vowels, which give éclat to the lower, would make the higher notes harsh and shrill. The neglect of this proceeding causes many voices to appear unequal; but, I repeat, it must be used with moderation and taste." [The vowels should also be harmonic with sung pitch.]

Apparently, there is a Law of Harmonic Compensation. 1) For low notes to be heard, there must be brightening which gives more overtones so that the voice can be heard, and 2) for high notes, the rounding places the energy in the lower harmonics. As a consequence there is greater purity of sound. When there is too much energy in the higher overtones, voices sound shrieky. Whether or not Garcia knew the law does not matter, he was able to describe the phenomenon.

Lilli Lehmann relates registers to an unfavorable "ah," (1914, p. 220).

"Italians who sing well never speak or sing the vowel sound ah otherwise than mixed, and only the neglect of this mixture could have brought about the decadence of the Italian teaching of song. In Germany no attention is paid to it. The ah, as sung often by most Italians of the present day, quite flat, sounds commonplace, almost like an affront. It can range itself, that is connect itself, with no other vowel, makes all vocal connection impossible, evolves very ugly registers; and, lying low in the throat, summons forth no palatal resonance. The power of contraction of the muscles of speech is insufficient, and this insufficiency misleads the singer to constrict the throat muscles, which are not trained to the endurance of it; thereby further progress is made impossible. In the course of time the tone becomes flat at the transitions. The fatal tremolo is almost always the result of this manner of singing.

Try to sing a scale upward on ah, placing the tongue and muscles of speech at the same time on ā, and you will be surprised at the agreeable effect. Even the thought of it alone is often enough, because the tongue involuntarily takes the position of its own accord."

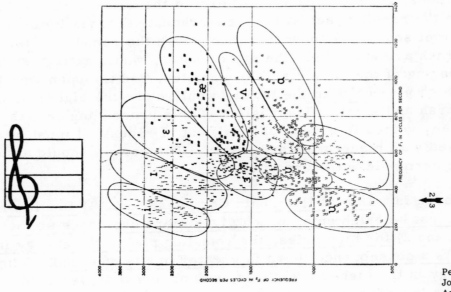

Peterson and Barney (1952)
Journal of Acoustical Society of
America. Vol. 24.

Fig. 44. Musical notation of R^1 frequencies of vowels as found
by Peterson and Barney (1952).

These are the frequencies of the lower vowel resonances, R^1, of 76 speakers,
men, women, and children as recorded by Peterson and Barney, p. 182,
Journal Acoustical Society of America, Vol. 24, No. 2, pp. 175-184, 1952. The
designs encompass all resonance values but 7 out of 760. It is mistaken to
think all voices have this latitude for vowel values. A study of the lower resonance, R^1, with a Vowel Resonator indicates that the values are very specific--
these have been indicated on page 57. Also the upper resonances have frequencies which are very specific. Of great value to us is the fact that vowel
values vary between men, women, and children. Please see Fig. 45. Resonance frequencies also vary with voice classification. BE SURE AND MOVE
THE ARROW OF THE CHROMATIC VOWEL CHART TO THE CORRECT
POSITION FOR YOUR PARTICULAR VOICE CLASSIFICATION. IF YOUR
VOICE DOES NOT RESONATE EASILY WITH THE VOWELS SHOWN, YOU MAY
NEED TO ADJUST THE ARROW UP OR DOWN SLIGHTLY. IN CASE OF
DOUBT, PLACE THE ARROW A SEMITONE LOWER.

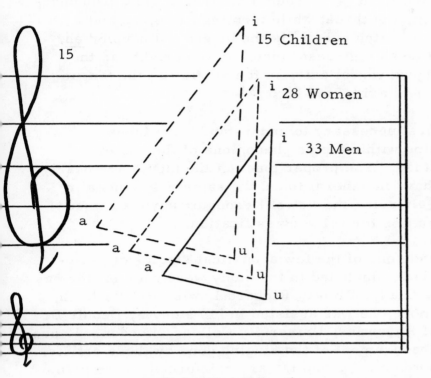

The upper (tongue channel) resonances of double vowels, R^2 and R^3. These values are within the frequency of the front cavity of the mouth heard when one whistles with the lips.

$$R^2, R^3$$

Vowels are differentiated by the upper resonances which lie above the treble clef <u>for all voices</u>. These frequencies must be heard in suitable contrast for perception of the vowels. (Musical notation based on Mol's 1956 realization of Peterson and Barney's frequencies.) JASA, March 1952, p. 182.

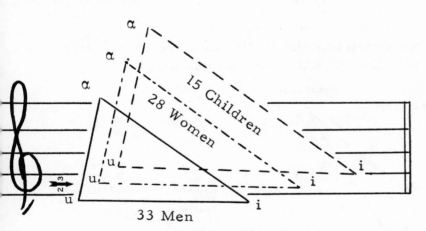

The lower (pipe) resonances of vowels, R^1 "Thumped frequency."

$$R^1$$

The musical notation of the lower resonances of Vowels has long been considered of importance for the fullness of tone in a voice.

Fig. 45. Vowels differ slightly for men, women, and children. (They differ similarly for the various voice classifications.)

(Cont'd from p. 214)
That was her way for inducing the front [a]. Thump the throat while pronouncing [i, e, ε, and a]. Then thump the throat while forming [u, o, ɔ, and ɒ].
[a] and [ɒ] may have the same R^1 pitch but [a] is the bright and coupled ah,
while [ɒ] is a single vowel and lacks high resonance. In the bright [a] the
tongue hump lies above the velopharyngeal axis, in the single [ɑ] the tongue
hump lies below the velopharyngeal axis. See Fig. 54.

To understand registers it is first necessary to understand the pitches of
vowels. Vowels are due to a pipe within a pipe phenomena of the voice.
Helmholtz (1885, p. 105) found that, "The proper tones of the mouth are nearly
independent of age and sex. I have in general found the same resonances in
men, women, and children." [By using the Vowel Resonator anyone can see
there is a difference in the variation for voice classification.]

Mackworth-Young (1953) has made one of the few acoustical studies of established professional singers to date. Included in the study were such singers as
Isobel Baillie, Astra Desmond, Gladys Ripley, Richard Lewis, Heddle Nash,
and Norman Walker. Furthermore, he was assisted in his study by Dennis B.
Fry, Head of the Department of Phonetics, University College, London. Hence
there was parallel scientific measurement of the singing done by these artists.
He indicated, p. 118, that the notes e^1, f^1, and $f\#^1$ are reinforced on the prime
in the male voice cavity but not in the female. The arrow on the Chromatic
Vowel Chart indicates the lowest vowel reinforcement.

The Registers and Posture. I have by now defined rather precisely that Vocal
Acoustics are involved with the manipulation of the spaces in the throat, mouth,
and on certain occasions above the soft palate. What are the manipulators
which bring about these changes of pitch which we are constantly monitoring by
feeling and listening?

Most important of all is the tongue which has the ability to move in five ways.
Van Riper and Irwin (1958), p. 377 illustrate this phenomena below.

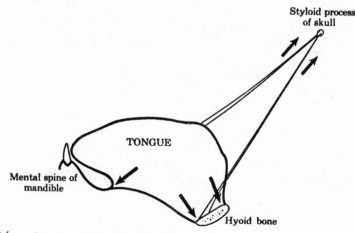

Styloid process
of skull

TONGUE

Mental spine of
mandible

Hyoid bone

C. Van Riper/J.V.Irwin, VOICE
AND ARTICULATION, ©1958, p.
37 Reprinted by permission of
Prentice-Hall., Englewood Cliffs.
N.J.

Fig. 46. Muscular Pulls Upon the Tongue.

The tongue may be 1) narrowed, and 2) widened in addition to 3) the forward, 4) up-back, and 5) downward actions as indicated in Fig. 46. Actually the arrows indicate to us the motions for the formation of the vowel triangle.

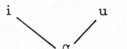 The hump of the tongue is pulled upward and forward to make [i]; the tongue is pulled upwards and backwards to form [u]; and the tongue is pulled down to make [ɑ]. [The feeling of openness in the throat for [ɑ] is an illusion.]

Certain actions of the tongue have been noticed in relationship to registers. William Shakespeare (1921, p. 20), of the Lamperti School was astonishingly knowledgeable of the functions of the extrinsic muscles of the larynx.

> "No one can fail to perceive, firstly that while singing a scale upwards in the chest register, and examining with the hand the floor of the mouth underneath the chin, we feel about this spot the contraction of a broad set of muscles increasing as we sing higher; secondly, that in the medium voice a less broad but still vigorous tension accompanies the notes as they ascend; and, thirdly, that on singing upwards the so-called head notes, only the slightest contraction is felt, and this of a delicate set of muscles in a line between the larynx and the point of the chin. In like manner by examining the muscles just above the breast-bone, the corresponding pull downwards will be observed.
>
> Thus the registers seem to be influenced by different sets of placing muscles; the latter through interchange of action balance the larynx in the exact position necessary to any note, high or low, loud or soft; simultaneously, the muscles inside bring about the infinite and remarkable modifications in the length and breadth of the vibrating vocal cords to which reference has already been made. The control over the placing, tuning, and register changes should be unconscious."

I have shown that placement is by ear, feel of vibration, and resonance developed into a knowledge of pronunciation gained through vocalisation of the vowel scales. Placement techniques can be heard and felt with the use of a Vowel Resonator. A singer "knows" by feel but cannot tell specifically what caused the tuning since it is a coordination of the breathing, phonating and resonating processes of the singing voice. The singer really knows; he does not gain his goals by permissiveness - decidedly not. He gains his technique by utilizing the sounds which are available to him by the harmonic series and vowel-pitch phenomena which are as impersonal as Newton's laws of motion. However, they do become very personal when they are abused.

The basis of the physiology of vocal acoustics is that the motions of the throat are brought about by the thought of vowel colors. Languages are made up of opposite vowels and in the process of using them and coupling them there is such flexibility and agility of movement that the throat does not have occasion to become tight or stiff. There can be no such thing as a stiff jaw if the vowel-tuning muscles are functioning correctly. Of course, singing in a wrong tessitura is disobedience of Nature's laws and one soon finds out that a song or aria should either be transposed or abandoned.

I cannot denigrate those teachers enough who desire to remain ignorant of the physical function of vowels. We may be oblivious of their action in speech without too much danger, however there is a vocal therapy for which only teachers of singing are qualified - THE TEACHING AND BUILDING OF THE SINGING VOICE. They should be allowed to have their way without the "butting in" from vocally unknowledgeable coaches, conductors, and stage directors. Some readers have noticed that I have reservations concerning some vocal coaches. The word "reservations" is weak; there should be some special kind of punishment for those who impose instrumental limitations upon the voices of singers. Frequently they discard those singers that work for them and who have been "used up." Then they audition for fresh new talent.

APPENDIX D - READINGS CONCERNING BREATHING TECHNIQUES

Most contemporary teaching of breathing has departed so far from the teaching of the masters that it is deemed best to give several of their statements concerning the breath and then to make a few observations. The teaching of Manuel Garcia II was on the <u>full</u> breath which involved a phenomenon of which we presently seem to be uncognizant.

The Breath

"No persons can ever become accomplished singers, until they possess an entire control over the breath - the very element of sound. In order that the lungs may freely receive external air, the chest must be sufficiently capacious to allow of their full dilatation; and in effecting this, the diaphragm - which is a wide convex muscle separating the lungs from the cavity of the abdomen - plays an important part. The action of breathing consists of two separate operations - the first being that of inspiration, by which the lungs draw in the external air; and the second, that of expiration, by which they give out again the air just inspired.

To insure easy inspiration, it is requisite that the head be erect, the shoulders thrown back without stiffness, and the chest expanded. The diaphragm should be lowered without any jerk, and the chest regularly and slowly raised. This double movement enlarges the compass or circumference of the lungs; first, at their base, and subsequently throughout their whole extent, leaving them full liberty to expand, until they are completely filled with air.

When the lungs have been gradually filled, without any jerking movement, they have the power of retaining the air without effort; this slow and complete inspiration is what the Italians term <u>Respiro</u> as contrasted with that slight and hurried inspiration which gives the lungs a slight supply, merely sufficient for a moment, and technically termed the <u>Mezzo Respiro</u>. In neither case, however, should the passage of the air through the glottis be attended by any noise, as, besides being offensive to the ear, it would make the throat both dry and stiff.

Of course the mechanical act of expiration is precisely the reverse of inspiration, consisting simply in effecting a gentle, gradual pressure of the thorax and diaphragm on the lungs, when charged with air; for if the movements of the ribs and of the diaphragm were to take place suddenly, they would cause the air to escape all at once.

We would remark, that by submitting the lungs to a particular exercise, their power and elasticity will greatly increase. This exercise consists of four distinct and successive practical operations now to be described.

First. - The pupil should gently and slowly inhale for a few seconds, as much air as the chest can well contain.

Secondly. - After taking a deep breath, the air should be exhaled again very gently and slowly.

Thirdly. - Fill the lungs, and keep them inflated for the longest possible time. And,

Fourthly. - Exhale completely, and leave the chest empty as long as the physical powers will conveniently allow. It must be confessed that all these exercises are at first extremely exhausting, and must be separately practised, after long intervals of rest. The two first, however, - namely, the gentle inspirations and expirations - will be more equally effected by nearly closing the mouth, in such a way as to leave only a very slight aperture for the passage of air. By these means, the pupil will acquire steadiness of voice, - a subject that we shall revert to hereafter. The breath influences the mode or character of vocal execution; being capable of rendering it either steady or vacillating, connected or unconnected, powerful or feeble, expressive or the reverse."

Garcia, The Art of Singing, Pt. I, ab. 1855, p. 10. Ditson.

The (1855) statement was essentially the same as that in the 1872 edition. Garcia's writings were exemplary in their definitiveness. His later editions (there were 11 in his lifetime) were abbreviations rather than extensions of that which he had written earlier. In his book, Hints on Singing (1894, p. 11), in question and answer form, he threw added light on the 1855 quotation:

1. He illustrated the rib structure and its action in inspiration.

2. Again he asked for a full breath - "the diaphragm must and does contract completely."

3. When this occurs the ribs raise, while the waist becomes thin - "stomach is drawn in." This inspiration is complete [full breath] and is called thoracic or intercostal.

4. <u>Of greatest importance - if the floating ribs are denied their action, the breath is clavicular.</u> This is the phenomenon overlooked by many teachers today.

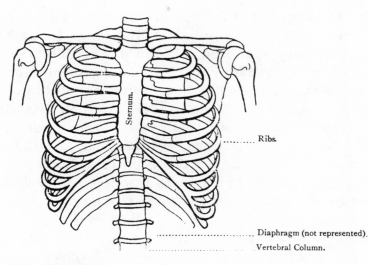

Fig. 47. Garcia's Rib Cage Diagram

The chest, a conical cage which protects the lungs, is formed at the back by the vertebral column, in front by the sternum, and on the sides by twelve ribs. Seven of these are united to the sternum, three are attached to each other by a cartilaginous border, and two are floating. This cavity is closed at the base by a large thin muscle, slightly convexed, called the midriff or diaphragm. It separates the thorax from the abdomen, and plays a most important part in the expansion and contraction of the lungs. (Garcia, <u>Hints on Singing</u>, 1894, p. 4.)

5. Referring again to Garcia's <u>Hints on Singing</u>, it is interesting to note that the fourth breathing exercise of the 1872 edition has been omitted - that of leaving the chest empty as long as the physical powers will conveniently allow.

6. Garcia stated that his method was essentially that of his father's, 1819.

His father's exercises were published within five years of his study with Ansani, believed to be a student of Porpora. It is not surprising to find agreement with Corri (1810, p. 11), who was a student of Porpora, "Take as much breath as you can, draw it in with moderate quickness, with suspiration, as if sighing, use it with economy, and at the same instant sound the letter A as pronounced by the Italian or Scotch."

The incomplete breath is the predominant breath of singers today without the added action of the floating ribs at the end of inhalation. Why is this important? Caruso (Marafiotti, 1922, p. 158) stated the symptoms of an incomplete breath:

> "The lungs, in the first place, should be thoroughly filled. A tone begun with only half-filled lungs loses half its authority and is very apt to be false in pitch. To take a full breath properly, the chest must be raised at the same moment that the abdomen sinks in. Then with the gradual expulsion of the breath, a contrary movement takes place.... It is this ability to take in an adequate supply of breath and retain it until required that makes, or the contrary, mars, all singing. A singer with a perfect sense of pitch and all the good intentions possible will often sing off the key and bring forth a tone with no vitality to it, distressing to hear, simply for lack of breath control.
>
> This art of respiration, once acquired, the student has gone a considerable step on the road to Parnassus...."

Commenting on Caruso's statement:

1. He leaves out the first phase of breathing - the diaphragm lowering which causes the stomach to slightly protrude. [The duality of the inhaling pattern must be taught.] Inhalation is in two patterns, the lowering of the diaphragm and the widening of the ribs followed by a thinning of the waist.

2. Is it not interesting that breathing and pronunciation are both involved with the "false pitch" of the voice? Vowel colors are involved with throat spaces, which are involved with proper inhalaation. Remember G. B. Lamperti (Brown, 1931, p. 91) said, "Tone and breath 'balance' only when harmonic overtones appear in the voice, and not by muscular effort and 'voice placing'."

I must compare the above statements with those of Francesco Lamperti who "followed the method of the old Italian School of Singing. Basing his teaching upon the study of respiration, he thoroughly grounded his pupils in the production of pure tone," Grove's Dictionary (1966). F. Lamperti considered his book (1890) to be based upon breathing. Now for what he said:

Q. What is meant by respiration?
A. It means the double action of the muscles of the thorax in receiving into and expelling air from the lungs.
Q. It is, then, an important thing that the singer should know how to take breath properly?

A. It is of the very utmost importance, for, if he has not a perfect mastery of the respiratory organs, he can neither develop the voice nor ever execute any piece of music artistically.

Q. How is a perfect respiration to be obtained?

A. By standing in the position, and observing closely the directions pointed out in Article III, and then inhaling the air, first through the nose, so that the lungs may dilate gradually and without strain; a breath thus taken may be held for a considerable time without fatigue.

Q. What is this gradual and complete respiration called?

A. A full breath. [Respiro]

Q. In singing an exercise or melody in strict time, should one always take a full breath?

A. No, only when it is interrupted by long rests; when this is not the case, and especially when written "allegro," one is obliged to breathe quickly, introducing only a small quantity of air into the lungs for the necessities of the moment.

Q. What is this instantaneous breathing called?

A. A half breath. [Mezzo Respiro]

Q. Is there any general rule for the duration of the breath?

A. No, a long or short breath depends upon the capacity of the lungs of the individual singer, and so it would not only be impossible, but useless, to fix the breathing places in vocal music.

Q. For how long can a pupil, well practised in this manner of breathing, continue a given note?

A. Up to twenty seconds, and sometimes more.

THE APPLICATION OF THE RULE FOR THE APPOGGIO OF THE VOICE

"By singing appoggiata, is meant that all notes, from the lowest to the highest, are produced by a column of air over which the singer has perfect command, by holding back the breath, and not permitting more air than is absolutely necessary for the formation of the note to escape from the lungs. By practice he will be able to do this without any effort, and so avoid those defects caused by straining the breath, such as frowning, contraction of the tongue, and a fixed expression of the eyes; for the voice will never be either well appoggiata nor capable of expression until the pupil is able to render his features calm and natural while singing.

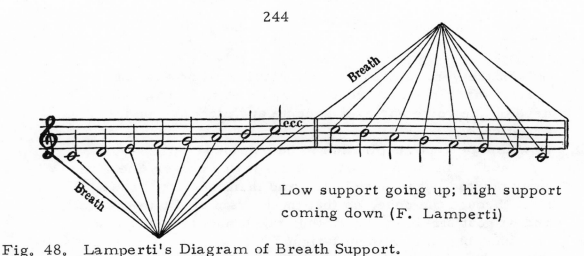

Low support going up; high support coming down (F. Lamperti)

Fig. 48. Lamperti's Diagram of Breath Support.

The student should hold his mouth natural and still while singing: it may be allowable in the very highest notes to open wider; but the difference should be very slight, and made without the least shock or sound of the air escaping. To avoid this, let him keep a firm hold upon the breath.

He should therefore, under the guidance of his master, and by dint of study and patience, strive to gain the power of retaining the mouth immovable; or, notwithstanding the beauty and strength of his voice, he can never become otherwise than a bad singer. [I take exception to this statement, movement for voice tuning should be allowed. BC]"

THE ATTACK OF THE NOTES

Q. To what should the pupil principally pay attention in singing his exercises?

A. To the attack of the notes and the control over the breath.

Q. How may he know that the sound has been emitted with a full respiration?

A. By measuring first the length of the respiration, and then that of the breath; as a breath slowly inhaled will last much longer than one hurriedly taken.

Q. How can you best give an idea of the right moment for attacking a note, so that it may have the proper quantity of breath for its support?

A. I should take the sign in use for crescendo, and placing it vertically, mark upon it the seconds for which the breath of an ordinary person may be sustained. [See Fig. 49.]

Q. Would it be prejudicial to attack it on the lower numbers, as 6, 9, and 12?

A. Certainly, as the sound thus emitted would be found wanting in steadiness and feeling.

Q. What are the advantages to be obtained by following the rules of Article VII. and the hints I have given here?

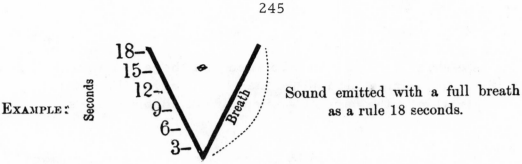

EXAMPLE:

Sound emitted with a full breath as a rule 18 seconds.

Fig. 49.   Duration of Inhalation.
Inhale for 18 seconds; sing for 18 seconds. (F. Lamperti)

A.   The fullest development of tone, the union of the registers, legato singing, sweetness of quality, security of intonation, an even agility, and a general elegance of execution, which qualities combined are necessary for good singing.

It is of the utmost importance that the pupil should, under the guidance of his master, study the true character of his own voice, so that he may not deceive himself as to its extension or character, and also that he may know what kind of music he ought to sing. One can easily see what is the true character of a voice by paying attention to the length of the breath on a given extension of notes, and up to what in these notes the singer can pronounce distinctly, and modulate their character, so as to convey the expression of love, hate, etc.

Q.   [Is the breathing of women different than that of men?]

A.   It is a mistake to suppose that the clavicular type of breathing is natural to women; on the contrary, it never exists in nature; that which has given rise to this erroneous impression is the following circumstance:

The pressure of the corset upon the abdomen, or in some cases the abnormal development of the stomach not permitting of the natural descent of the diaphragm, the respiration becomes lateral; the movement of the ribs and breastbone causes the rise and fall of the bosom, thus leading one to believe that the breathing is clavicular; but it will be seen that there is no movement of the collar-bones, and so we may be sure that the natural type of respiration in the case of women, if not abdominal, is lateral.

The voice is the sound produced by the passage of the air expelled from the lungs through the larynx.

To sustain a given note the air should be expelled slowly; to attain this end, the respiratory muscles, by continuing their action, strive to retain the air in the lungs, and oppose their action to that of the expiratory muscles which at the same time, drive it out for the production of the note. There is thus established a balance of power between these two agents, which is called the lutte vocale, or vocal struggle. On the retention of this equilibrium depends the just emission of the voice, and by means of it alone can true expression be given to the sound produced.

G.B. Lamperti (1905, p. 5) quotes Prof. L. Mandl, "Singing-voices were preserved much better and longer by the old Italian method, as taught by Rubini, Porpora, etc., than by our modern methods, which teach (or at least permit) clavicular breathing. And those teachers who favor diaphragmatic breathing can likewise show the best results."

F. Lamperti (1890, p. 12) stated:

> "For purposes of study, the pupil should make use only of the 'timbre aperto' [open timbre] and warned the singer "to be careful lest, by inattention to the rules in respiration, he should confound this with singing bianco [white] and sguaiato [graceless, awkward]."

> "The open quality," as Duprez observes, "should be produced by the vowel A, as in the word anima. It should be formed in the bottom of the throat, care, however, being taken that it does not change into O; since such an inflection, though it might give to the voice a more full and rounded character in a room, would render it smaller and without brilliancy in a theatre." [There is a modification of this in the Caruso Vowel Scale.]

The above quotation indicates that proper breathing assists in giving the correct throat opening of the Italian A, probably by tracheal pull resulting from the lowering diaphragm. If the breathing is not correct, the A can become white.

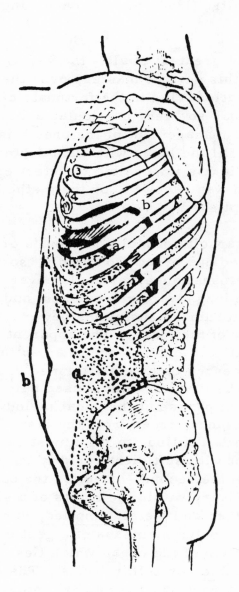

<u>Inhalation</u>. When diaphragm descends to position <u>a</u>, waist extends to position <u>b</u>.

<u>Exhalation</u>. When waist thins to position <u>a</u>, diaphragm rises to position <u>b</u>. (The concept of G. B. Lamperti.)

Garcia felt the waist thinning and slight chest rising began at the end of the full inhalation. F. Lamperti thought that there were contra-pressures between the descending action of the diaphragm and the waist thinning action. This would cause a slight bulging outwards of the area between the navel and the sternum, called the epigastrium, during singing.

Fig. 50. Lamperti's Concept of Diaphragmatic Breathing

The Half Breath (Mezzo Respiro)

I will discuss the half breath, or Mezzo Respiro, mentioned by Garcia and
F. Lamperti. I will quote W. B. Rockstro (1894, p. 8), concerning its use by
Jenny Lind:

> "One great secret - perhaps the greatest of all - the key to the
> whole mystery connected with this perfect mastery over the
> technical difficulties of vocalisation - lay in the fortunate cir-
> cumstance that Signor Garcia was so "very particular about
> the breathing." For the skilful management of the breath is
> everything; and she learned to fill the lungs with such dexterity
> that, except with her consent, it was impossible to detect either
> the moment at which the breath was renewed, or the method
> by which the action was accomplished.

> Her chest had not the natural capacity of Mdlle. Alboni's or
> Signor Rubini's; but she renewed her breath so rapidly, so
> quietly, so cleverly, that the closest observer could never
> detect the moment at which the lungs were replenished; and,
> by the outside world, her extraordinary sustaining power was
> attributed to abnormal capacity of the lungs. The apparent ease
> with which she attained this difficult end was due to an artfully-
> studied combination of the processes technically termed "costal"
> and "clavicular breathing"; in the first of which - used only
> after the completion of a distinct phrase of the vocal melody -
> the lower part or "base" of the lungs, freed from the last
> remains of the previous breath is refilled, to its utmost capacity,
> without undue precipitation, yet with sufficient rapidity to answer
> all practical purposes; while in the second - used for the continua-
> tion of phrases too long for delivery within the limits of a single
> inspiration - the lungs are neither completely emptied, nor com-
> pletely refilled, but replenished only, by means of a gentle
> inhalation, confined to that portion of the organ which lies
> immediately beneath the claviculae, or collar-bones. The skill
> with which these two widely different processes were inter-
> changed, when circumstance demanded their alternate employ-
> ment, was such as can only be acquired by long and unwearied
> practice, untrammelled by prejudice either for or against any
> special method whatever; and it is not too much to say, that it
> was to the sustaining power, acquired by this careful manage-
> ment of the breath, that Mdlle. Lind owed her beautiful
> pianissimo, and that marvellous command of the messa di voce
> which enabled her to swell out a crescendo to its utmost limit,
> and follow it, without a break, with a diminuendo which died

away to an imperceptible point, so completely covering the end
of the note that no ear could detect the moment at which it
faded into silence.

Within the last few years, an attempt has been made to
connect the term, clavicular breathing, with a mode of filling
the lungs, pernicious, to the last degree - a process which, we
need scarcely say, was never practised, either by Mdlle. Lind
or Rubini, whose method of breathing seems to have been closely
analogous to, if not absolutely identical with her own. True
clavicular breathing is not only a perfectly legitimate process,
but one quite indispensable to the accomplished vocalist."

I will only say there are two breaths; the full breath and the half breath, and
that they were both used by historical artists of the 19th century. We would do
well to utilize both of these techniques today.

In conversation, the abdominal muscles are quite lax. In singing, they are
working. In conversation, after the inhalation the lungs recoil. The phase of
inhalation and exhalation in sleep is about 1 to 1.5; in singing 1 to 20 or 30.
The art of breathing is the control of air flow.

Fricative Inhalations

It is well to know the proper actions of breathing, but if the actions can always
be gained indirectly that method should be used. This is because the artist will
need to be thinking of his musical interpretation and acting when he is on the
opera or concert stage. The proper action of inhalation has been gained by
various teachers by the use of fricative inhalations.

1. Inhaling through pursed lips was utilized by Garcia in the Art
   of Singing quoted in this chapter, and Hints on Singing (1894).

2. Louis Bachner (1944, p. 122), a world reknowned teacher of his
   time, used "the hand brought up to the nose, with the lower portion
   of the palm pressing lightly against the nostrils." The breath was
   then taken against this resistance. He had great success and was
   the teacher of Sigrid Onegin, Heinrich Schlusnes, and Marjorie
   Lawrence among others.

3. I have noted the glottal fricative used by Paola Novikova in her
   teaching, p. 19 of this text. Also gained by this was a larynx
   lowered by the breathing. It can be used stage center anywhere
   in the world. The Bachner inhalation cannot be used on the stage;
   the pursed lips' inhalation of Garcia might be used at times.

The Flexible Breath

In the terminology of violinists, I have been talking primarily of the use of the full length of the bow (breath). This is necessary for legato passages (and for the resonance of the total vocal pipe in singing). There are several other musical uses of the breath. One of the most important is similar to the bouncing bow of the violinist. How is this done? Many contemporary teachers use the panting device for securing the flexibility of the diaphragm followed by such exercises as the G. B. Lamperti (1905, p. 20) exercise which is very favorable for head voice in women.

Fig. 51. Lamperti's Staccato Exercise.

Also the gymnastic exercise is an excellent one to keep the voice from becoming too heavy. Such articulations are necessary for all voice classifications.

<u>The Bernoulli Effect</u>. I cannot depart from the discussion of breathing without discussing a principle which was stated by Bernoulli in 1738 one year after Farinelli, the most acclaimed of the castrati, departed from public life to join the Spanish court. Surely the great singing of the castrati was involved with this phenomenon of air flow.

If a person takes two sheets of paper, holds them 1/4th inch or so apart and blows through them, what happens? The person who has not tried the experiment will probably say that the sheets of paper will be blown apart. What occurs is that the two pieces of paper are drawn into vigorous vibration. The velocity of air through the paper causes a cycle of reduction of pressure drawing the sheets of paper together, followed by the air blowing them apart. Taylor (1958) and Vennard (1967) have envisioned that the Bernoulli Effect occurs when the vocal cords are being adducted on the attack and during the time the breath stream is moving. The evidence is overpowering when one considers that two vocal cords can begin vibrating when they are apart and that in the messa di voce they can touch each other while they are moving (soft explosions), can be pressed together for sharp explosions, and can then return to a whisper without one bit of evidence of any kind of a break. This is brought about by three factors: 1) correct resonator echoing; 2) even adduction of the vocal cords; and 3) a masterly control of the breath flow. The slit between the vocal cords can be small with a fast velocity of the air through the cords, or the vocal cords can slap in every cycle with small air flow. This is the crux of the art of singing - the incredible teamwork of resonator, vibrator, and energizer. These are the bases by which the artist accomplishes his creative work in vocal performance.

Glottal Closure and Air Flow in the Messa di Voce. When C and C are brought together, the vocal cords are adducted. When C and C are separated, the cords are abducted. B is the direction of the breath flow. The vocal cords can be vibrated while they are apart by the breath flow, giving a velvety quality of tone with few harmonics. The wave form would approximate

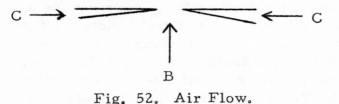

Fig. 52. Air Flow.

C and C can be pinched together giving a biting, incisive tone, rich in overtones with a wave form which would approximate ⌁⌁⌁. The triangular wave exists in bowing a stringed instrument. Two variables are present, 1) the pressure of the bow on the string, and 2) the speed of the bow across the string. This is probably the reason Mancini (1777, p. 99) used the term, "draw out the voice." The concept is helpful.

When C and C are pinched together too much, the voice gives a grating sound. When they are not approximated enough, the breath rushes through the cords

too fast and there is a breathy sound. From 𝄞 upwards in the female

voice, called Head Register, the cords are usually not completely adducted. When they are completely adducted there is a metalic sound, which is of artistic use on certain occasions. When this closure is overdone the voice is referred to as being brassy. The female middle voice is frequently breathy and usually needs to be trained in vocal cord adduction so that there is a closed

glottis. Below 𝄞 for all voices, concert pitch, the messa di voce is usually from open glottis to closed glottis to open glottis. The air flow through the glottis will proceed from the ⌇ wave to the ⌇ wave, and return to the ⌇. At the same time, the cavities will proportionally enlarge for the forte and become smaller for the pianissimo, while the vowel color (not quality) will remain the same. For example, the favorable vowel color of [ʊ] is being sung. The singer will begin a small mouthed [ʊ] on the pianissimi-crescendos at the same time he is proportionally enlarging the cavities and then follow with the diminuendo to the original small mouthed [ʊ]. Thus both the breath and the cavities are at play in the messa di voce. The variability of vocal cord thickness, cavity volume and breath pressure are essential or the tone will feel as though it is stuck. The messa di voce was one of the great training devices of the vocal masters and was called "The Soul of Music" by Corri (1810, p. 14). Advanced singers will learn how to sing the pianissimo with large cavities on certain notes for mysterious effects. There are many variations but the basis of all vocal expression in singing is the messa di voce.

Belts. Dr. Joal stated (1895, p. 92) that in the classic Italianate singing, the singer could excite more pleasure and enthusiasm by means of trills, messa di voce, singing line, and embellishments than by violent efforts of passion. This demanded a great art of breathing. It was based on the open Italian vowels. In dramatic singing there is more decibel output and the louder sounds take greater pressure. The perceptive eye will note that the heroic singers are frequently belted or girdled. There is an historical background to this. Joal in his book dedicated to Jean de Reszke, has much to say about the use of belts by singers (p. 126). This causes a costal or thoracic type of respiration which increases the power and solidity of the voice. One singer stated that the voice was fatigued much less after singing with a belt. Some artists used a band of flannel for purposes of slightly compressing the abdomen, the result being that their voices were better sustained. Another, after having been taught diaphragmatic breathing with poor results, constructed a belt which obliged him to enlarge the lower part of the chest [flexible ribs]. His voice had a return of strength. Joal concluded that costal breath:

> "...is employed by the majority of singers, advised by the most renowned artists, and recommended by the old Italian masters, who have carried to such a high degree of perfection the art of singing."

Sbriglia, the teacher of Jean de Reszke, Edward de Reszke, Pol Plançon, and Lillian Nordica designed a belt which he called the Sbriglia Belt. I have never been able to find a picture or obtain a description of its design. I know the purpose of a belt and how it assists in singing. Franco Corelli uses one (N.Y. Times, Feb. 8, 1970, p. 56) "for support under his chest." Placido Domingo (N.Y. Times, Feb. 27, 1972) wears a sturdy elastic supporter around his waist against which he presses all the way out for high notes, "for the middle register halfway and for pianissimo he lets it relax."

Let me say that one of the great pictures in Eisenstadt's "Witness to our Time" is that of the heroic tenor, Lauritz Melchior, in an enormous corset that extended from his hips to halfway up on his rib cage with 5 straps that could be adjusted independently. The evenness and density of his vocal scale was no doubt related to the advantage that this device gave him.

I know of women artists who have said they have liked to sing with tight girdles, although their remarks are not in print. However, there are many pictures of the prima donnas at the turn of the century who were not only corseted but cinched to give the "wasp waist" in vogue at that time. Some singers feel that a belt reminds them of good posture and makes them "feel like a singer." A well-known American baritone who was a student of de Reszke said that he did not recommend the use of a belt to him but that several of the European singers with whom he sang used them.

In conclusion, as the diaphragm lowers on a deep breath, there is a downward pull on the trachea which lowers the larynx. It is my belief that the use of a belt or elastic band around the body reduces the trachea pull and leaves the larynx in a better position for singing middle and high notes than does a deep breath without a belt. A belt is almost a guarantee that the breath will be thoracic. It seems that there is a mechanical advantage gained from its use by dramatic singers. Also, there is a possibility that the voice is slightly raised in tessitura.

What is inspiration? During speech we inhale in the mood of the idea which we will immediately express. As on the stage where the eye leads the action, in singing the inhalation prepares the delivery. The inspiration (imagery of an idea) of what one is going to say, and the inspiration (inhalation) of the breath are so closely related that they seem to occur at the same time and in the same motion. I must state the thesis that, in singing, the inhalation should form the voice for the expression of the musical phrase which follows. When this occurs, with the play of resonate vowel colors, there can be dramatic truth while the musical instrument of the voice is being played. When both tone and expression are present, singing is a delight. One without the other is not enough because the senses are insufficiently stimulated. Never overlook the emotional power of the varying airflow over the vocal cords, that which is mechanistically called "the Bernoulli Effect."

F. Lamperti concludes his book by urging students to make a careful study of respiration. "Let him always bear in mind this important truth, he who has the best command over his breath is the best singer." With the added knowledge of harmonic pronunciation, the singer should be spectacular.

APPENDIX E - OPEN YOUR MOUTH! (Correctly!)

The statement has been made a million times by teachers of singing. It is frequently done without a knowledge of what the Italians discovered and without a knowledge of vocal acoustics. First let me give a few quotations of the masters, followed by an acoustical explanation.

Mancini (1777, p. 89), stated: "Upon the evening of the mouth depends the clearness of the voice." He later stated, "I have finally fixed a general rule... every pupil must shape his mouth for singing, just as he shapes it when he smiles. The upper teeth show a little, and are slightly separated from the lower ones." [This is probably the silver AH resonated on Notes #40, #41, #42, #43, etc.] He indicates that the exaggerated opening of the mouth gives a voice which is throaty, since the fauces are under strain, and lacking in clearness and facility. He states that the person will sing "...with a suffocated, crude and heavy quality."

Corri in the Porpora tradition wrote in 1810, p. 11, "Open the Mouth in an oblong form, as smiling, so that the lower lip may not rise above the Teeth, which otherwise will damp and weaken the tone of the Voice."

Garcia wrote (1847, Part II Paschke tr., 1970, p. 7):

> "The Italian [a], [ε], and [e], and in general all the open and
> rounded vowels should be produced without the participation of
> the lips. The narrow and dark vowels like the [o], [ø], [u],
> and [y] are the only ones which want the lips brought together.
> These procedures, at the same time as they favor the emission
> of voice and add ease and clarity of articulation, prevent those
> abrupt transitions from one timbre to the other which resemble
> the barking of a dog."

He makes a further definition of mouth form, p. 17, "If the lips are flattened against the teeth, the voice will be better and the words more clear." Distinguishing diction in sombre timbre is somewhat like taking pictures on a cloudy day - there is a lack of contrast and the images (vowels) do not stand out clearly. Also, p. 7, he stated, "In order to perfect that equality so necessary among all the tones of the voice, we advise maintaining always the same separation between the jaws for all vowels without exception." To bring this about, he suggested the placement of a little piece of wood or cork laterally between the teeth. [This position differs from those found with the Vowel Resonator.]

Today's international stars, as seen and heard on television from the great opera houses and festivals, indicate that the lips are positioned more roundly, as found by the Vowel Resonator. This is an important change from the mouth position advocated by the early master teacher of singing.

Lilli Lehmann made a very definitive statement for us (1914, p. 220), "The pleasing expression of the mouth requires the muscular contractions that form the bright vowel ah." She does not speak of a relaxed Ah - the correct "ah" required a muscular effort in the throat and by the lips.

It is necessary to have the pleasing expression of the face these days for singing on television and in intimate situations. No longer will facial contortionists be cast unless the hall is so large that the sound is so important that sight is irrelevant.

Caruso stated (1922, p. 157-8), "It is necessary to open the sides of the mouth, at the same time dropping the chin well, to obtain a good throat opening. In taking higher notes, of course, one must open the mouth a little wider, but for the most part the position of the mouth is that assumed when smiling.... If one is well versed in the art, one can open the throat perfectly without a perceptible opening of the mouth, merely by the power of respiration."

Conclusion: The masters were all speaking of an /a/ which would give a cantilena. Garcia indicates that if the wrong vowels are used the vowels do not join and that the transitions between the vowels sound like the "barking of a dog." A rather derisive statement. Lilli Lehmann says the wrong /a/ connects with no other vowel. The basic thought seems to be to sing on the bright vowel which has its own chiaroscuro. It is in midposition and connects with the Front vowels as well as the Back vowels.

Man's physiological and acoustical nature has not changed since the time of these writers. Many teachers have been overly permissive in their teaching of singing which has allowed us to wander from the principles discovered and rediscovered in the past. Those singers who rediscover and develop a natural technique will be rewarded by their own throats. When using the Vowel Resonator above c^2 two resonating positions are possible - one with the jaw very low, the other with the cheeks raised and the jaw less open. The singer has two positions from which to choose - the more close one for low notes and the more open for high notes.

APPENDIX F - SPECTOGRAMS OF VOWEL RESONANCES

Notice that the lower resonances stay the same in examples a, b, and c. This is the basis of coupling. Keep the low resonance in all vowels but alternate them.

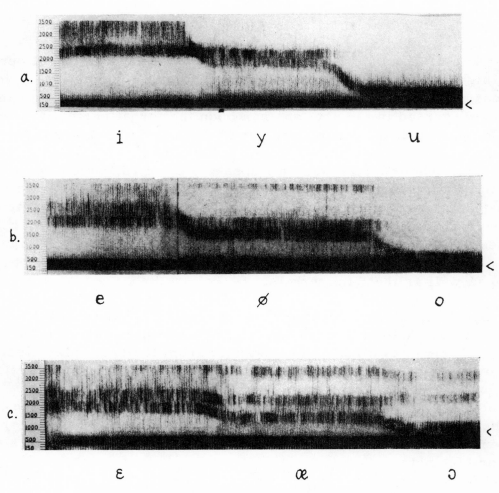

Spectrograms showing the lowering of formant 2 frequencies, either by lip rounding: [i]–[y], [e]–[ø], [ɛ]–[œ]; or by tongue backing: [y]–[u], [ø]–[o], [œ]–[ɔ]. (Scale is disposed for reading measurements at center of formants.)

Reprinted by permission of the
Modern Language Association of
America from Vol. LXVI, Sept.
1951, #5.

Fig. 53. Delattre, P. Publications of the Modern Language Association of America, Vol. LXVI, Sept. 1951, #5.

APPENDIX G - COVERING - CLEAR AND SOMBRE TIMBRE

What is covering?   This is a question which is frequently asked of a teacher of singing. By use of the Chromatic Vowel Chart this question can now be specifically answered as to the why and how.

First of all, let's look at the history of the phenomenon. It appeared in the person of Gilbert-Louis Duprez upon the stage of the Paris Opera in a performance of "William Tell" in 1837. His singing was given the name of voix sombre. The new style created a furore with the public and Adolphe Nourrit, a pupil of Manuel Garcia's father, departed for Naples to learn the new technique. He was less than satisfied with it and committed suicide. It is not surprising that Garcia wrote on clear and sombre timbres since he was very closely associated with their artistic use.

Garcia presented his "Memoire on the Human Voice" to the French Academy in November of 1840. It was accepted by the Academy after he had demonstrated the principles and it appeared in the minutes of April, 1841. These principles were the basis of his "Complete Treatise on the Art of Singing, " [Part I] published that same year, 1841. He makes the following statements concerning registers and timbres (Paschke's tr. 1970, p. xxxix):

"We have observed that when the voice passes through each register completely, the larynx behaves very differently in its movements according to whether the series of tones belongs to the clear timbre or the sombre timbre.

When the voice rises in the chest register from the lowest tone to the highest tone, if the timbre is clear the larynx occupies in the first moment, a position a little lower than that of rest; then, by regular ascending movements, it follows the voice in its rise, carrying itself slightly forward. When the voice reaches the extreme of which it is capable in that register, the larynx moves against the jaw by a very pronounced rocking motion, which one can verify by touching. The notes produced in this last period of the ascension of the larynx are thin and strangled; at the last limits of the compass, the head tips back a little in order to facilitate the elevation of the larynx.

The same movement is reproduced when the voice passes through the falsetto and head registers in the clear timbre; the larynx takes for its point of departure the same low position as for the lowest note of the falsetto, then it climbs by

very slight movements, very small, which correspond to the
elevation of the tones. As soon as the voice arrives at the head
tones the larynx rises rapidly to the position of deglutition
[swallowing]. In this last period the tones are thin and shrill.

But if the voice, passing through the chest register, keeps the
sombre timbre for all the notes, the larynx remains fixed a
little below the position of rest. The lowering becomes especially apparent, when the individual seeks, by a last effort, to
exaggerate the timbre and to give to his voice all the volume of
which it is capable; in this last hypothesis, the larynx remains
immovably fixed in the lowest position for the entire compass of
the register. One is obliged to facilitate this position by leaning
the head forward a little. The distinction of the timbres begins
to be perceptible only toward d.

When the larynx produces the falsetto register in the sombre
timbre, it again takes the same position as that above, and
keeps it unvaryingly, especially if one tries to increase the
volume of the voice. As for the head tones, the larynx almost
always produces them while rising rapidly. One could not prevent these movements; trying to do so to swell the voice would
be a dangerous and often useless effort. [Please notice the
last statement - it is self explanatory.]"

Garcia was in agreement with prior findings. Luchsinger and Arnold (1965,
p. 103) state:

"In 1840 Diday and Petrequin were able to demonstrate that
open singing of an ascending scale is accompanied by laryngeal
elevation and shortening of the resonance tube. In contrast,
covered singing is characterized by low positioning of the larynx
following a deep inspiration.... Through this lengthening of the
resonance tube, covered singing is richer in sound than is open
singing." [A lower R^1 is used in coupling with the high resonance of a, æ, ɛ, e, ɪ, i, œ, ø, ʏ, and y].

Luchsinger and Arnold, p. 103, quote Pielka's (1912) study of "open" and
"covered" (or closed) vowels: "Below c^1 male singers can sing all vowels
with perfect purity. [I would say Note #17.] The vocal organ is then in open
position, mainly through elevation of the larynx. Above this neutral point at
c^1, the technique of covering is needed to produce pure vowels. The shifting
of the vowel color to darker types through the covering technique is achieved
chiefly through the lowering of the larynx...."

Pielke observed the prominence of the second harmonic during open singing [see Vowel Scales ② between Notes #18 and #23], while covered singing showed a weak second harmonic. Conversely, covered singing was characterized by a strong fundamental [see Vowel Scales ① between Notes #18 and #23] and a rich spectrum of higher harmonics.

To sing open (or clear) timbre use Vowel Scales ②. To sing very closed, use Vowel Scales ①. To sing voix mixte use Vowel Scales ①.5 which reinforce both the fundamental and second harmonic.

It will be noted that the vowel couplings indicated in Green allow the singer to sing in his clearest timbre and yet avoid the hiatus at changes of register. If a singer attempts to go upward on [ɑ] from any of the ah's which are numbered ①, ②, ③, or ④ he is courting disaster. Vowel values at these spots are reserved for climax notes and are not to be used prior to ascending. In the words of Garcia, at these points, "the voice reaches the extreme of which it is capable in that register, the larynx moves against the jaw by a very pronounced rocking motion." If one goes any further in that register the notes are "thin and strangled."

Luchsinger & Arnold (1965, p. 103), report the confirmation by R. Schilling (1925) of the lowered position of the larynx in covered singing. "Furthermore, it could be shown that the essence of covered singing consisted in elevation of the epiglottis [found in u and ɯ] and widening of the... space between the tongue base and the epiglottis." [Widened and lowered by the down and widening pull of the omo-hyoid muscles and lowered by the "tracheal pull."]

The Velopharyngeal Axis. Much more needs to be known about the action of the velopharyngeal muscles and their action in relation to singing, see Fig. 54. Garcia (1894, p. 11) when speaking of timbres said:

> "The timbres may be divided into two classes, the clear (bright), or open, and the dark or closed. These two opposite qualities are obtained principally through the agency of the larynx and the soft palate. The movements of these two organs are always in a contrary direction. The larynx rises when the soft palate falls, and when the larynx falls, the soft palate rises. The high vault produces the dark timbres, the lower arch the clear ones. The arch rises when we are in the act of yawning, and falls when we are in the act of swallowing."

My interpretation would be that there was a pull of 3 (and 4) against 2 (and 1) in Fig. 54. The tongue continually crosses this axis with the hump being in front of the axis for Front and Umlaut vowels and the hump being behind the axis for the Back vowels. This continual play across the velopharyngeal axis allows the throat to be free in speech. The crossover exercises are most helpful in training the singing voice.

Probably the greatest variable in the throat is the fronting and backing of the tongue over the velopharyngeal axis as indicated by Fritzell (1969) in The Velopharyngeal Muscles in Speech. Acta oto-laryngologica, Supplementum 250,

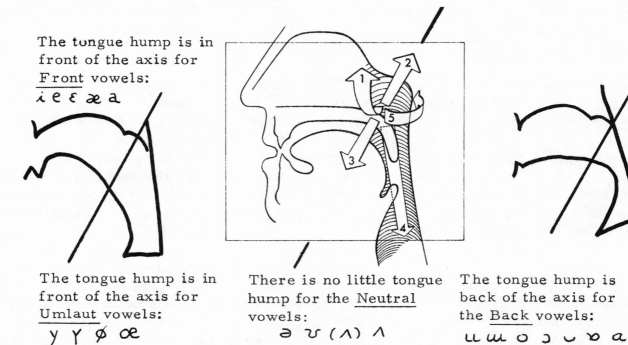

The tongue hump is in front of the axis for Front vowels:

i e ɛ æ a

The tongue hump is in front of the axis for Umlaut vowels:

y ɣ ø œ

There is no little tongue hump for the Neutral vowels:

ə ʊ (ʌ) ʌ

The tongue hump is back of the axis for the Back vowels:

ɯ ɯ o ɔ ʊ ɒ a

Fig. 54. The Velopharyngeal Axis

THE GARCIA PRINCIPLE OF CLEAR AND SOMBRE TIMBRES, CHIAROSCURO.

In the strictest sense languages are systems of sound color. Cogan (1969, p. 76), stated, "Languages are timbral systems of considerable complexity and subtlety. They consist of a variety of attacks (consonants) and sustained timbres (vowels and some vowel-like consonants)." Garcia in his writings from 1840 until 1894 wrote extensively on the timbres of the voice. In 1894 he extended his theory of timbre "from the most open (or bright) to the most closed (or dark) to utilize three vowels of the French language:

> The Italian A approximates to o when darkened
> " " E " " eu in French when darkened
> " " I " " u in French when darkened
> " " O " " u in Italian when darkened

His table "shows what change each vowel undergoes in passing from clear to dark." He said the process should be inverted. The table transcribed phonetically would be:

A when darkened approximates to [ɔ] or [ɒ] and when clear returns to
[ɑ] or [a].

E (open) when darkened approximates to [œ] and when clear returns to
[ɛ].

E (close) when darkened approximates to [ø] and when clear returns to
[e].

I when darkened approximates to [y] and when clear returns to [i].

O when darkened approximates to [u] and when clear returns to [o].

Figure 55 is a notation of this definition of timbres which has only to do with the alteration of the upper resonance. In my observations the lower resonance also seems to be involved. The higher combination vowels [ɒ, ɑ] of R^1 will give clear timbre; the lower combination vowels of R^1 [o and u] will give sombre timbre. G. B. Lamperti and Garcia both used the term chiaroscuro. The words chiaro and oscuro (spelled with a and u) are descriptive of what occurs in vowel coloring. A combination vowel towards [ɑ] will give chiaro (clear timbre); a combination vowel towards [u] will give oscuro (sombre timbre). Garcia referred to "chiaroscuro" in the paintings of the Spanish Velazques who was influenced by the Dutch Rembrandt. What was the secret of what has been called the "Rembrandt light?" Van Loon (1937, p. 377) answers the question:

"Merely the realization, suspected before by others but never
put into execution, that darkness is merely another form of
light and that every color is just as much subject to the law of
vibrations as the sound of a note played on a violin."

Or sung by a voice, I would add. Figure 55 is a musical notation of the vowels in the Clear and Sombre timbres. Not to be outdone by Rembrandt, I have indicated the frequencies of the pitch for the centers of each of the vowel colors indicated.

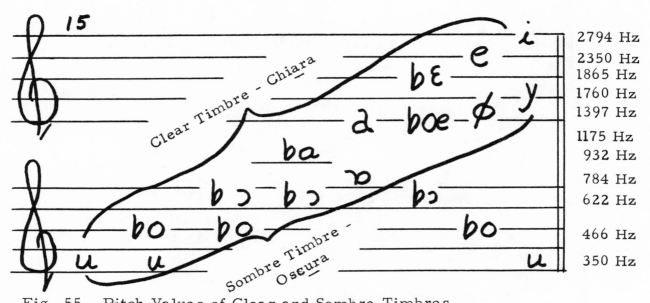

Fig. 55. Pitch Values of Clear and Sombre Timbres.

Conclusion: The term register is taken from the stops or pipes of the organ - a pipe phenomenon. In the human voice the registers are due to the phenomenal relationship of the pitch of the total pipe, between the glottis and the front of the mouth, and sung pitch. Covering is a method by which the human voice

changes its coupling so that the [musical notation] notes can be sung with a dramatic

quality of voice [vowel scale ①] as opposed to the lyric [vowel scale ②]. Both of these are phenomena of Harmonic Resonation shown in the Chromatic Vowel Chart.

APPENDIX H – CONNECTIONS OF TONES

Garcia (ab. 1872, p. 12) stated that connections of tones on any vowel can be accomplished in five different ways. They are as follows:

1. Gliding or slurring. To glide or slur (con portamento) is to conduct the voice from one note to another through all intermediate sounds. The time occupied by a slur would be taken from the last portion of the note quitted; and its rapidity will depend on the kind of expression required by any passage in which it occurs. This dragging of notes will assist in equalizing the registers, timbres, and power of the voice.

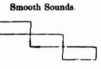

Slurred Sounds.

This technique should be carefully used with taste. When overdone it is a mark of a bad singer.

2. Legato. To sing legato means to pass from one note to another in a neat, sudden and smooth manner, without interrupting the flow of voice; yet not allowing it to drag or slur over any intermediate sound. ...the breath "must be subjected to a regular and continuous pressure, so as intimately to unite all the notes with each other." The notes should be equal in power, value and timbre to unite with each other, according to Garcia.

Smooth Sounds.

3. Marked. Marked connections of notes are indicated > > > >. To mark sounds is to lay a particular stress on each, without detaching them from one another: this will be attained by giving a pressure to the lungs; and by dilating the pharynx, as if repeating the same vowel for every note in the passage, - which is in effect done.

Marked Sounds.

a a a a

Marked vocalization helps to bring out the voice, and to correct the habit of gliding notes. Dull voices have no better method of articulating notes. It is, besides, a principle resource for giving color and effect to florid passages.

This is basically for use in diatonic scales. Marked sounds are indicated by points and a tie.

4.   <u>Detached, Staccata.</u> To detach sounds is to utter each individually by a distinct stroke of the glottis, and to separate them from one another by a slight pause. If, instead of leaving them immediately, they receive a slight prolongation, a kind of echo is produced. The first of these is indicated by dots; the second by dashes over the notes, which is equivalent to

Besides the eclat which these accents impart to a passage, when used with taste, they help to give elasticity to stiff throats.

5.   <u>Aspirated.</u>   "Aspirated notes allow the <u>breath to escape</u> between them, detracting from their purity, and very rapidly exhausting the lungs."

> "These four ways of vocalizing, should be exercised on every vowel in turn through the entire compass of the voice, with varying degrees of power, at all rates of speed, and by introducing suspensions.
>
> This comprehensive mode of study enables the organ to pass with promptness and flexibility through all varieties of intonations: it equalizes the vocal instrument, and, without straining it makes its whole extent familiar to the pupil."

What more could be added to this statement concerning tonal connections - very little except the utilization of favorable vowels, vowel couplings, and vowel modifications.

<u>Breath and the Connections of Tones.</u> Just as the many articulations of a violin are involved with the use of the bow in relationship to the vibrator (string), so are the articulations of singing involved with the breath and its relationship to the vibrator (vocal cords). Garcia summarizes his chapter on articulations in singing by describing the subtle relationships of the breath and the vocal cords.

<u>Co-action of the vocal cords and breath.</u>

> Dragging of the voice: - Lungs, - equal and continued pressure of air.
> Glottis, - gradual changes in the tension of the lips of the glottis.
> Smooth vocalization: - Lungs, - equal and continued pressure of air.
> Glottis, - sudden changes in the tension of the lips of the glottis.
> Marked agility: - Lungs, - continued and accented pressure of the air.
> Glottis, - sudden changes in the tension of the lips of the glottis.
> Detached agility: - Lungs, - alternately pressed and in repose, which
> corresponds - Glottis - to the alternating and sudden tensions of the
> glottis.
> Aspirated vocalization: - Lungs, - continued pressure.
> Glottis, - alternate contractions and distensions; escape of air
> before the sounds.

<u>Articulation, colorings and artistry.</u>   Too frequently beautiful singing, <u>bel</u>
<u>canto</u>, has been thought of as being only legato. Of course singing line, canti-
lena, is the basis of singing but if only the legato articulation is used, a
singer's performance soon becomes boring. The more the singer masters the
various articulations and timbres the more attractive his or her singing will
become.

<u>Portamento.</u>   I cannot leave the Appendix on Articulations without stressing the
tasteful use of the Portamento. Corri (1810, p. 3) said

> ... "the <u>portamento di voce</u> is the perfection of vocal music; it consists
> in the swelling and the dying of the voice, the sliding and blending one
> note into another with delicacy and expression.... <u>Portamento di voce</u>
> may be justly compared to the highest degree of refinement in pronun-
> ciation in speaking.... It was the particular excellence of Farinelli,
> Pacchiarotti, Raaff and others of the first eminence."

Henry Pleasants, the well known musical critic, has stated that critics have
driven a wedge between the singer and his audience. I believe that they have
been absolutely damaging to singers by being super-critical of anything that
sounds like a <u>portamento</u>. We have almost come to the place that the Italians
are the only ones who can connect tones. We have even come to the place
where the Appoggiatura is usually unconnected. This is poor singing because
it lacks in elegance. Garcia (1894, p. 63) stated

> "Q. What are the characteristics of the <u>portamento</u>?
> A. Energy (a) and grace (b). Applied to the expression of powerful
>   feelings, it should be strong and rapid; less so for moderate or
>   tender sentiments."

It is an embellishment which should be subject to good taste.

APPENDIX I - THE TRILL

<u>Trill</u>. No book on singing should be written without including the technique of a <u>trill</u>. I will simply include the statement of Lilli Lehmann (1914, p. 258) since it is the most effective device I have found. The alternating between [e] and [i] may be related to the tongue trill of brass instruments where the alternate forming of vowels brings about a trill. This changes modes of vibration when played on high pitches.

Trill

"There still remains the trill, which is best practised in the beginning as follows: always from the upper note to the lower one.

Fig. 56. Lilli Lehmann's Trill Exercise.

ā and ē are placed very closely against each other, nearly pinching, and held tight; the larynx kept as stiff as possible and placed high. Both tones are connected as closely, as heavily as possible, upward nasally, downward <u>on</u> the larynx, for which the <u>y</u>, again, is admirably suited. They must be attacked as high as possible, and very strongly connected with the chest. The trill exercise must be practised almost as a scream. The upper note must always be strongly <u>accented</u>. The exercise is practised with an even strength, without decrescendo to the end; the breath pressure acts more and more strongly, uninterruptedly to the finish.

Trill exercises must be performed with great energy, on the whole compass of the voice. They form an exception to the rule in so far that in them more is given to the throat to do - always, however, under the control of the chest - than in other exercises. That relates, however, to the muscles.

The breath vibrates <u>above</u> the larynx, but does not stick in it, consequently this is <u>not</u> dangerous. It is really a gymnastic exercise for the muscles.

The exercise is practised first on two half, then on two whole tones of the same key (as given above), advancing by semitones, twice a day on the entire compass of the voice. It is exhausting because it requires great energy; but for the same reason it gives strength. Practise it first as slowly and vigorously as the strength of the throat allows, then faster and faster, till one day the trill unexpectedly appears."

APPENDIX J - DIFFERENCE TONES

Difference tones are definitely related to the way we hear the singing voice. This is because the Vocal Pipe is in the neighborhood of 6-1/2 inches long, varying with voice classification. [Since sound travels at 1080 ft per second, and the lowest 1/4 vibration to be resonated would have a wave length of 24 inches or 2.2 ft, the lowest fundamental frequency which can be resonated would be about 490 Hz (vibrations per second) which is about b above middle c.] Because of various factors, I have found the lowest pitch that can be resonated is nearer to f above middle c. [The first note below that is what has been called "the break."]

We hear tones below that pitch by a physiological and psycho-acoustical phenomenon known as "difference tone." Perhaps this can be best understood by comparing the speaker of a transistor radio [which plays the low pitches but does not reinforce them] and an expensive speaker which has a "tweeter" and a "woofer." With the latter there is a feeling that the tone is more "real" than it is on a transistor radio, although, it does give the illusion that the lower pitches are being heard.

The phenomenon is more easily explained than understood. Alexander Wood in his book ACOUSTICS (1960, p. 482) states that Helmholz showed that the structure of the drum of the ear has the asymmetric character necessary for the production of these [difference] tones, and the fact that the middle ear shares this character has been established by Stuhlmann. This prepares us for the fact that the quality of musical notes may be considerably modified by this property of the ear. Analysis of the air vibrations corresponding to certain notes shows a surprising feebleness of the fundamental. It may carry only 1 per cent of the total energy, yet it defines the pitch of the note and is the only constituent tone which is ordinarily heard. It may be noted, however, that if the note consists of the harmonic series of partial tones [1, 2, 3, 4 etc. times the fundamental frequency], then the first order difference for each successive pair of partial tones has the frequency of the fundamental. Thus the quality of the note as perceived by the inner ear may be something entirely different from the quality as revealed by an analysis of the air vibrations external to the ear, and in particular the fundamental may be greatly strengthened.

Corroboration of this view comes from experiments by Fletcher [Journal American Society Acoustical Vol. 9, p. 119 (1937)] using ten different vacuum tube generators adjusted to give the frequencies 100 to 1000 at intervals of 100 Hz. By suitable switching arrangements any individual components could be eliminated. When they were all impressed upon the receiver, a full tone resulted with a definite pitch corresponding to 100 Hz. The elimination of the 100 cycle component produced no appreciable effect. The note still appears to have a pitch corresponding to 100. Even with the first seven components eliminated, leaving only 800, 900 and 1000, the pitch corresponded to a frequency of 100.

[For pitch values see the numbers on the Chromatic Vowel Chart.] Any three successive components were sufficient to give the tone a pitch corresponding to 100, and with four consecutive components the fundamental was very prominent. When a piece of music is produced with all frequencies below 300 is suppressed, the quality is affected to an astonishingly small degree." THIS IS THE AREA OF "THE BREAK!"

The simplest explanation of these results is that the mechanism of the ear displays a non-linear response to external applied forces. [When a sinusoidal wave strikes a membrane and causes it to vibrate in like fashion the vibration is called linear; when a sinusoidal wave strikes a membrane and it does not vibrate sinusoidally because of a load and has work to do the inner ear greatly amplifies the energy in air.]. Then the vibration of that membrane is called nonlinear. This non-linearity produces aural tones.... Békésy maintains that aural overtones are almost certainly produced in the cochlea and difference tones in the middle ear, since their loudness is altered by differences of air pressure and muscle contraction in the ear passages.

Backus THE ACOUSTICAL FORMATIONS OF MUSIC (1969, p. 109) states, "If the reader has gained the impression at this point that we still do not know very much about what constitutes tone quality, he is perfectly correct. Further research will uncover more aspects of the problem, and we may hope that it will also provide some answers. In particular, it may someday be possible to determine what it is that differentiates "good" tone by a musical instrument from one that is not "good." On this subject we are quite ignorant."

We know that people hear the quality of voices differently - look at the diversity in scores in NATS Auditions and other similar events. Aural taste may depend on what the judge hears! Theory teachers know that some ears are good for melodic dictation, others for harmonic dictation, etc. Is that due to the individual assymetry in the ear? We know from the National Auditions of NATS held in Portland, Oregon in 1968 in which all of those in attendance were polled according to placement of winners that the men chose different winners than the women! Moral--if you audition and you are not chosen, there may be others who will like your voice for the role or musical activity with which they are connected.

I would like to add that 100 Hz is about the low A of the Bass voice. To resonate this tone would require a tube about 30 inches long and a bell 10 inches in diameter - WHAT A MOUTH, and WHAT A FACE!

What does this mean to the singer? It means that he is not supposed to imitate other voices because what he hears is partly created by his ear. Instead he should sing the overtones of his voice in such a way that his/her individual voice will sound in the most natural and healthy way. What the singer hears in another voice, in person or on a record, is part illusion; and what he hears and feels from his/her own voice is also an illusion because the ears are placed in such a strange place and the hearing which the singer does have is largely by bone conduction. The singer's feedback is mainly the kinesthetic feel of vibration on the mucous membrane of the mouth and the vibration in various parts of the head. A feedback from the larynx itself usually means something is wrong, hence the statement, "The Italian singer has no throat."

This also means that a singer does not need to employ as "fat" a sound as he/she thinks is needed to give a full sound. The quality of the tone he/she communicates is partly psycho-acoustical. The psychological part is also involved with our natural senses of communicating emotion and feeling. This is a guide to the teacher individualizing voices - place the lower vowel resonance peak on an harmonic of sung pitch. The quality of that individual's voice will reveal itself. G. B. Lamperti said that the individualization of voices was missing in his time. This we must achieve!

VIBRATIONS OF THE VOCAL CORDS

Please see pp. 98, 99 for the different types of vibration of the vocal folds. The collisions in <u>Sharp Voice</u> are the type which occur in Chest Voice - Male and Female. The type shown in <u>Soft Voice</u> can occur in about any register, the kind shown for <u>Falsetto Register</u> applies mainly to female Head Voice and to Sotto Voce in most registers, Male and Female. The play from one form of vocal cord vibration to another is employed in the <u>messa di voce</u>.

APPENDIX K - THE RADIOGRAPHY OF VOWELS AND ITS ACOUSTICAL CORRELATIONS

Dr. Pierre Delattre's "La radiographie des voyelles françaises et sa corélation acoustique" was published in the French Review, Vol. 42:1, pp. 48-65, 1968. An English translation was prepared for publication but was not accepted because it was felt to be too elementary. This happens to be just what we need as a bridge to understand the physical positions and tunings of the vowel elements of language in speech. Motion picture X-Rays of singing indicate the throat is continually tuning in singing but the positions indicated on page 274 will serve as a point of departure. Delattre's speech synthesis was part of a team effort of Delattre, Liberman, Cooper and Gerstman at the Haskin's Laboratory and their "new frontier" publication occurred in 1962. The value of speech synthesis is that various theories of speech can be tested and validated or rejected. His work was entirely with two vowel resonances. My efforts in singing have been involved with 1, 2, 3, or 4 plus a fixed resonance. The singing voice simply does not act on two resonances. This sound is heard on the blatant, pushed [e] vowel heard in many male voices on Notes #20, #21, and #22. The voice will work successfully only when 3 movable resonances are worked, period. That has been my observation over a period of years. Those who wish to train the voice in terms of two vowel resonances will be placing an unnecessary limitation upon the singing voice. In other words, some great colors of singing will be missing. Furthermore, the characteristic resonance of [i] and German [e] are involved with this resonance. That Delattre was a pioneer in the field of language research is attested by the text, "Papers in Linguistics and Phonetics to the Memory of Pierre Delattre." The Hague and Paris, Mouton and Co., 1973. It was my privilege to have been associated with him and it has been my honor to carry on a part of his work. Dr. Delattre has used the term vowel formant rather than vowel resonance.

THE RADIOGRAPHY OF VOWELS AND ITS ACOUSTIC CORRELATIONS
Pierre Delattre
University of California
Santa Barbara

How could one speak of vowels without recalling the phonetics lesson in Molière's Le Bourgeois Gentilhomme:

> PROFESSOR OF PHILOSOPHY: . . . There are five vowels or
> voices: A, E, I, O, U.
> MONSIEUR JOURDAIN: I understand all that.
> P. OF PHIL.: The vowel A is sounded by opening the mouth very
> wide, -- A.
> M. J.: A, A. Yes.

P. OF PHIL.:   The vowel E is sounded by bringing the lower jaw
    to the upper jaw, -- A, E.

M. J.:   A, E; A, E.   Bless me!   How fine that is!

P. OF PHIL.:   The vowel I is formed by bringing the jaws still
    closer together, and stretching the corners of the mouth
    toward the ears, -- A, E, I.

M. J.:   A, E, I, I, I.   That's true.   Hurrah for science!

P. OF PHIL.:   The vowel O is sounded by opening the jaws and
    drawing in the lips at the two corners, -- O.

M. J.:   O, O.   Nothing could be more true.   A, E, I, O, I, O.
    It is admirable!   I, O; I, O.

P. OF PHIL.:   The mouth must be opened exactly like a round O.

M. J.:   O, O, O.   You are right.   O, -- ah!   what a fine thing it
    is to know something!

P. OF PHIL.:   The vowel U is sounded by bringing the teeth
    together without entirely joining them, and protruding the
    lips outwardly, while bringing them narrowly together with-
    out actual contact: O, U.

M. J.:   O, U, U; the truest thing that ever was, -- U.

P. OF PHIL.:   Both your lips should be stretched out as if you
    were making a grimace; so that if you should ever want to
    make a face at any one and ridicule him you have only to say
    "U".

M. J.:   U, U.   True enough.   Ah!   why didn't I learn that in my
    youth?

In reading this celebrated passage one is surprised to find that the distance
which separates popular notion from scientific truth is the same today as in the
17th century.   For Monsieur Jourdain's Professor of Philosophy, "There are
five vowels or voices: A, E, I, O, U," pronounced [a, e, i, o, y] as in
French sa, ses, si, sot, su.   In 1968, for the bourgeois from Philadelphia as
well as the factory worker from Detroit, the number of vowels has not changed.
Ask either one to recite the English vowels, and he will respond with: A, E,
I, O, U, pronounced [éi, i, ái, óu, ju] as in English bay, bee, buy, bow, boo.

In French, as in English, there are in the majority of dialects not five but
fifteen vowels; that is to say, fifteen classes of vocalic sounds (syllable nuclei)
capable of effecting a change of meaning by simple substitution.   The following
sequences of minimal pairs, in which the vowel alone changes, will serve as an
illustration.   For French, lit, lut, loup, les, leu,[1] lot, l'air, l'heure, l'or, là,
las, lin, l'un, lent, long.   For English: keyed, kid, could, cooed, cade, curd,
ked, cud, code, cawed, cad, cod; file, foul, foil.[2]

The Professor of Philosophy knows perfectly well that each vowel in a given
language has a distinctive sound because the mouth assumes a different shape
for each one.   To make Mr. Jourdain understand that, the Professor of

Philosophy limits his description to the outwardly visible organs -- to the widening of the jaw angle: "The vowel A is sounded by opening the mouth very wide . . . The vowel E is sounded by bringing the lower jaw to the upper jaw," and to the rounding of the lips: "The vowel U is sounded by bringing the teeth together without entirely joining them, and protruding the lips outwardly, while bringing them narrowly together without actual contact: U."

Mr. Jourdain was delighted by these summary notions of phonetics. How much greater his wonder would have been had the Professor of Philosophy placed him in front of an x-ray tube and shown him on a television screen what takes place inside his mouth, from the incisors to the pharynx and from the velum to the larynx, during the articulation of these same vowels. Thanks to the recent invention of light intensifiers it is possible today to photograph almost invisible radiographic images (reducing exposure to radiation to an infinitesimal degree) -- the intensifier increases the intensity of the images by a factor of 3000 and makes it visible to the camera. This is done in the same way as when the amplitude of acoustic waves is increased in a radio to make them audible to the ear.

In a well equipped laboratory of phonetic research, any bourgeois gentilhomme, whether curious or scientifically minded, can not only study on a television screen the articulatory gestures, but make a film of these movements and analyze them at leisure. Thanks to special projectors, he can see the film at normal speed, while hearing the speech sounds that were automatically recorded on the film, or see it in slow motion without losing the sound. He can even stop at each frame without time limitations and trace sketches of interesting images.

It was by tracing cineradiographic film images projected on opaque glass that the vowel profiles of Figure 57 were obtained. Note that these profiles do not involve posed photographs, but a selection of frames from cinematographic images made during the actual and natural pronunciation of words, and showing the most characteristic movement of vocalic opening. The speaker for these films is a Frenchman raised in the Loire valley, and without dialectal peculiarities. In this figure, therefore, we find vocal cavity shapes that are sufficiently representative of Northern French. Now let us see what they can teach us.

We shall first glance briefly at Figures 57 and 58, then we will examine in turn the different ways of classifying the vowels from an articulatory, acoustic, and perceptual viewpoint. We shall see that one classification is purely practical, whereas the others have the advantage of explaining the relation between the physical aspect (acoustic) and the physiological aspect (articulatory).

Figure 57 presents the articulatory aspect, exclusively, and Figure 58 the acoustic aspect. The articulatory positions of Figure 57 are, therefore, those which produce the resonance note of Figure 58, and the notes in turn are responsible for the perceptual distinction among vowels.

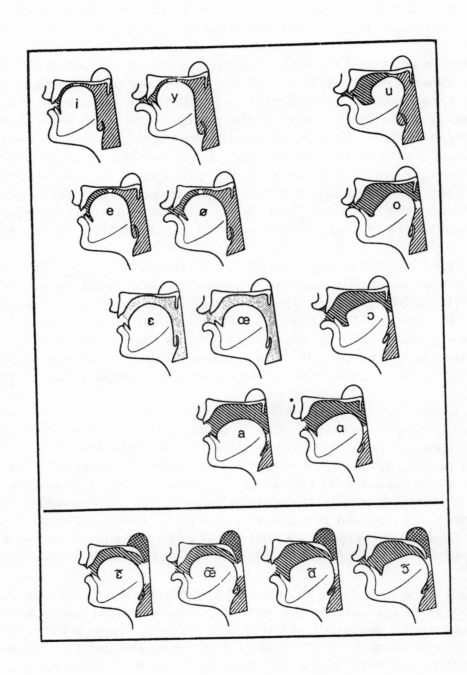

274

(Spaces of the throat in speech.)

Fig. 57.

DELATTRE DIAGRAMS

Permission granted by French
Review to reprint from Vol.
42:1, 1968

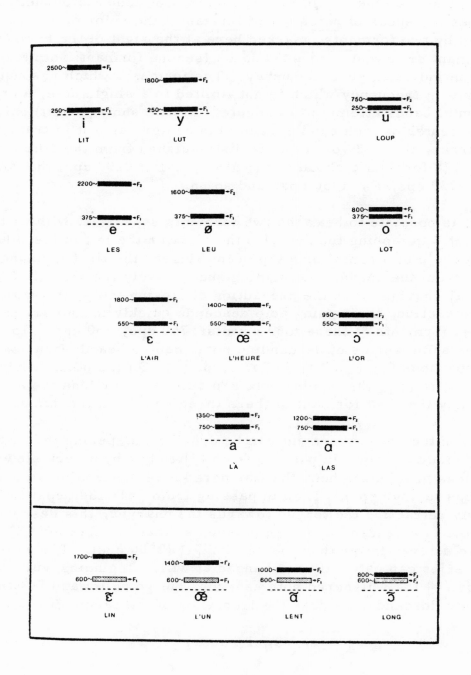

("Pitches" of the vowels in speech.)

Fig. 58.

DELATTRE DIAGRAMS

Permission granted by French Review to reprint from Vol. 42:1, 1968

Acoustics of Vowels

The horizontal bands of Figure 58 represent acoustically the two main resonance notes of the mouth, viewed as a single cavity limited by the lips at one end and the vocal cords at the other.[3] In the terminology of acoustic phonetics, however, one does not speak of notes but of formants; the color of a vowel is characterized by two formants, marked here at the right of the horizontal bands, F_1 (first formant or lowest formant) and F_2 (second formant from the bottom). The dotted line indicates zero frequency. The formants which resonate in the oral cavity have a frequency which is not limited to a single note, as the width of the horizontal bands attempts to indicate. But we show (at left) only the frequency of the center of each band. Using this center value it is traditional to say, for instance, that the vowel [e] is distinguished from the others by a musical chord (a formantic chord): F_1: 375 cps, F_2: 2200 cps; the vowel [a] by a chord: F_1: 750 cps, F_2: 1350 cps, and so on.

Moreover, it is possible to hear the two formants separately without the help of any instrument. In tapping the neck, to the right or the left of the Adam's apple with the help of a pencil or a tap of the finger, the first formant is very well isolated from the second. Assuming successively the articulatory positions of [a, ɔ, o, u], having taken the precaution of closing the glottis with a slight laryngeal contraction, the tapping note descends quickly in four frequency-steps as do the first formants of these four vowels: 750 cps, 550 cps, 375 cps, 250 cps. The same series of descending notes can be heard when assuming the successive positions [a, ɛ, e, i] or [a, œ, ø, y]. On the other hand, passing from [ɛ] to [œ] to [ɔ], the tapping note remains more or less the same; correspondingly the first formant of these three vowels is the same.

The isolation of the second formant can be done by whispering the vowels in a quiet, well-isolated room. In passing from [i] to [y] by a very slow rounding of the lips, it is possible to hear the whispered note descending almost a fifth (from 2500 cps to 1800 cps). Then in passing from [y] (1800 cps) to [u] (750 cps) by slowly retracting the tongue towards the pharynx, this descent of the whispered note is extended beyond an octave, so that the note for [u] (750 cps) is almost two octaves lower than the one for [i] (2500 cps). The ascending or descending series can naturally be changed at will. Beginning with [a], going toward [i] or [y] the whispered note ascends, but going toward [u] the whispered note descends, as does the frequency of the second formant.

Vowel Theory

In producing a vowel, man combines, therefore, two acoustic functions: a source and a resonance -- the source (at the vocal cords) produces a complex tone in a very wide frequency-band, and the resonance (in the cavities above the vocal cords) filters this complex tone allowing only the passage of narrow frequency-bands (formants) which coincide with the resonance notes of the resonator (or resonators) formed by the mouth from the vocal cords to the lips. In spoken-aloud speech, the source is represented by the vibrating vocal cords producing a rich series of harmonic tones (all pure, or sinusoidal), all simple multiples of the fundamental tone (melody or intonation of speech); the formants, then, are the result of only those harmonics which the filtering process of the oral cavities have let pass. In whispered speech, the source is represented by tightened and immobile vocal cords producing a white noise (non-periodic sound) in a very wide frequency-band when the air from the lungs is forced through the glottal slit; the formants, in that case, are narrow bands of noise which the filtering process of the oral cavities have let pass.

What counts in vowel perception is, therefore, not the harmonics (since there are none in whispered speech) but the formants, or frequency-bands, determined by the shape of the mouth. Whether the formants are composed of periodic sound as in the harmonics of the vibrated voice, or of non-periodic sound (turbulent), as in the noise of the whispered voice, they always fulfill their linguistic function in distinguishing between one vowel and another.

Formants of Men, Women, and Children

Generally, formant frequencies are cited as absolute values. This is not altogether correct. The frequencies of Figure 58 are those of a man with average pitch, that is to say of approximately 120 cps. The formants of women are slightly higher -- on the average from 5 to 15 percent higher according to the vowel; those of children are up to 25 percent higher still. These differences are due to the dimensions of the oral cavities which are smaller for women than for men and still smaller for children. From the perceptual viewpoint the human ear is accustomed to identifying the vowels in relation to pitch. On the average, the female voice is higher than the male voice by about an octave (about 240 cps instead of 120 cps for men), because the feminine vocal cords vibrate approximately twice as fast. If a high voice pronounces, for example, an [a], we understand [a] only if the formants are slightly higher than those of a low voice for the same vowel. The following experiment on the speech synthesizer is based upon this perception theory. In synthesizing the word pomme [pɔm] with a fundamental according to a male voice, the two vowel formants are at 550 cps and 950 cps respectively, as for the [ɔ] in Figure 58. To the degree that the fundamental is gradually raised without changing the formant frequencies, the meaning of the word tends to change from pomme with an open [ɔ] to paume [pom] with a closed [o]. The meaning of the word becomes ambiguous if the fundamental has been raised to a point between one and two octaves. In order to re-establish the vowel color that corresponds to pomme, the frequency of the two formants must be slightly raised. This experiment is favored by the fact that the two formants rise almost in parallel fashion in going from [ɔ] to [o].

X   X   X

After these fundamental notions about the acoustic properties of vowels, let us return to Figure 57 which presents their articulatory aspect.

We must first identify in our sketches the organs which come into play in the formation of a vowel. Let us proceed from left to right. The lips can be flat against the teeth or protruded, and they can be spread or rounded according to whether the corners of the lips are distant from each other or close together; they follow in other respects the widening of the jaw angle. In French, the widening implies the flattening of the lips; the rounding, the protruding of the lips.

The upper and lower incisors are located respectively in the upper maxillary and lower maxillary bone (mandible). We can see in the drawings, inside the chin, the tip of the lower maxillary. When the mouth opens, this maxillary pivots on its point of attachment to the skull (condyle of the mandible), while the upper maxillary remains immobile. This condyle is visible by x-ray, just to the right of the cushion of Passavant which forms the point of contact between the velum and the pharyngeal wall, when the velic passage is closed to prevent nasalization.

To the right of the upper lip, in the drawings of Figure 57, is a bone, which is attached to the upper maxillary and which extends more than half way through the palate to the point where a thickening is seen. From here to the right-hand extremity the palate is formed by a muscular membrane and is called the soft palate or velum. In the x-rays of the oral vowels of Figure 57, one has the impression that the velum ends in a right angle; in reality, the wide end of the velum lies against the vertical wall of the pharynx to permit closure of the velic passage so that the nasal and oral cavities can communicate; and the appendage which hangs vertically is the projection, called "uvula," which can be seen between the tonsils when opening the mouth widely to say Ah. This uvula vibrates and periodically touches the tongue during the pronunciation of the uvular R.

With the nasal vowels, seen at the bottom of Figure 57, this same velum lowers for the opening of the velic passage and permits the small rhino-pharyngeal cavity (indicated by the cross-ruled area) to combine its resonance with that of the oral cavity for the distinctive effect of nasality.[4]

The vertical line to the right is the wall of the pharynx. The pharynx is the rear part of the mouth, or, more simply, the throat. Its forward boundary is the root of the tongue which forms a vertical wall for [i] and a pharyngeal constriction for [a].

The horizontal line which defines the base of the pharynx represents, for four-fifths on the left side, the vocal cords (between which is the glottis). These cords, in the center of the larynx, are at the upper end of the trachea which conducts the air pressure from the lungs, pressure which is controlled by the intercostal muscles.

To the right of the vocal cords, extending from the pharyngeal wall, is the narrow entrance to the esophagus which takes food to the stomach. The little flap which rises against the base of the tongue is the epiglottis whose role it is to cover the glottis during the process of swallowing and to direct the food toward the esophagus.

Finally, the tongue, key to phonation because of the variety of forms it is able to assume, is generally divided into tip, blade (upper side adjacent to the tip), dorsum (front, back) and root. We mean by root that part which faces the pharyngeal wall, by dorsum that which faces the palate, and by tip that which faces the incisors or the alveoles; but it is possible, in retroflex sounds, to see the tip move toward the palate.

The Tongue-Hump: Inadequacy of the Phonetic Triangle

The first phoneticians, from Paul Passy, creator of the phonetic alphabet, to Daniel Jones, his successor as president of the International Phonetic Association, established the traditional phonetic triangle based upon the highest point of the tongue.

In order to envision this triangle, one has only to imagine that the articulatory profiles of [i], [a], and [u], (Figure 57) are superimposed in such a way that the palates coincide. Then the highest point of the tongue, in relation to the palate, forms a triangle with [i] at upper left, [u] at upper right, and [a] at bottom center. The other vowels can be inserted more or less arbitrarily between [a] and [i] or between [a] and [u]. According to Figure 57, the vowels [e, ø, ε, œ] would each have their highest point of the tongue close to the [a-i] line, and the vowels [o-ɔ] would have theirs close to the [a-u] line.

This phonetic triangle has rendered great service in the field of historical phonetics. It explains with rare simplicity the tongue positions in two dimensions: front-back and high-low (or closed-open if one thinks in terms of the separation of the jaws which accompanies the lowering of the tongue). Unfortunately, the articulatory triangle has shortcomings with respect to the acoustics and the perception of vowels. First of all, it only takes into account the tongue; consequently it classifies [y] at the same point as [i] (these two vowels having nearly the same tongue position), [ø] at the same point as [e], etc. Furthermore, and this is more serious, it does not indicate what is most relevant to linguistic perception -- the highest point of the tongue has no direct relationship with the frequency of the acoustic resonances which distinguish vowels from one another perceptually. For the identification of vowel [a], for instance, it is not the low level of the tongue-hump which counts acoustically, but rather the pharyngeal constriction which is formed between the root of the tongue and the wall of the pharynx. It is the place and narrowness of this constriction which is critical. This constriction separates the mouth into two cavities each of which favors a certain resonance (without being entirely independent as long as they communicate). It is, therefore, as we shall see later when considering the mouth as a cylinder, the distance which separates this constriction from the other constrictions at the lips and at the glottis which explains the frequency of the first and second formants.

The x-rays of Figure 57 fortunately allow us to make other classifications better related to the now known acoustic reality of vowels.

Tongue Constrictions

Starting with the profile, in Figure 57, and proceeding to the right, one can observe that the tongue constrictions circle the walls of the mouth -- the constriction of [a] is low in the pharynx, that of [ɑ] is a little higher, toward the middle of the pharynx, those of [ɔ] and [o] are higher still, in the upper portion of the pharynx; for [u] the constriction reaches the velum, for [y] and [i] it advances up to the hard palate, for [ø] and [e] it widens and draws back slightly toward the pharynx, from where the [a] constriction started.

As for [œ] and [ɛ], these vowels have, so to speak, no constriction. For them, the mouth assumes the shape of a cylindrical tube of somewhat uniform diameter. The tube for [ɛ] is the shorter and more open of the two. It is for [œ], the neutral vowel, that the mouth best resembles the simple shape of a uniform tube. Figuratively speaking, one can consider the vowels [œ] and [ɛ] as a bridge between those which have a constriction at the palate and those which have one at the pharynx, thus closing the circle of vocalic constrictions.

The nasal vowels (lower row in Figure 57) have this in particular that they always form their tongue constriction at the pharynx, just below the tip of the lowered velum. We shall see later the significance of this fact.

Lip Constriction

The constrictive play of the lips, although less varied than that of the tongue is also very important. As one can see in the profiles of Figure 57, it is principally the labial constriction (rounding) which changes [i] to [y], [e] to [ø], [ɛ] to [œ], [ɛ̃] to [œ̃], and [ɑ̃] to [ɔ̃] and, at least partially, modifies [a] to [ɑ]. This labial constriction is, therefore, comparable in importance to the displacement of the tongue constriction along the walls of the pharynx and palate which plays the principal role in changing [y] to [u], [ø] to [o], [œ] to [ɔ], and [a] to [ɑ].

Velic Constriction

The velum when lowered forms a constriction called velic which contributes greatly to the change from [ɛ] to [ɛ̃], [œ] to [œ̃], [ɔ] to [ɔ̃], and [ɑ] to [ɑ̃]. We intentionally say "contributes" because the articulatory position of the nasals is quite different from those of the corresponding orals, as is well shown in the x-rays of Figure 57. Thus, the front cavity for [ɔ] is more like the one for [o] than like the one for [ɔ]; the back cavity for [ɑ̃] bears more resemblance to the one for [ɔ] than to the one for [ɑ]. Moreover, duration plays a certain role in the nasal/oral distinction.

Glottal Constriction

Finally, the vocal cords themselves form a constriction, whether in the position for vibration or for whispering. One becomes aware of this when tapping the throat close to the Adam's apple in order to hear the resonance note of the first formant for [ɛ], for example. During this procedure, if one opens the glottis as if for breathing, the resonance note disappears, or becomes so low that one can no longer discern it. Such deterioration of the resonance process occurs because the pharyngeal cavity has now been lengthened by the trachea and the volume of the pharyngeal cavity is immeasurably increased.

Furthermore, the glottal constriction plays a role when falling or rising with the entire larynx -- lowering the larynx increases the total length of the mouth cavity or of the pharyngeal cavity. One sees in Figure 57, for instance, that the glottis is considerably lower for [u] than for [ɑ].

Resonance Cavities and Formants

The tongue constrictions which we have just described tend to divide the mouth into two resonance cavities. Theoretically, since these cavities communicate, they do not resonate separately, and each modification of one of the two affects the frequency of both. But practically speaking, one may consider the frequency of the first formant as related to the back cavity (pharynx) and that of the second formant to the front cavity. The more narrow the constriction the more negligible is the element of error. (In the x-rays of Figure 57, we distinguished between front and back cavities by using different hachures.)

The resonance formula which applies here is simple: the larger the cavity and the smaller and longer its opening, the lower its note of resonance; and conversely. Let us add immediately that due to the play of compensations, a cavity of little volume and small opening (two opposing effects) can have the same frequency as a cavity of large volume and large opening (also two opposing effects).

Correlations Between the Back Cavity and the First Formant

According to Figure 57, the back cavities for [i] and [y] (top row) have almost the same large volume and small opening (tongue constriction). Accordingly, in Figure 58 the first formants of these two vowels have about the same frequency.

The same observation applies to the vowels [e] and [ø]: their back cavities are similar as are their first formants.

It also applies to the nasal vowels [ɛ̃, œ̃, ɑ̃, ɔ̃] (bottom row); their back cavities are similar (Figure 57) as are their first formants (Figure 58).

In the series [u, o, ə, ɑ] the volume of the back cavity decreases regularly. The frequency of the first formant, however, increases in this same order, thus illustrating the fact that the smaller the cavity, the higher its resonance note. The series [y, ø, a] and [i, e, a] illustrate the same law. Note here that the [a] type vowels have the smallest back cavity and of all the vowels the highest frequency for the first formant. (The fact that the back cavity of [u] and [o] is smaller than that of [y] and [ø], respectively, although their first formants hardly differ, is attributable to the lowering effect of the front cavity which is large and closed, hence has a low resonance frequency.)

Correlations Between the Front Cavity and the Second Formant

In examining Figure 57, we will first make comparisons among certain profiles. In passing from [i] to [y], the rounding of the lips considerably reduces the opening of the front cavity and slightly increases its volume. Theoretically, both effects should contribute to lowering the resonance note of this cavity. Figure 58 shows, in fact, that in passing from [i] to [y], the frequency of the second formant is considerably lowered.

In passing from [y] to [u] the retraction of the tongue constriction increases the volume of the front cavity which should lower the resonance note of this cavity even further. Figure 58 shows, in fact, that in passing from [y] to [u] the frequency of the second formant is greatly lowered.

The same logic can be applied to the second row of profiles, but with less pronounced effects. Let us compare [e] to [ø]. The rounding of the lips for [ø] lessens the opening and enlarges the volume of the front cavity. This should theoretically lower its resonance note. Accordingly, the second formant is lower for [ø] than for [e].

Let us compare [ø] to [o]. The retraction of the tongue constriction for [o] increases the volume of the front cavity. This should result in a lower resonance note for [o] than for [ø]. Thus, as is shown in Figure 58, the second formant is lower for [o] than for [ø].

The influence of the lips is again visible in the nasals. In comparing [ɛ̃] to [œ̃], we see that lip rounding reduces the opening and increases the volume of the front cavity. Accordingly, a lowering of the second formant frequency appears in Figure 58.

Let us compare [ɑ̃] and [ɔ̃]. Lip rounding strongly reduces the opening of the front cavity. This correlates in Figure 58 with a lowering of the second formant frequency (in spite of a slight decrease in front-cavity volume).

Let us now compare the front cavity of the vowels which are at the three corners of the triangle.

The front cavity of [i] is very small and since the corners of the lips are spread, the opening of the cavity is medium. It is natural, therefore, that the second formant of [i] be higher than for any other vowel.

On the contrary, the front cavity for [u] is large and its opening very small. One should, therefore, expect the second formant of [u] to be very low; it is, in fact, the lowest of all, but followed closely by [o] (which is distinguished from [u] by the first formant more than by the second).

What can now be said about [a]? It offers a case of compensation. Whereas for [i] there is a concordant effect between the smallness of the front cavity and the largeness of the opening, and for [u] a concordant effect between the largeness of the front cavity and the smallness of the opening, for [a] there is an opposing effect between the largeness of the front cavity and the largeness of the opening. The fact that the front cavity for [a] is very large (which should result in a very low note) is largely compensated for by its immense opening (which causes the frequency to rise). Thus, we have an explanation for the second formant of [a] being intermediate in relation to [i] and [u].

The Chord of the Two Resonance Notes

A brief look at the cavities of the vowels in Figure 57 should now enable us to predict the formant frequencies of those vowels.

The vowel [i], formed by a very large and closed back cavity and a very small and open front cavity, should be characterized by the combination of a very low and a very high note. The vowel [u], formed by two cavities which are both large and closed, should be characterized by two low notes. The vowel [a], formed by a small and closed back cavity (two opposing factors), and a large and open front cavity (again two opposing factors) should be characterized by two medium notes. These assumptions are confirmed in Figure 58.

The resonance notes of the other oral vowels can be explained by the intermediate positions they have in relation to the above three.

All the nasal vowels have a medium and slightly closed back cavity with a resonance note that is comparatively high (according to the scale of the first formants). They are distinguished from one another by the front cavity which is medium and open for [ɛ̃], medium and closed (corners drawn together) for [œ̃], large and open for [ɑ̃], large and closed for [ɔ̃]. This should produce four different resonance notes ranging from middle-high for [ɛ̃] to low for [ɔ̃]. Figure 58 confirms that assumption -- the nasal vowels are distinguished from each other by their first formant alone.

The nasal vowels, by lowering the velum, add a third cavity to the resonance system. This nasal cavity acts upon the back cavity (pharyngeal): it damps the resonance, and even cancels some of its harmonics by means of counter-resonance. The perception of nasality is, thus, simply the result of an un-balance in the relative intensities of the formants -- the first formant is now much weaker than the second. (To show this lowering of the first-formant intensity these formants are shaded in gray, in Figure 58, in contrast to the solid black of their oval counterparts.)

The Mouth Seen as a Tube

In the two sections on the correlation between mouth cavities (front, back) and formants (second, first), we intentionally did not examine the particular aspect of the vowels [ɛ] and [œ] for which the mouth is not clearly divided into two cavities. In order to explain the frequency of the formants of these two vowels, we have to call upon a totally different theory which, though more exactly applicable than the others, is too demanding from the viewpoint of mathematical knowledge to be more than summarily presented here.

According to this theory, all vowels are explained as modifications of a neutral vowel which is produced in a cylindrical tube of uniform diameter. (We can see in Figure 57 that for [œ] and [ɛ] the shape of the mouth resembles that of a tube.) In a long, uniform tube, the resonance frequency depends solely upon the length of the tube, not upon its width or its volume. From a tube of 17.5 centimeters (average length of a man's mouth) closed at one end (the glottis) and open at the other (the lips), result resonances of 500 cps (first formant), 1500 cps (second formant), 2500 cps (third formant), 3500 cps (fourth formant), etc., which correspond to one-quarter of a wave length, three-quarters of a wave length, five-quarters of a wave length, etc., of a 17.5 cm tube in which the speed of sound is 3500 cm per second. The frequencies of 500 cps and 1500 cps are close to those of the first two formants of [œ]: 550 cps and 1400 cps or of [ɛ]: 550 cps and 1800 cps.[5]

Here you have to recall your first physics course of long ago. The resonance of one-quarter of a wave length (first formant) forms a node at the closed extremity (glottis) of the tube and a loop (anti-node) at its open extremity (lips). The resonance of three-quarters of a wave length (second formant) forms two nodes and two loops, one node at the closed extremity (glottis), one loop at one-third of the tube length, one node at two-thirds of the tube length, and one loop at the open extremity (lips). The formant frequency of every vowel can be found by applying the following laws separately to its two lowest modes of resonance (one-quarter of a wave length and three-quarters of a wave length): The frequency of a mode of resonance rises or falls according to whether the constriction approaches a node or a loop, respectively. Thus, the pharyngeal constriction of [ɑ] (see Figure 57) is near a node (near the glottis) of the first mode of resonance (one-quarter of a wave length); hence, the first formant is higher than for the neutral vowel, that is to say, higher than 500 cps. This pharyngeal constriction is at the same time near a loop of the second mode of resonance (three-quarters of a wave length); hence, the second formant is lower than the one of the neutral vowel, that is to say, lower than 1500 cps. Accordingly, the formant frequencies of [a] are approximately 750 cps and 1300 cps (Figure 58).

For [e] -- another example -- the palatal constriction is near a loop of the first mode (near the lips); hence, the first formant is lower than 500 cps. At the same time, the [e] constriction is near a node of the second mode of resonance; hence the second formant is higher than 1500 cps. Accordingly, the formants of [e] are approximately at 375 cps and 2200 cps, in Figure 40.

Distinctive Acoustic Features

According to Figure 58, a vowel can be distinguished from another one by one, two, or three acoustic features.

A single distinctive feature. Example: [e] is distinguished from [ø] by the frequency of the second formant alone. This condition exists in all the rows of Figure 57 -- the vowels of the same row are distinguished from one another solely by the frequency of the second formant. Thus, acoustically speaking, [i] is distinguished from [u] by a single feature, [ɛ̃] from [ɔ̃] by a single feature: the second-formant frequency. This creates a problem since, from the traditional viewpoint, such vowels are distinguished from one another by at least two articulatory features: the rounding of the lips and the retraction of the tongue! In perceptual terms, a question arises which has not been answered: Does the brain perceive the color distinction between two vowels directly by means of the formant-frequency waves which strike the ear drums, or indirectly by reference to the articulatory features which produce those formant frequencies?[6]

The distinction 'nasal vowel/oral vowel' can also be considered as principally determined by a single acoustic feature, the intensity of the first formant, as long as the nasal vowel approximates the formant frequencies as its oral counterpart. This is to a certain extent the case for the pairs [ɛ/ɛ̃] and [œ/œ̃] but much less for the pairs [ɔ/ɔ̃] and [a/ɑ̃].

<u>Two distinctive features</u>:   From one row to another row, in Figure 39, the oral vowels are generally distinguished by two acoustic differences. Thus, the formants composing [y] are at 250 cps and 1800 cps, those for [ɔ] at 550 cps and 950 cps. In two particular cases of Figure 58, however, the distinction seems mainly attributable to the first formant alone. These are the pairs [y/ε] and [u/o].

<u>Three distinctive features</u>:   Except in the cases mentioned above where a nasal vowel has an oral counterpart, all nasal vowels are distinguished from oral vowels by three acoustical differences: the frequency of the first formant, the frequency of the second formant and the intensity of the first formant.

Let us mention a fourth feature (but merely in passing, since in French it is either unstable or secondary). Vowel <u>duration</u> distinguishes <u>maître</u> from <u>mettre</u>; besides, it contributes to the distinction of <u>paume</u> from <u>pomme</u>, <u>tâche</u> from <u>tache</u>, of <u>cinq</u> from <u>sec</u>, but then, duration is conditioned by vowel color, hence, not separately distinctive.[7]

It goes without saying that the auditory confusion between two vowels is reduced in direct proportion to the number of features which separate them. Thus, in a crowded room where everyone is speaking at the same time, <u>bulle</u> is more easily confused with <u>boule</u> than with <u>balle</u>.

Thus, in French, four acoustic features serve to distinguish fifteen vowels from one another: the frequency of the first formant, the frequency of the second formant, the intensity of the first formant and the duration of the two formants. The acoustic facts are very clear; the articulatory facts and their role in perception are unfortunately less clear.

X   X   X

Let us summarize. Using x-rays of vowels taken from cineradiographic films of speech which show the entire oral cavity from the vocal cords to the lips, we have confronted the traditional vowel classifications with new descriptions justified by these x-rays. It has enabled us to show that the vocalic formants which are responsible for the perception of vowels have no direct relationship to the highest point of the tongue (traditional classification), but are explained (a) by the place of constriction in the mouth and (b) by the shape and volume of the two main mouth-cavities (front and back) or (c) by envisaging the mouth as a uniform tube and the vocalic positions as modifications of the tube through the formation of constrictions.

Thus, the examination of cineradiographic frames serves to explain the real relationship that exists between the acoustic aspect and the articulatory aspect of vowels, and allows one to judge objectively the superficial notions passed on by tradition.[8]

FOOTNOTES

[1] Medieval term for wolf, retained in the expression à la queue leu leu.

[2] The Professor of Philosophy's error, like that of Rimbaud in the sonnet Vowels, stems from the confusion between 'letters' and 'vowels'. In writing the 15 different vocalic sounds of French, one makes use of only 5 characters -- the Latin letters a, e, i, o, u -- which explains the chaos of our spelling and the difficulty which our poor children have in learning it.

[3] In French Review for May, 1948 (Vol. 21, pp. 477-484) appear spectrograms of oral vowels of a French speaker, made on the first spectrograph from the Bell Telephone Laboratories, in the spring of 1947. They mark an historic date; the very first publication of spectrograms with a linguistic intent, and they have been reproduced in PMLA for September, 1951 (Vol. 66, pp. 864-875) and in Studies in French and Comparative Phonetics, The Hague, Mouton, 1966, p. 239.

[4] For an acoustical, articulatory and perceptual discussion of nasality, see French Review, October, 1965 (Vol. 40, pp. 218-223).

[5] We have not mentioned the third formant because it varies only slightly -- it remains near 2500 cps for all the vowels, except for [i] where it reached 3000 cps. The third formant, thus, is not distinctive, or at least only slightly. The higher formants have really no linguistic function -- rather they determine the quality of the voice.

[6] For a discussion of this question, see: "Acoustic or articulatory invariance?" Glossa (Vol. 1:1, 1967, pp. 3-25).

[7] The problems of vocalic duration are discussed in French Review, October, 1959 (Vol. 32, pp. 547-553), in Studies in French and Comparative Phonetics, The Hague, Mouton, 1966, pp. 105-141, and in Comparing the Phonetics Features of English, German, Spanish, and French, Philadelphia, Chilton Books, 1965, pp. 63-66.

[8] The research reported herein was performed pursuant to a contract with the U.S. Department of Health, Education, and Welfare, Office of Education.

Reprinted by the kind permission of Dr. Genevieve Delattre.

BIBLIOGRAPHY

Aikin, W. A. The Voice, An Introduction to Practical Phonology. New York: Longmans, Green, 1927.

American Academy. "A recommendation for the correction of pitch involving the performance of music from 1620-1820." NATS Bulletin, Dec., 1974.

Appelman, D. Ralph. The Science of Vocal Pedagogy. Bloomington, Indiana, University Press, 1967.

Backus, John. The Acoustical Foundations of Music. New York: Norton & Co., 1969.

Bartholomew, Wilmer T. Acoustics of Music. New York: Prentice Hall, 1942.

Bell, Alexander Melville. Visible Speech: the Science of Universal Alphabetics.

Benade, Arthur H. Fundamentals of Musical Acoustics. London: Oxford, 1976.

Benade, Arthur H. Horns, Strings, and Harmony. Garden City, New York: Doubleday & Co., 1960.

Benade, Arthur H. "The Physics of Brasses." Scientific American, July 1973, p. 24.

Beranek, Leo. Music, Acoustics and Architecture. New York and London: John Wiley and Sons, Inc., 1962.

Biancolli, Louis. The Flagstad Manuscript. New York: G. P. Putnam's Sons, 1952.

Boone, Daniel R. Voice and Voice Therapy. Englewood Cliffs, N. J.: Prentice Hall, 1971.

Brodnitz, Friedrich S. Vocal Rehabilitation. Rochester, Minn.: Whiting Press, Inc., 1959.

Brower, Harriette. Vocal Mastery (Talks with Master Singers and Teachers). New York: F. A. Stokes Co., 1920.

Brown, William Earl. (G. B. Lamperti) Vocal Wisdom. Boston: Crescendo Publishers, 1931.

Caruso, Enrico. (See Fucito.)

(Caruso) Marafiotti, P. Mario. Caruso's Method of Voice Production. Austin, Texas: Cadica Enterprises, 1950 (former copyright by D. Appleton & Co., 1922).

Chiba, T. and M. Kajiyama. The Vowel, Its Nature and Structure. Tokyo: Phonetic Society of Japan, 1958.

Coffin, Berton. "The Instrumental Resonance of the Singing Voice." NATS Bulletin, Dec., 1974.

Coffin, Berton. "The Relationship of Phonation and Resonation." NATS Bulletin, Feb., 1975.

Coffin, Berton. "The Relationship of Breath, Phonation and Resonance in Singing." NATS Bulletin, Dec., 1975.

Coffin, Berton. "Articulation for Opera, Oratorio, and Recital." NATS Bulletin, Feb., 1976.

Coffin, Berton. Overtones of Bel Canto. Metuchen, N. J.: The Scarecrow Press, 1980.

Coffin, B., Errole, R., Singer, W., Delattre, P. Phonetic Readings of Songs and Arias (The Singer's Repertoire Series). Metuchen, N. J.: The Scarecrow Press, 1982.

Cooke, James Francis. Great Singers on the Art of Singing. Philadelphia: Presser, 1921.

(Corelli) Honan, Wm. H. "A Champion Tenor Defends His Title." New York: New York Times Magazine, Feb. 8, 1970.

Corri, Domenico. The Singer's Preceptor. London: 1810. Facsimile by E. Foreman in The Porpora Tradition. Champaign, Ill.: Pro Musica Press, 1968.

Curtis, H. Holbrook. Voice Building and Tone Placing. New York: D. Appleton & Co., 1909.

(Delattre) Valdman, Albert, Editor. Papers in Linguistics and Phonetics to the Memory of Pierre Delattre. The Hague and Paris: Mouton and Co., 1973.

Delattre, Pierre. "Acoustic cues for the perception of initial w, j, r, l in English." WORD, 13, 1: 24-43, 1957.

Delattre, Pierre. "Change as a correlate of the vowel-consonant distinction." Studia Linguistica. Vol. 18, 1965.

Delattre, Pierre. Comparing the Phonetic Features of English, French, German, and Spanish. Heidelberg: Julius Groos Verlag, 1965.

Delattre, Pierre. "La radiographie des voyelles françaises et sa corrélation acoustique." The French Review, 42, 1: 48-65, 1968.

Delattre, Pierre. Studies in French and Comparative Phonetics. The Hague: Mouton and Co., 1966.

Delattre, Pierre. "The Physiological Interpretation of Sound Spectrograms." Publication of the Modern Language Association of America, Vol. LXVI, #5, Sept., 1951.

Delattre, Pierre. "Vowel Color and Voice Quality (An Acoustic and Articulatory Comparison)." Chicago: NATS Bulletin, Oct. 1958.

Delattre, P., Liberman, A. M., Cooper, F. S., Gerstman, L. J. "An Experimental Study of the Acoustic Determinants of Vowel Color; Observations on One and Two-Formant Vowels Synthesized from Spectrographic Patterns." New York: Haskins Laboratory, reprinted from WORD, Dec. 1952.

Delattre, Pierre, Liberman, A. M., Cooper, F. S. "Formant transitions and loci as acoustical correlates of place of articulation in American fricatives." Studia Linguistica. Vol. 15, 1961-62.

DeReszke, Jean (Chapter by Walter Johnstone-Douglas on "Jean DeReszke's Principles of Singing" in the book - Jean DeReszke - Clara Leiser.) New York: Minton, Balch & Co., 1934.

(DeReszke) Leiser, Clara. Jean DeReszke. New York: Minton, Balch & Co., 1934.

Domingo, Placido. My First Forty Years. New York: Alfred A. Knopf, 1983.

(Domingo) Walker, Gerald. "The More I Sing, The Better I Sound." New York: New York Times Magazine, Feb. 27, 1972.

(Ellis, A.) See Helmholtz, H. L. F.

Emmons, Shirlee. Schumann-Heink, Ernestine, Pt. II, NATS Bulletin, May/June 1984.

(Flagstad) Biancolli, Louis. The Flagstad Manuscript. New York: G. P. Putnam's Sons, 1952.

Fletcher, H. Speech and Hearing in Communication. New York: Van Nostrand, 1953.

Fritzell, Björn. The Velopharyngeal Muscles in Speech. Göteborg: Orstadius Boktryckeri Aktiebolag, 1969.

Fucito, Salvatore and S. Beyer. Caruso and the Art of Singing. New York: F. A. Stokes Co., 1929.

Garcia, Manuel (del Popolo Vicente). Exercises Pour la Voix. Paris: Petit, 1821.

Garcia, Manuel II. The Art of Singing, Part I. Boston: Oliver Ditson, ab. 1855.

Garcia, Manuel II. A Complete Treatise on the Art of Singing, Part I. Translated by Donald V. Paschke. New York: Da Capo Press, 1984.

Garcia, Manuel II. A Complete Treatise on the Art of Singing, Part II. Translated by Donald V. Paschke. Comparison of 1847 and 1872 editions. New York: Da Capo Press, 1975.

Garcia, Manuel II. Hints on Singing. London: Ascherberg & Co.; New York: Schuberth & Co., 1894. Available in H. Klein 1911 revision from Chappell, London, 50 New Bond St., W 1, London, England.

Garcia, Manuel II. Memoire on the Human Voice. Paris: 1841. Translated & copyrighted, Donald V. Paschke, Eastern New Mexico University, Portales, N. M., 1970.

Garcia, Manuel II. "Observations of the Human Voice!" London: Royal Society, 1855.

Garcia, Manuel II. Traite Complete de l'Art du Chant, in two parts. Paris: Heugel, 1872.

Garcia, Manuel II. Trattato Completa dell'Arte del Canto, Part I. Milano: G. Ricordi, 1949.

(Garcia, Manuel II) See McKinlay, M. S.

Gatti-Casazza, Giulio. Memories of the Opera. New York: Charles Scribner's & Sons, 1941.

(Harvard Dictionary) Apel, Willi. "Combination Tone, " 1967, p. 164.

Helmholtz, Hermann L. F. On the Sensations of Tone (fourth and last edition). New York: Dover Publications, Inc., 1954 (new); 1877 (old); 1885 (A. Ellis trans.).

Henderson, W. J. The Art of the Singer. New York: Scribner's Sons, 1910.

Herbert-Caesari, E. The Voice of the Mind. London: Robert Hale Ltd., 1963.

Hines, Jerome. Great Singers on Great Singing. Garden City, N. Y.: Doubleday, 1982.

Honan, Wm. H. (See Corelli)

(Horne, Marilyn) The New York Times Magazine, Jan. 17, 1971.

(Horne, Marilyn) Musical America, May 1970.

Husler, Frederick and Yvonne Rodd-Marling. Singing: The Physical Nature of the Vocal Organ. London: Faber & Faber, 1965.

Husson, Raoul. Physiologie de la Phonation. Paris: Masson et C^{1e}, 1962.

IPA. The Principles of the International Phonetic Association. University College, Gower Street, London, WC 1 E 6 BT.

Jackson, Chevalier. "Myasthenia laryngis observations on the larynx as an air column instrument. " Archives Otolaryngology, Vol. 30. p. 434. 1940.

Joal, Dr. On Respiration in Singing. London: F. J. Rebman, 1895.

Jones, Daniel. An Outline of English Phonetics. New York: Dutton, 1940.

Kay, Elster. Bel Canto and the Sixth Sense (The Student's Music Library Series). London: Dobson Books, Ltd., 1963. Chester Springs, Pa.: Dufour Editions, Inc., 1963.

Kolodin, Irvin. "The Legendary Lily. " Saturday Review, June 24, 1972.

Kolodin, Irvin. "Richard Tucker." Opera News, Apr. 12, 1975.

(Kraus, Alfredo) Opera. London, Jan. 1975.

Lamperti, Francesco. The Art of Singing (Revised, edited, translated,
    J. C. Griffith), Vol. 1587, Schirmer's Library of Musical Classics.
    New York: G. Schirmer, Inc., 1890.

Lamperti, Giovanni Battista. See William Earl Brown.

Lamperti, Giovanni Battista with Maximilian Heidrich. The Technics of Bel
    Canto (translated, Th. Baker). New York: G. Schirmer, Inc., 1905;
    Berlin: Albert Stahl.

Lamperti, Giovanni Battista (recorded, William Earl Brown). Vocal Wisdom
    (Enlarged Edition, Supplement edited by L. Strongin). Dresden: Notes
    to W. E. Brown, 1891-1893. New York: Arno Press, 1931 and 1957.

Large, John. "Acoustic-Perceptual Evaluations of Register Equalization."
    NATS Bulletin, Oct. 1974.

Lehmann, Lilli (translated, Richard Aldrich). How To Sing (Meine Gesangs-
    kunst). New York: Macmillan Co., 1902 and 1914.

Leiser, Clara. Jean DeReszke and the Great Days of Opera. New York:
    Minton, Balch & Co., 1934.

Lombardi, Gioacchino. "Equipment of the True Vocal Teacher." The
    Musician, March 1940.

Luchsinger, Richard and Godfrey E. Arnold. Voice-Speech-Language (Clinical
    Communicology; Its Physiology and Pathology). Contributor, Fritz
    Winckel. Vienna: Springer-Verlag (German), 1949. London: Constable
    & Co., 1959. Belmont, California: Wadsworth Publishing Co., 1965.

Lunn, Charles. The Voice, Its Downfall. London: Reynolds, 1904.

Mackworth-Young. What Happens in Singing. London: Newman Neame, 1953.

McKinlay, M. S. Garcia the Centenarian. New York: D. Appleton & Co.,
    1908. Reprint by Da Capo Press, Inc., New York, 1976.

Mancini, Giambattista. Practical Reflections on the Figurative Art of Singing.
    Boston: (translation of the 1777 edition), The Gorham Press, 1912.

Marafioti, P. Mario. Caruso's Method of Voice Production. Austin, Texas: Cadica Enterprises, 1950.

Marchesi, Mathilde. Marchesi Vocal Method, Pt. I & II, Opus 31. Schirmer Library Series. New York: G. Schirmer, Inc., 1905.

Merrill, Nathaniel. "Opera's Tightrope Walker," New York Times Magazine, March 14, 1969.

Miller, Dayton C. The Science of Musical Sounds. New York: Macmillan Co., 1916.

(Musical America) See Horne, M.

Nathan, Isaac. Musurgis Vocalis. London: Fentum, 1836.

(New York Times) See Horne, M.

(New York Times) See Novikova, P.

Nilsson, Birgit. "Nilsson on Wagner." Opera News, Oct. 10, 1970.

(Novikova). "Novikova Taught Singers." New York Times, Aug. 24, 1967.

Opera (Kraus, A.).

Opera News (Kolodin).

Opera News (Nilsson).

Paget, Sir Richard. Human Speech. New York: Harcourt Brace & Co., 1930.

(Paschke, D.) See Garcia, M. II.

Pellegrini-Celloni, Anna Maria. Grammatica O Siano Regole Per Ben Cantare. Rome: 1817.

Peterson, G. D. and H. L. Barney. "Control Methods Used in a Study of the Vowels." Journal Accoustical Society of America, Vol. 24, No. 2, March 1950, p. 175-184.

Pleasants, Henry. The Great Singers. New York: Simon and Schuster, 1966.

Potter, R. K., G. A. Kopp & H. G. Kopp. Visible Speech. New York: Dover Publications, 1966.

Rockstro, W. B. Jenny Lind, A Record and Analysis of Her Method. London and New York: Novello, Ewer & Co., 1894.

Russell, G. O. and J. C. Cotton. Causes of Good and Bad Voices. Washington, D. C.: National Research Foundation and Carnegie Institute of Washington, catalogued, 1959.

Saturday Review (Kolodin).

Scripture, E. W. Researches in Experimental Phonetics. Washington, D. C.: Carnegie Institute of Washington, 1906.

Scripture, E. W. "Vowel Vibrations and Vowel Production." Nature, No. 3593, p. 619, Oct. 1, 1938.

Shakespeare, William. Plain Words on Singing. London and New York: G. P. Putnam's Sons, 1924.

Shakespeare, William. The Art of Singing. Boston: Oliver Ditson, 1921.

Spinney, L. V. A Textbook of Physics. New York: Macmillan, 1943.

Stockhausen, Julius. Method of Singing. London: Novello, 1884.

Sugg, James Ferrell. "Comparisons in historical and contemporary viewpoints concerning vocal techniques." Waco, Texas. Thesis, Baylor University, 1973.

Tosi, Francesco. Observations on the Florid Song. London: J. Wilcox, 1723. (Available in reprint from William Reeves Bookseller, London, W.C. 2, England.)

Vennard, William. Singing, the Mechanism and Technic. New York: G. Fischer, 1967.

Viardot, Pauline. An Hour of Study; Exercises for the Voice. Vol. 399, Book I, Schirmer's Library of Musical Classics. New York: G. Schirmer, Inc.

Waengler, Hans-Heinrich. Atlas of German Speech Sounds. Berlin: Akademie Verlag, 1968.

Waengler, Hans-Heinrich. Instruction in German Pronunciation. St. Paul: EMC Corp., 1966.

Walton, J. Harold. The Larynx. Summit, N. J.: CIBA, 1964.

Winckel, F. "How to Measure the Effectiveness of Stage Singers Voices."
Folia Phoniatrica 23: pp. 228-233, 1971.

Winckel, F. (Luchsinger and Arnold). Chapter III, "Phoniatric Acoustics."
Voice-Speech-Language. Belmont, California: Wadsworth Publishing
Co., Inc., 1965.

Winckel, Fritz. "Space, Music, and Architecture." CULTURES, Vol. 1,
No. 3, 1974. UNESCO and la Bacconnière, Paris.

Witherspoon, Herbert. Singing. New York: G. Schirmer, Inc., 1925.

Wood, Alexander. The Physics of Music. London: University Paperbacks,
Methuen, 1962.

GLOSSARY OF TERMS AS USED IN THIS TEXT

ACOUSTICS

fundamental - the component having the lowest frequency of a complex

vibration. In singing this is the sung pitch.

harmonic - a tone whose rate of vibration is a precise multiple of that of a

given fundamental tone.

harmonic undertones of a resonator - sung pitch on any note which has over-

tones that will energize the vocal tract. These pitches are below the

resonator at the 8ve, 12th, double 8ve, double octave 3rd, double octave

5th and triple octave. This phenomenon occurs on vowels below the

underlined Vowel diagonal of the Chromatic Vowel Chart. In singing this

means - that the vowel pitch is in harmonic relationship to the sung pitch

below. (Based on Helmholtz, p. 110)

Hz - is a convenient term for vocal frequency since we must use it to state

the frequencies of both the vocal cords and the vocal tract. The vocal

range is very low (75-1400 Hz), while the consonant spectra go as high

as 8000 Hz. The vowel spectra for all voice classifications are con-

siderably lower (between 3300-4000 Hz).

non-harmonic overtones - sounds which have a non-periodic, non-harmonic

relationship to the sung tone such as husky, noisey sounds.

overtones - any of the higher tones which accompany the fundamental tone

produced by a musical instrument.

partials - any of the pure, or harmonic tones forming a complex tone.

Phantom Fundamental - The sung pitch which is not reenforced by the vocal
tract but which is heard by the presence of any three consecutive
overtones. (Based on Fletcher.)

resonance - intensification and prolongation of a sound by reflection.
Resonance occurs when a resonator is in tune with the vibrator or
vibrators.

resonant - resounding; re-echoing; increasing the intensity of the sound.

resonator - a tube or cavity for producing resonance or increasing sound by
resonance.

vowel formants - areas of resonation which differentiate the vowels. In these
areas, certain harmonics of the sung pitch (fundamental) are amplified.

PHONETICS

/a/ vs ⌊a⌋ and the others. In brackets - the specific colors of the phenomenon
/a/.

Broad frequency bands - broad energy bands of both harmonic and non-harmonic
sounds. These exist in speech because of the presence of all overtones,
harmonic and non-harmonic. The harmonic sounds are amplified in good
singing; the non-harmonic are reduced in energy, purifying the tone.

closed syllable - a syllable which ends with a consonant.

close vowel - vowels which have the lower frequencies of R^1.

Emission - sound emitted, the creation of sound waves. The term "vocal
emission" is a far better term than "vocal production."

Narrow frequency bands - exist in good singing where the non-harmonic

overtones are neutralized by the harmonic overtones. (A focused tone.)

open syllable - a syllable which ends with a vowel.

open vowel - vowels which have the higher frequencies of R^1.

Transmission - The carrying of sound waves by air or electronic device.

PHYSIOLOGICAL TERMS

Air chamber - same as above. Also the air chamber of the chest which,

although it has compressions and rarifactions of the air, is not classified

as a resonator - and cannot be heard with the aid of a RadioEar -

headphones hook-up.

Air passage - The pipes from the vocal cords to the front of the mouth and

the passages through the nostrils.

channel - the same as groove, diagonal, pipe or tube. A composer about a

castrato, "Why all the piping?"

groove - singing up and down a diagonal. When the voice is in the right

groove it goes up easily.

Horn from vocal cords to lips - in the voice it is the vocal tract.

Piping - "to play on the (vocal) pipe" - WEBSTER. Singing up or down the

resonance tubes on the Chromatic Vowel Chart.

Resonance Tracking - singing either up and down the diagonals (resonance

pipes) on the Chromatic Vowel Chart.

Resonance tube - the various diagonals on the Chromatic Vowel Chart.

Two part trumpet - When the nasal passages are used <u>with</u> the mouth passage

the voice becomes a "two part trumpet" (Witherspoon).

Tunnel - The vocal tract from the vocal cords to the orifice of the mouth.

Vocal tract - the tube between the vocal cords and the lips.

Vocal tube - the resonator between vocal cords and lips.

PSYCHOLOGICAL

hear - to become aware of (sounds) by the ear.

kinesthetic - to sense the position, movement, etc. of parts of the body,

perceived through nerve end organs in muscles, tendons, and joints.

REGISTERS

Chest Register - the register below "the break" in which reenforcement is by

overtones of the sung pitch.

Falsetto - an artificial way of singing in which the voice is placed in a

register much higher than that of the natural voice. See Vowel Chart.

Head Register - a type of vibration which comes into the voice between c^2 and

$f\#^2$ that has a purer sine wave quality.

Male Head Voice - high notes of the Male Voice which are reenforced at the

octave. Easily shown with a Vowel Resonator.

Middle Voice - the register above the Chest Voice in female voices.

Mixed Voice - a "mezzo tint" in which the sung pitch and second harmonic are

equally reenforced. Indicated by diagonal ⑴.5 on the Chromatic Vowel

Chart.

Piccolo Register - a register above the Whistle Register comparable to the

sonics of a trumpet.

Upper Voice - the term I have used for Male Voices on diagonal ②on the

Chromatic Vowel Chart.

Vowel Register - A register in which the frequency of the puffs from the

vocal cords is the same as that from the vocal tract.

Whistle Register - a register in the treble voice which is probably created

by vortex vibration.

SYMBOLS

Ⓕ   means vocalises or exercises for Female Voices

Ⓜ   means vocalises or exercises for Male Voices

⒡ⓡ   means vocalises or exercises for Female Voices with Vowel Resonator

⒨ⓡ   means vocalises or exercises for Male Voices with Vowel Resonator

$_2\!\downarrow\!_3$ is the arrow on the Vowel Chart which is moved for various voice
classifications.

⟩⟨   means exercises through the passaggio for Female Voices

⟩⟨   means exercises through the passaggio for Male Voices

Hz means cycles per second, cps.

INDEX

INDEX

INDEX

INDEX